The Impossible Child

The Impossible Child

David A. Lane

Trentham Books
in association with
The Professional Development Foundation

First printed in 1990 by Trentham Books Limited

Reprinted 1992

Trentham Books Limited
Westview House
734 London Road
Oakhill, Stoke-on-Trent
Staffordshire ST4 5NP

British Library Cataloguing in Publication Data
Lane, David
  The Impossible Child
  1. Schools, Students. Behaviour problems. Treatment
  I. Title
  371.8'1
  ISBN: 0 948080 26 4

Designed by Trentham Print Design, Chester
Printed in Great Britain by BPCC Wheatons Ltd, Exeter

The Professional Development Foundation

The Professional Development Foundation is a non-profit research trust limited by guarantee and registered in England (No. 2172915).

It specialises in the promotion of practitioner generated research. Through a network of advisors in higher education and other professionals, it provides consultancy, research support and professional development programmes. Both independent projects and cooperative schemes with other professional and academic institutions are undertaken. It assists with the publication of work relevant to the promotion of professional development.

The Foundation has been involved with the field of behaviour problems for many years and has provided a wide range of programmes for schools. Its publication in conjunction with Trentham Books of the first UK book on *Bullying in Schools* in 1988, generated substantial interest and raised the profile of this issue.

The Foundation supported the research on which the publication of *The Impossible Child* was based. This interest has continued and currently training courses are offered to schools to develop policies in relation to this area.

Details of the range of services available to organisations in the public sector are available from the Foundation.

Studio 21, Limehouse Cut, Morris Road, London E14 6NQ.
Telephone: 071-987 2805

David Lane is Director of the Professional Development Foundation and Visiting Professor at the University of Syracuse, New York State.

Contents

PART ONE

UNDERSTANDING THE IMPOSSIBLE CHILD

CHAPTER ONE

The child who would not be ignored

The Impossible Child

'It was not my intention to study the impossible child. He intruded himself into my work, and would not be ignored.'

This is how I started an earlier book about the Impossible Child and it reflects the way in which my interest developed. I was involved in a wider study of response to intervention for learning and behaviour problems, but the Impossible Child (who turned out to be male *or* female) refused to be ignored. My colleagues and I were trying to devise new ways of working with problem behaviour in schools, seeking to provide a service to schools in the London Borough of Islington. Teachers interested in our research would present cases of children they said we should look at.

'Your research may be alright for most kids, but it will never work with John M....., he is just impossible. We have tried everything and he just does not respond.'

It soon became clear that the qualities necessary to be labelled as impossible consisted of a minimum of two. Firstly, the child had to present behaviour disturbing to the teacher. This might be blatant or more subtle but its quality was found in the way in which it made life difficult for the teacher. Children seen as disturbed, as 'clearly needing psychiatric help' were not defined in such a way. Being disturbing, so that the teachers' sense of their own competence was affected, provided the essence of the quality. Secondly, all attempts at making the pupil change through punishment, sympathy, psychology, child guidance, or residential placement had to have failed.

They simply did not respond to what was traditionally offered by way of intervention. They became the focus for increasing professional frustration and came to be seen as bloodyminded, unmotivated, or just downright impossible.

These children contributed greatly to the degree of stress generated in any educational setting. They also contributed greatly to our problems in trying to establish credibility for the service that was offered at the Islington Educational

Guidance Centre. Successful attempts to work in a school-focused way with a broad range of children were undermined by the example of just one such child. Working well with ten children seen as difficult in a school counted for nothing to the teacher tearing her hair out with rage at the latest antics of Jack or Jill Impossible.

We wanted to succeed with our vision of creating a support service for schools that would enable schools to recognise their own contribution to solving the problem of disruption. This left us with no choice. We had to look at this category — the 'Impossible Child'.

The Emergence of the Sin Bin

Understanding why it was so important to consider this problem requires some familiarity with the debate on disruptive behaviour in schools in the 1970s.

Concern about the problem of disruption in schools was rising and, in response, a trend was developing to exclude increasing numbers of children. It was the age of the 'sin bin'. Of course, Education Authorities did not call their new off-site units for disruptive pupils 'sin bins' (although one or two did so initially) but they came to be associated with this label. Unfortunately, the popular press were not entirely inaccurate in applying this term. As both Topping and Quelch (1976) and HMI (1978) pointed out, the units were often ill-conceived and often used haphazard criteria for admission and discharge.

The peak year for establishing exclusion units nationwide was 1974, and it was in that year that I was appointed to start the Islington Centre (née Hungerford). We set out to do something different. Essentially we tried to persuade schools that the problem of disruption was not about deprived (or bad) children or families, nor to do with special needs requiring special facilities, but was essentially a problem of how a school generated and managed behaviour. It was the school's concern. Sending children off to units or clinics to have their brains fixed was not the answer. In this period which, it must be remembered, was pre-Warnock (1978), Rutter, et. al., (1979), Galloway, et.al. (1982), Reynolds (1982), Tattum (1982), Mortimore et. al. (1988), etc., it was not a message many wanted to hear, or would believe even if they heard it. (The tale is told elsewhere, Lane, 1990).

We were arguing for normality, not pathology. However, those schools prepared to work with us found that they could generate valuable change. Many teachers, psychologists, inspectors, social workers, parents, attended our workshops and conferences as we hawked the ideas around the country. If they listened, they found that some parts of our message made sense. Some greeted us with derision and hostility. We realised how our pupils must have felt. But, we listened to the ideas that numerous practitioners shared with us and we shared with them. As a result, an increasing belief emerged that prevention and a school-focused approach were possibly a real alternative.

That was all fifteen years ago. Perhaps it does not matter any more for after all, are we not all school-focused now? Unfortunately it does matter. In 1976 the Prime Minister initiated a great debate on education, looking at disruption and the national curriculum. A decade later, the same debate was once again upon the teaching profession. A national enquiry into discipline in schools was launched, (Elton, 1989). In spite of a decade of Warnock (1978), as Tomlinson (1982) predicted, exclusion is still the order of the day. Ainscow and Tweddle (1988) who themselves did much in their earlier book (1979) to enhance the quality of the debate, can still refer in 1988 to the idea of looking at the school's role in learning difficulties as 'controversial'. They argue that learning difficulties are still seen as something the child has. Practice has become more school based but not necessarily school-focused. The location has changed but not necessarily the philosophy. It is as if we and all the other practitioners who spent the last decade moving in the other direction never checked to see if anyone else was accompanying us (for example Lawrence, 1973, Gillham, Galloway, Burden, Daines, etc. featured in Gillham, 1981, or Widlake, 1986, or Coulby and Harper, 1983, or Topping, 1983 and numerous other unsung teachers featured in Lane and Tattum, 1990).

The Elton Report (1989) can refer favourably to the work of behaviour support teams of the type pioneered in Islington, but as Moses, Hegarty and Jowett (1988) point out, there are few such teams and a conference of professionals working in behaviour support in 1988 (BSC, 1988) can still refer to the same problems we experienced in 1975. Supporting children with behaviour problems is still an unpopular idea.

There have been changes over the last decade; some major gains have been made. School based work is certainly much more common, but school-focused work, in which the emphasis is on the role of the school in interaction with the child, is still having to justify itself. The reality is that the research reports do little to offer comfort to the teacher struggling with the day-to-day realities of school life. The solutions preferred by teachers reporting to the Elton enquiry were centred on smaller classes, tougher sanctions and counselling for difficult youngsters. Changing teaching styles, curriculum and school climate were favoured by only two in ten.

Campaigning for school-focused work remains a necessity.(Lane and Tattum, 1990) Fortunately, the Elton Report strongly favoured whole-school approaches, as well as school-focused support teams.

The Paradox of the Impossible Child

Successive staff at the Islington Centre worked with some 3,000 children. All but a minority stayed in school. We actively supported and trained others to do the same. The original volumes on the work (Lane, 1978) were used as training manuals on our courses (and those in other centres) to train people in school-focused work. The paradox of the Impossible Child remained. The contradiction between our work on changing schools and the concern with a specific group was not lost on many of our critics. The picture on the cover of the original volumes, of a child breaking the 'impossible' label, contrasted with the impression given by research which looked at individual differences. Our concern with individual differences was not the same as a concern with special needs. We rejected the concept of special needs and instead argued for a dimensional approach, with the whole dimension contained within normality. But we were left with a problem. Teachers would present children to us and say that the particular child was impossible. This included teachers who supported our efforts, worked extremely hard to keep pupils in school and who recognised their own role in generating difficulties. They wanted to support their pupils, but found that they could not. What were we to do, ignore their plea? Claim they were mistaken? We could not. So we set out to examine the problem and see what lessons could be learned which could be translated back into the school. We studied the Impossible Child.

In doing so, we were at risk of promoting the myth that there was such a thing as an Impossible Child, a syndrome, to be uncovered and remedied. To overcome that risk, we published the training manuals on a restricted access basis. You had to attend a course to get them, order them through local psychological services, or from a course tutor at a college. It was felt that by training individuals in the use of the ideas we could overcome any difficulties. More than one thousand people obtained the manuals. Services in several parts of the country and abroad used the ideas. To some extent we were successful, due partly to the fact that few training alternatives to our workshop series on school-focused work, which started in 1975, were available. Mostly, it was due to the sense of struggle that we found among many practitioners who were trying out similar ideas on their own and who were happy to share experiences with us.

The position subsequently changed dramatically, and a flood of books on disruption appeared. Few addressed the paradox that even when teachers tried to use the numerous packages of ideas available, some children would continue to drive them crazy. Our message was, unfortunately, a complex one. It involved a range of factors of influence. Consequently, we never believed that a packaged approach was possible, and we never offered one. Even our manuals, on social skills, cognitive skills, stress management, contracting, and many other techniques (Lane, 1972, 1975, 1978), remained for workshop use only.

The issue as we saw it was not just one of a problem in the child, family or school, but an interaction which required analysis of each factor in combination. Establishing that a group of factors was present did not mean that we believed that they were unchangeable. The pattern we saw underlined the situation as it existed, and we presented ideas for change. Working in the context of providing a service and at the same time researching the issues, did cause difficulty. We could not ask teachers to wait five years for the results of our outcome studies before offering advice. We had to make judgements about techniques which could impact on remission (Lane, 1983). It was possible in spite of this to offer a service seen as highly effective and an example of good practice (Topping, 1983, HMI, 1980).

The Impossible Child, as he or she appeared to us at the time, did present a number of problems in our attempts to promote 'School-Focused Analysis and Intervention'. Part of the outline formulation from 1978 is worth repeating, since it illustrates the contradiction.

A Picture of the Impossible Child

On the basis of a study of twenty one factors and sample of around 200 pupils (split into smaller samples for each study), a provisional pattern emerged. The pattern is quoted directly from the earlier volume.

The child is male in the quote, because the majority referred for help at that time were male. In subsequent research the pattern was found to be more complex and the language was adjusted accordingly. For the purposes of this book, however, where all the specific case studies are of boys, the male pronoun will be used.

The basic picture of the impossible child established is that of one of a small minority of pupils who present behaviour disturbing to the teacher and general hostility to adults and who do not respond to the help traditionally offered. They tend not to think about the consequences of their actions, are tough-minded and emotionally stable, although some may be highly emotionally unstable.

These characteristics make them less likely than other pupils to acquire socially appropriate behaviour. Their behaviour is to some degree constitutionally predisposed but the form the behaviour takes is shaped by the negative experiences (or lack of positive experiences) the individual encounters.

The impossible child is, and has been throughout his school life, labelled as different and is negatively conditioned by those responsible for him to respond by violence and disruption. He has a social skill/informational deficit. He does not know how to behave even if he wanted to.

This picture presents a view of the child as one who starts with a disadvantage which in turn is then shaped and maintained through experiences in school.

The framework for intervention suggested at that time strongly argued for change not just in the child but in the response to him by his environment. Teachers were asked to look at their role and play their part. The generalised picture presented was balanced by a plea for individual analysis and intervention based on the context. The pattern described the way it was, not how it must be. Lack of access to appropriate learning experiences (Lane, 1974) and not special needs, were being observed.

The contradiction between this picture, which pointed to features of the child and the message we had spent some years purveying to schools, certainly confused at least one Deputy Head. (".... but isn't all this talk on problems the child has the exact opposite of everything you have said in the past. Are we no longer to concentrate on defining the behaviour we see, the context in which it occurs, and then change it!). The confusion was understandable. We were still saying 'define in context', but we were also exploring other ideas to meet the particular problems of this group.

There were a number of problems with this early research, involving as it did small samples, but enough of a case was made for further research to be viable. It appeared that there were pupils presenting difficulties in school who were not responding to the techniques available. Of the thousands of children who eventually became part of the school-focused work of the Islington Educational Guidance Centre, only a few hundred formed part of this group. But they were a very important part and contributed much to both the frustration and pleasure of us all. Who were they and how did they acquire the 'impossible' label?

Definition of the Impossible Child

The pupils were variously described by their teachers. Some were called impossible, some would be described in other terms which implied impossibility. Such vague terms are, however, of no use in a research study. They need to be defined, to be classified in some way.

Traditionally, classification of problems in children has relied on psychiatric models. These classifications have often been based on small samples without appropriate controls. They have used medical models of physical disorder, in which a basic causation is postulated which when discovered will lead to a cure. This was even applied to physical disorder and is totally inadequate, as Mac-Kieth (1972) has pointed out. Attempts to improve this situation (Rutter, 1965, 1976) have not always been viewed as successful (Stott, 1975). For example, Wolff (1977), refers to agreement on broad groupings but also to the absence of clearly defined sub-groupings. Attempts to improve this situation through statistical clustering has produced a confusing array of categories. Thus we have from Hewitt and Jenkins (1964) Socialised Delinquency and Unsocialised Aggression and from Conners (1970), Aggressive Conduct Disorder and Anti-social Reaction. The different ratings which emerge with each study and the lack of correlation often obtained between the diagnoses of clinicians, does little to inspire confidence (Eysenck and Eysenck, 1975, Cattell, et.al., 1974).

An alternative classification system, which has been widely used in the U.K., is Stott's evolutionary model. It is argued that the consequences of behaviour, that is, the changes that the individual is able to establish in relation to the environment, provides meaningful units of analysis (Nissen, 1954).

Stott, in using this idea, assumes that if a behaviour fails to yield an advantage to the individual, it becomes maladaptive. Most anti-social acts in the long run will fail to yield such advantages. The classification of these maladaptive behaviours in Stott's system covers under-reactive behaviours such as unforth-comingness, withdrawal and depression, and over-reactive behaviours, such as inconsequence and hostility. The well established statistical basis for this system (*The Bristol Social Adjustment Guide*, Stott, 1971), provides a possible structure for looking at the pupils in this study, although the use of the label 'maladjusted' was rejected.

However, as discussed earlier, it is not simply the behaviour of the pupils which marks them out, but also its continuance in spite of attempts to change it. It would not be sufficient simply to look at groups of children who differ on BSAG scores and assume that the highest scorers are those who would be seen as impossible.

To be useful, a definition would also have to take account of the findings of several researchers who have indicated that behaviour problems are often temporary and will 'spontaneously remit' within two years (Rachman, 1971). In an earlier study (Lane, 1976), it had been indicated that most improvement in therapy occurred in the first year, with little change after that.

If we start with those children seen by their teachers as impossible, but add the ideas above, a workable definition emerges:

A pupil who obtains a score indicating maladjusted, over-reactive beha-viour disorder as defined by the BSAG; who has exhibited problems for not less than two years and who has received qualified specialist help over a period of not less than one year but who has not shown any improvement as judged either by responsible professionals or statistically.

This was the definition used in the early studies.

The Prevalence of the Impossible Group

The above definition is ours, but does it relate to other studies? It cannot be directly related. Figures for conduct disorders (Rutter, et.al., 1970, Stott, et.al.,

1975), psychiatric disorders (Rutter and Graham, 1966) or maladjustment (Davie, et.al., 1972), provide some indication of a rate between four and thirteen percent. The Impossible Child is likely to be a sub-group within these figures. Several teachers had suggested that the problem affected about one percent of pupils. The population that had to be used to find 100 pupils for the later studies, suggests that one percent is about right.

So, maybe the impossible one per cent makes sense — it certainly has a journalistic ring to it — but getting to these figures is the end product of a great deal of filtering through the views of teachers and researchers. An important labelling process has taken place.

Who Defines Whom

The term 'maladjusted' carries certain implications. We used the cut-off score for that category (on the BSAG) but rejected the term. In the research reports it appears, but not in the day to day case study material. The power of such labelling is nevertheless very real. Simply to say we reject the term is not enough. A child is referred by a parent, teacher, or some other agent. The question of how the referral happens, the label used and the point at which this label is removed, is not a neutral issue.

A number of factors will influence referral decision. These include resource differences between areas, attitudes of teachers towards their role, and the attitudes of support services (Fitzherbert, 1977). In looking at referrals made via the Educational Social Work Service, Green (1980) discovered that frequently children with similar problems varied greatly in the way they were processed and labelled. The theories that the practitioners used to understand problems did influence the decisions made. An attribution process was happening (Lane, 1989) with sometimes unfortunate consequences for the child, in, for example, court appearances (Lane, 1985). A child may be labelled and remain labelled when no objective data for the continuation of the difficulty any longer existed (Lane, 1976).

A teacher may refer because the child is, and I quote:

'The most violent aggressive pupil it has ever been my misfortune to teach'.

The label applied carries with it the attitude of the referring agent. That attitude is absent from any system of classification of the child's behaviour, yet it will vitally affect referral decisions and the long term outcome, as Green and Fitzherbert demonstrate.

Three aspects of this require attention.

1. Early intervention or Red Tagging?

The Warnock Committee (1978) recommended early identification of children with problems so that help could be offered. Yet, as several writers have pointed out, there can be negative consequences in being picked and 'red tagged' early in life (Scheff, 1966, Clarizio, 1968, Scheff and Sundstorm, 1970, Ullman and Krasner, 1975). Even without professional intervention most behavioural difficulties ameliorate, so why mark the child out? Individuals can be led to view their behaviour in terms of a sick role, through a process which is supposedly for their own good, but which may operate as a control mechanism (Ford, et.al., 1982, Adams, 1986, Lane and Dryden, 1990).

The relationship between the actor, the behaviour and an observer who is in a position of power who can apply the label is crucial to this tagging process.

2. Power Relationships in the Expert, Transplant or Support Role

The idea of experts intervening for another's good forms the cornerstone of much therapy. However, there are alternative ways to view the relationship. Cunningham and Davis (1985) describe the expert model, in which the professionals view themselves as in control of the decision making process, a consumer model in which the professional assists clients to make their own decisions and a transplant model which lies somewhere in between. This raises a number of questions about the roles played by service providers.

If a consumer model is seriously to be preferred, then the power relationships must be addressed and the process through which a definition emerges must be one of social exchange, not expert labelling.

3. Defining Problems Through Social Exchange

A number of issues were apparent in the way the process of defining problems emerged for the Islington Centre. The idea that a number of agents had the power to impact on the decision was recognised and taken into account (based on earlier work, Lane, 1972, 1974). The child was seen as one of those agents and therefore his view was incorporated. We were operating within the framework of 'exchange theory' through contracted work (Lane, 1972). Thus the process by which definitions emerged was one of negotiation between the parties involved. In order to deal with power inequalities, an 'open file' system was instituted, borrowed from earlier work (1973) which two of the staff (David Lane and Fiona Green) had originated elsewhere (see Lane and Green, 1990).

This negotiation could conflict with the mechanism discussed above for defining the Impossible Child. To resolve this, the use of a teacher-directed technique such as the BSAG had to be reconstructed within the exchange framework. Several studies were undertaken to look at this and the use of the BSAG as a self-report device for children emerged. These proved successful (Lane, 1975, Lane and Hymans 1982) and therefore a self-report BSAG was included in some of the studies undertaken for the research and also in the practice of the Centre. This led on to the possibility of negotiating definitions

9

of problems through the use of discrepancy between the views of the parties on the BSAG together with the individual's view of where he or she was and where they wanted to be.

Performance Discrepancy as a Definition

An individual becomes defined as a problem through an awareness that something is wrong. This may be through feedback from others or from themselves but the individual gains a personal sense of performance error.... this is not how it should be, feel, look, act..... The forms of feedback available may include BSAG, checklists, self observation, but something can only be defined as a problem when the performance error is recognised.

Three elements received particular attention in the performance discrepancy framework. One, the actual behaviour that constituted the error, had to be defined and agreed. Two, the objective to be met, that is the new behaviour to be attempted had to be agreed. Three, the role each of the parties involved were to play, had to be agreed.

Any process of investigation thereby became a social exchange in which each party negotiated definitions and knew where they stood.

Exploring the Paradox

The attempt to look at the Impossible Child represented what many saw as a distraction from the main vision of the Islington Educational Guidance Centre, which was to create a school-focused model of analysis and intervention, (EGC, 1975, Lane, 1986).

However, teachers continued to present such children to us and some attempt to explore the nature of their impossibility became inevitable. We were originally looking at the definition from the teachers' perspective but there was a contradiction between that and the negotiated practice of the Centre. This meant that we would also need to look at the pupils' definitions and also at the process by which a shared definition (that is, a shared concern) could emerge if change was going to be possible.

The pupils themselves also held views on the problems which formed an important part of the process of change. They also had views on the research itself. Their comments are reported at various points throughout the text.

This study attempts to incorporate the various contradictions and provide a structure for working with the Impossible Child. We start the process of this study through exploring in a traditional way the literature for some potential explanations. But it will not be long before the Impossible Child intrudes and refuses to be ignored any longer.

CHAPTER TWO

Theories of causation

Introduction

The position of the Impossible Child was marked by two features, the behaviour itself and its resistance to change. This chapter considers the first feature in terms of explanations for the occurrence of behaviour problems. The second aspect will be considered in terms of theories of remission.

There is a vast literature devoted to explanations of why individuals develop behaviour disorders. The literature on aggression and anti-social behaviour (conduct disorders/delinquency) is very extensive. This work probably represents a useful starting point. A general introduction to some of the ideas which were current when the work on the Impossible Child first started will be provided. More recent research will be included where it provides answers to some of the questions posed.

Explanations available tend to fall into broad divisions which see behaviour in terms of either cultural or individual difference.

Cultural explanations for aggression and delinquency

The tendency to aggression is thought to be of evolutionary value, basic to the survival of the species, and based on a natural response to frustration. Yet societies differ enormously in their degree of expression of aggression (Whitting and Child, 1953). Similarly, it has been argued that there are considerable variations between social classes in the degree to which they tolerate or encourage aggression (Klein, 1965). Simple frustration theories have therefore given way to a variety of ideas, from ethology, social learning theory and cognitive models. (Howitt, et.al., 1989)

In the same way that aggression varies according to culture, delinquency is a cultural artefact. It is defined by law. A delinquent is someone caught and convicted, and the distinction is very important, since convictions and sentencing decisions are subject to a variety of influences which include characteristics of the offender (White/Black, Rich/Poor) and the moral judgements of the judiciary (Lane, 1985, Parker et.al., 1989). The role of cultural factors in delinquency has long been argued (Shaw and McKay, 1942, Cohen, 1955).

The most important single contribution from the sociological literature is the understanding that some degree of deviant or criminal behaviour is a normal rather than an abnormal state of society.

Crime is present not only in the majority of societies of one particular species but in all societies of all types... Everywhere and always there have been men who have behaved in such a way as to draw upon themselves penal repression... From the beginning of the nineteenth century statistics enable us to follow the course of criminality. It has everywhere increased. There is then, no phenomenon that presents more indisputably all the symptoms of normality, since it appears closely connected with the conditions of all collective life (Durkheim, 1938).

Setting aside the social implications of such theories, it is clear that explanations of deviant behaviour must include the fact that such behaviour is learnt, is normal, not pathological and is maintained by the current situation. Whatever predisposition of genetic/environmental influence there might be, it is what the individual learns and the outcomes that accrue, which determine the type and frequency of the behaviour occurring. However, simply to argue that cultural factors are important is not enough; the mechanism involved needs to be established.

Five ideas will be considered:
1. Delinquent Neighbourhoods
The assumption that delinquent behaviour relates to the existence of poverty and neighbourhoods which generate anti-social behaviour is one of the earliest of cultural theories. The studies of Burt (1925), Thrasler (1935), Shaw and McKay (1942), consistently emphasised the relationship. Unfortunately, inroads into dealing with poverty have not resulted in a reduction in deviance. Indeed the rising trend of delinquency noted by Durkhiem has continued and delinquent behaviour is very widespread among the young (Rutter and Giller, 1982).

Cohen, (1955) Merton, (1949) and Cloward and Ohlin (1961), in different ways saw juvenile crime as both a reaction to working class youths' frustration and as a part of a working class sub-culture, thereby serving an adaptive function. Halleck (1967), however, has argued that while the delinquent behaviour of adolescents is certainly incongruent with the goals of middle class adults, they are also alien to the working classes who are similarly disturbed by the unreasonable nature of juvenile crime. Robbins (et.al.,1966) has pointed out that anti-social behaviour in childhood is equally predictive of adult disturbance in all classes, and therefore its so called adaptive function must be questioned. The fact that in the long term most working class youths do not remain delinquent, and the remarkable similarity in the type of offences committed by working and middle class youths (Nye, 1958, Herskovitz, et.al., 1959), makes cultural transmission theories less tenable than they used to be. However, this is not to say that poverty does not lead to deprivation, only that the cultural infection theory lacks support. In a major report based on ten years of accumulated research, Brown and Madge (1982) concluded that all the evidence suggested that cultural values are not important for the development and transmission of deprivation. They also quote West's (1979) research for the same project as concluding that the role of delinquent sub-cultures can be largely discounted.

Cultural theories probably have little to offer as potential explanations for the Impossible Child. However, research into bullying behaviour has pointed to the role of peer groups and power/affiliation issues (Askew, 1988, Roland, 1988). This aspect will be taken up below.

It may be towards individual and family influence rather than broad cultural factors that the attention has to be directed.

2. Delinquent families and socialisation

Alternative theories are those which see anti-social behaviour as arising from patterns within families. The early pioneering study was that of the Gluecks' (1950), in which they compared 500 delinquent and non-delinquent youths. There were a number of problems with the study but many of their conclusions were reflected in later studies. Argyle (1964), reviewing the main results of a number of studies, pointed to the role of parental discipline, the absence of a parent or parental conflict and delinquency in the parents as important. A major emphasis on the role of the mother in early studies (Bowlby, 1951), gave way to consideration of the role of the father. Andry (1960) implicated the inadequacy of role relationships between father and son in delinquency. Family pathology models represent, in part, a recognition of the importance of the models to which an individual is exposed in shaping behaviour patterns.

Trasler (1964) attempted to integrate sociological and psychological models. He argued that experience within the family constitutes the opportunity to learn skills and confidence in interpersonal relationships and is also a means of acquiring social and moral training. Individuals whose early experience is unsatisfactory, inconsistent or unrewarding will be deprived of opportunities for acquiring either social anxiety and other motives or the techniques of social interaction. An individual whose social skill learning has been deficient will be comparatively invulnerable to social pressure and therefore will remain under-socialised.

13

This concept has potential application to the dual aspects of the Impossible Child in explaining the occurrence of difficulties and resistance to change.

A whole variety of family factors have been potentially linked to difficulties. These include child rearing patterns, socio-economic circumstances, family composition, family size, birth order, and family break-up. The interpretation of such data has proved both controversial and difficult but a multiple set of measures may have to be included in any study (Brown and Madge, 1982). Recently, Ellis (1988) has reviewed over five hundred studies internationally which look at demographic correlates of criminal behaviour. It is argued that there is a universal sense of what constitutes criminal behaviour and this is based on the role of the victim. For crimes involving a victim seven universal demographic correlates are presented — intactness of parent's sexual/marital bond, family size, race, social status, urban/rural residency, age and sex. The difficulties with this area are illustrated by the fact that even with the comprehensive coverage of the literature undertaken by Ellis, major studies which present a contrary view, such as those of Stott, (et.al., 1975) are not mentioned.

3. Delinquent schools

During the 1960s there was an increasing emphasis on the role of the school in promoting anti-social behaviour or low expectations in pupils (Willmott, 1958, Musgrove, 1964, Partridge, 1966, Hargreaves, 1967). Power and his associates (Power, et.al., 1969) pointed to differences between schools in fostering delinquent attitudes. This study in particular was influential and led to a spate of interest in the role of the school. Schools, in the way they are organised, through conflicts of role, the weight placed on achievement, attitudes of teachers in promoting conflict or cooperation, the content of lessons and the operation of rewards, can greatly influence behaviour, attendance and the learning that takes place (Lane, 1973, 1976, 1978).

The role of the school has recently received far more attention. The work of Reynolds (1982), Rutter (et.al.,1979), and Mortimore (et.al.,1988) has been very important in refocusing the debate on the role of the school. From our perspective, however, the studies by Galloway and his associates (Galloway, et.al.,1982) are highly relevant in their concentration on disruptive pupils. They point among other things to the way in which organisational problems in the school contribute to disruptive behaviour and how some forms of support for the child may actually increase difficulties. Support groups may function as ways of removing the evidence of tension within a school. The relationship between schools, disruptive behaviour and delinquency, is a complex one worthy of attention but much of the data is difficult to interpret. It does appear, as a Home Office research review indicates, that some practices in schools influence the progression from minor misbehaviour to delinquency. (Graham, 1988)

Thus it is not just the school attended which matters but patterns of interaction within it. Understanding those patterns may be very useful in explaining the problems of the Impossible Child.

4. Discrimination and language.

Discrimination in society is clear and obvious and whole groups can receive adverse treatment (Brown and Madge, 1982). However, the possibility of selective labelling of children from different ethnic minorities, and the consequent placement of them in special education, has concentrated attention. A number of suggestions that black children were over-represented in units for disruptive children did raise questions about differences between groups in levels of difficulty (West et.al., 1986). The arguments about racial differences in behaviour have a very long history and show no sign of going away. Recently, a theory which links racial differences to evolutionary genetics has appeared (Rushton, 1988). The evolutionary perspective presented links all species of animals in a reproductive framework. A review of this evolutionary perspective by Zukerman and Brody (1988) under the title of 'Oysters, rabbits and people', criticises Rushton's article for its logic, the credibility of some of its sources, selectivity from the literature and from data within studies, and for failing to consider diversity within sub-groups. Flyn (1989), has presented a further detailed criticism of the research on which the evolutionary perspective is based. As Gould (1981) has pointed out, the use of 'science' to present members of ethnic minorities in a negative light has a long history. Psychology in particular has a poor image (Jones, 1979).

That language can have a powerful effect on how children are seen and labelled in schools was clearly established by Eggleston (et.al., 1985). The level of representation of pupils in groups labelled as especially difficult requires consideration in spite of the sensitivity of the issue. The possibility of pupils being referred for special education on grounds of racial differences rather than any objective difference in behaviour cannot be ignored. West, (et.al., 1986) referred to the over-representation of pupils classified as Caribbean in centres for pupils with difficulties, and an under-representation of Asian pupils. Surveys by the Inner London Education Authority (1988), confirm this pattern. They argue for greater vigilance by teachers in referral. Data was obtained from the Islington Centre for the ILEA survey: however, we could find no evidence of over-representation in our sample, but the pattern of under-representation of Asian pupils was reflected.

It could very well be that positive action by the ILEA has had an impact, and the widespread over-representation which was believed to exist in the 1970s

15

has now largely disappeared. The impact of ILEA policies to tackle discrimination deserves careful study.

5.   The labelling of the child.

As Becker (1963) pointed out, "Social groups create deviance by making the rules whose infraction constitutes deviance and by applying those rules to particular people and labelling them as outsiders.".

If we apply this thinking to our consideration of the Impossible Child, it becomes clear that whatever it is that counts as 'impossibility' is not a simple quality present in the act of deviance itself, but rather the end product of a process of response by others to the act, which results in the gradual alienation of the individual from sources of support. We see this in the fact that, to be labelled. the child has both to behave in a given way and to fail to respond to attempts by professionals to come back into the 'fold of the righteous'. Coser (1956) refers to the positive function of such conflict for the 'in group'. Attempts to bring the individual back have the effect of strengthening existing bonds and values but where the attempt fails the individual's exclusion serves as a restatement of the 'in group' values.

The existence of a deviance amplifying effect which drives a child to more, not less deviance has been outlined by Wilkins (1966). A detailed study of life in school provided further evidence of the effect of such processes (Hargreaves, et.al., 1975). Some teachers are able to insulate the child from deviance, other teachers provoke it. Hargreaves quotes Tannenbaum (1938) who shows how a gradual shift occurs in which first the individual's acts are defined as evil but later the individual comes to be defined as evil. The person becomes the action described.

The function served by placing the child in an out group may have to be considered. Galloway (et.al., 1982) has already referred to some possibilities, including the issue of removing evidence of tension within the school.

The question also arises as to why a child should accept an out group label. Hullett, (1966) has incorporated the symbolic interactionism of Mead (1934) with the concept of goal achievement in order to argue that an individual will adopt another's attitude about self, if an advantage can be gained by doing so. Possible advantages for the child could be considered.

Of course, this raises the whole issue of the beliefs of the teachers about the child but also about the children's beliefs about themselves and the situation. The child's view is often invisible. There are exceptions (for example, Hammersley and Woods, 1984), and Galloway and his colleagues sought pupils' views. Our Impossible pupils had a number of views about why they behaved as they did, why they were seen as they were seen, and the prospects for recovery. The interaction of these contradictory attributions was illustrated in a case study recently published (Lane, 1989). The various parties were acting in accordance with predictions based on their beliefs about causation. Changing those proved very difficult.

Social learning, aggression and anti-social behaviour

Traditional formulations of aggression focus on concepts such as inhibition, drive or guilt deficit, for example Dollard's (et.al., 1939) view that frustration leads to aggression. An alternative position (Bandura and Walters, 1959) sees aggressive behaviour as normal behaviour which has been negatively labelled by some person in authority. Aggressive behaviour can be placed in such a view within the larger category of assertive behaviour (Patterson, et.al., 1967). So defined, it is normally occurring behaviour which may or may not receive a negative response. It is nevertheless governed by standard principles of learning and no elaborate pathological theories are needed to explain it. An individual learns to behave aggressively because it is reinforcing to do so.

Walters and Brown (1964), for example, trained different groups of children to hit a large plastic doll, rewarding the children with marbles. Children who received training in hitting the doll were later paired with those who had not been trained and rated in a second game by naive observers on aggression. Those who were trained were considerably more aggressive than those who were not. Can these children be considered abnormal, or viewed as individuals with more aggressive drives or impulses, or is it more accurate to say that they had learnt that under certain conditions it was more appropriate to behave in a given way?

There are numerous experimental studies supporting the value of such learning principles applied to behaviour problems (Ullman and Krasner, 1975). It is not as simple as it appears, however, for some behaviours are harder to change than others and there do appear to be limits on conditionability even in well controlled animal experiments (Rachlin, 1976). Recent research in animal conditioning and learning theory indicates that 'conditioning is neither a simple nor well understood process' (Dickinson, 1987). Bandura(1969) has pointed out that it is generally easier to disinhibit (allow someone to do something previously prevented) than to inhibit a response pattern by vicarious means. The reasons include the fact that behaviours that are often punished by adults are often immediately reinforcing for the child. In such cases little modelling is required to overcome the effects of prior suppression. Contemporary theories, as Dickinson pointed out, may have to allow for the observation that inappropriate behaviours and beliefs may arise through conditioning experience.

Thus if the alternative behaviours open to the Impossible Child are not as immediately reinforcing as those it is hoped to replace, little change will occur. Learning is more effective when behaviours are being taught rather than inhibited and also when a child can identify with a model who is a source of

17

reinforcement. In such a case the pupil is more likely to accept the views of the model. Perhaps for our pupils, the models available to them have not been reinforcing. If they have learnt that people are not reinforcing but punishing, they could punish back.

Ullman and Krasner (1975) have developed such a theory to explain extreme forms of anti-social behaviour. They argue that the behaviours are seen in a person largely unaffected by the factors that control most people's behaviour. In particular, other people do not seem reinforcing to them, and thus they show poor social judgement and frequently break rules and promises.

People with such a life pattern find it difficult to predict the effects that their own behaviour will have on others because those others do not provide adequate, consistent feedback on what constitutes appropriate behaviour. Thus they do not learn acceptable attitudes about themselves or others. Behaviour is treated as if it were inconsequential; attending to the social situation or other people's feelings is therefore pointless, since no consistent learning is possible from it.

For example, the family experience of the individual might be one of severe punishment or punishment based on the adults' shifting moods rather than on consistent objective principles related to the child's behaviour. The result is that the individual learns that people are sources of punishment, to be avoided, rather than sources of reinforcement to be sought.

Such an explanation, taken together with the Hargreaves/Tannebaum framework, might go a long way to explaining aspects of the Impossible Child. However, the issue of the consistency of such patterns would require discussion (Ajzen, 1988, Howitt, et.al., 1989).

But not all children faced with similarly difficult circumstances respond in the same way. Something else may be involved. One possibility lies in differences in conditionability.

Genetic, Individual Difference and Congenital explanations

Although the learning principles discussed above are well established, it is necessary to explain why some individuals respond more readily than others to some learning situations. There does appear to be some evidence to support the idea that individuals vary constitutionally in responsiveness to conditioning.

Theories of causation also include genetic and constitutional concepts. The early ideas that physical characteristics were important concomitants of deviant behaviours (Sheldon, et.al., 1949, Lombroso, 1917) have largely disappeared. A modern variant, the concept of 'minor physical abnormalities', has appeared instead. High rates of 'MPA's' have been found in various groups of children presenting behaviour problems, and these features are usually evident from birth

(Quinn and Rapaport, 1974). Genetic studies also point to inheritance factors playing a part in determining the level of disturbance (Shields and Slater, 1960).

It is also commonly argued that there is a relationship between gender and aggression. Physical aggression, for example, bullying, is more common in boys. (Munthe and Roland, 1989). This is partly the result of learned sex roles, but, since even young children vary on this dimension, (Sears, et.al., 1957) and since animal research has indicated that injecting male sex hormones into animals makes them more aggressive (Suhl, 1961), it may be partly constitutional. Nevertheless, it is apparent that aggressive fathers will serve as models to their sons. Parents who do not generally permit aggression but who also do not punish it when it occurs, produce less aggressive children than parents who do punish aggression (Sears, et.al.,1957).

More sophisticated studies, based on brain wave activity, have shown that delinquents in general do not differ from non-delinquents but certain groups who often commit offences do differ on such measures (Michaels, 1955, Volavka, 1987). Of interest are the increasing number of studies which link arousal levels in the brain with response to punishment (Hare, 1971). It is argued that some individuals do not change their behaviour in anticipation of punishment in the way that other individuals do, and thus the threat of punishment has no impact. Ellis (1987), in a review of numerous studies in this field, argues strongly for the link with arousal. This view would point to the importance of including individual differences in personality in any consideration.

The personality models of both Cattell and Cattell (1969) and Eysenck and Eysenck (1975) provide a framework to consider this issue. In an earlier study (Lane, 1976) extensive use had been made of the Cattells' model. However, the Eysencks' model provided a number of precise hypotheses which could be tested as explanations for the occurrence of difficulties and their continuation. The prediction they make is that behaviour problems are more likely in extraverted, emotionally unstable children who are also toughminded. A large number of studies have been undertaken to test this prediction. The results have not always been consistent but do show some correlation at the extreme but not for mild disorders (Rutter and Madge, 1976, Eysenck and Gudjonsson, 1989). The concept will be discussed in more detail in the next chapter, but the increasing research into arousal patterns and behaviour disorders does provide ample reason for including differences in personality types as one possible explanation for the Impossible Child.

The argument that there might be constitutional 'personality' differences has been extended to the possibility of congenital involvement. Stott (et.al., 1975), looked at cultural theories but could find no evidence to support them. They did, however, argue that three factors might be relevant:

1. Poorer nutrition, greater social stress, and poorer health among pregnant women.

2. A greater prevalence of family stress during childhood.

3. A cultural pattern which favours tolerance of others' weakness rather than one which trains children to adhere to abstract moral principles.

In their study of approximately 2,500 pupils, they found a number of factors associated with higher levels of behaviour problems. These included gender differences, a pronounced tendency to ill health, and motor impairment. On the basis of this they argued for a multiple congenital impairment conception.

Girls were less subject to this condition than boys and various morbid conditions such as poor motor coordination, speech defect, respiratory difficulties etc., were associated with behaviour problems.

A common origin was suggested, based on neurological dysfunction. This was linked to social class through the greater likelihood that mothers suffering severe hardships would experience stress in pregnancy. It was argued that the likelihood of 'pre-natal insult' having an effect was determined by the genetic constitution of the embryo and the mother. Pre-natal stress proved noxious by triggering genetic predispositions.

The strength of Stott's data make it difficult to ignore the possibility of some congenital explanation and therefore the health of the pupils becomes a factor to take into account.

What should we take into account ?

There are clearly a range of potential explanations. At the individual level, gender differences and the role of arousal and personality need to be considered. Health and possibly the occurrence of minor physical abnormalities will also have to be included. A link between social class, higher levels of problems and health difficulties would be of interest. Cultural factors are likely to prove more difficult but the existence of problems within the family at some level has to be examined, and several aspects of the role of the school are worthy of further examination. More difficult will be consideration of the way labels and beliefs impact on the child. The child's own view of these factors cannot be ignored.

Discovering factors that make it more likely that children will have difficulties is not an easy task. Unfortunately, it is made still more difficult since factors which lead to problems may not be the same as those which maintain them (Yule, 1978). It is not just the existence of problems that we have to explore but also factors which relate to remission from them.

A more detailed consideration of the problem of remission is necessary. It is to that task that we now turn.

CHAPTER THREE

The concept of remission: a review and introduction to the field

Remission: is it spontaneous?

One way in which the Impossible Child is a problem is because of lack of response to attempts at change. Understanding change processes has received most attention through the concept of remission. The term is used to describe recovery from illness but has been extended to include change in response to psychological therapies.

Remission is what this chapter is about. It attempts gradually, and somewhat haltingly, to feel its way towards a determination of the areas that must be included in any attempt to understand the *process* of recovery or change in behaviours seen as problematic in children, that is, of remission. Unfortunately, much of the literature on remission has been directly or indirectly dominated by Eysenck's concept of spontaneous remission (Eysenck 1952), and in effect centres on the dispute as to whether or not Eysenck was right.

The central role played by Eysenck is reflected in this review of the field. In part this means an inevitable medical bias. However, some sense of this context does need to be understood. At the end of this chapter, the following question can be asked:

What do we need to consider if the process by which some children who present behaviour difficulties improve (remit) and others do not, is to be understood?

Intoxicating hope and sober reflections

The last fifty years have seen enormous progress in medical services. It has been a time of intoxicating hope. The development of antibiotics and the advances in provision of child health care services seemed to open up the possibility of answers to all our problems. The 1950s and 1970s in particular, marked by spectacular successes in surgery and technological innovations, have led to rising public expectations of what is possible. As MacKeith (1972) points out, the public often wants magical solutions which involve no effort on their part. The faith of the public in healers continues unabated, as does the demand for services. Yet from time to time, someone takes a sober look at our achievements and finds them seriously wanting. An editorial in the medical journal *The Lancet* (1971) points out that the 1960s were a decade of 'therapeutic triumphs achieved for the few at great cost'. Indeed, a comparison of health statistics indicates that all the advances of the last half century put together, have added very little to life expectancy, incredible as it may seem. Such advances as there have been owe much to simple (though careful and painstaking) developments in public health e.g. sewage works, inoculation, clean air legislation, and little to complex technologies of individual professional intervention. It appears to be a 'heresy that medicine is about curing people ... most of it is not: medicine is about alleviation with occasional and very rewarding episodes of curing' (MacKeith 1972).

Thus it is not to individual therapies that we should look for major change but to public health and social policy.

A similar pattern can be traced in the field of psychological disorders. The last half of the century has seen an unparalled rise in the provision of psychological services. The first child psychiatric services date back to this period (in the children's department of the Maudsley Hospital and the child guidance clinics).

Yet, as Mainard (1962) pointed out, Eysenck (1952) caused consternation by exposing the similar heresy that psychotherapy is a cure for all our psychological ills. His famous (some would say infamous!) paper underlined once again the fact that simple relationships do not exist. One cannot identify disorder, apply psychotherapy and effect a cure.

Eysenck reviewed studies totalling more than 7000 cases of patients treated for neurotic disorders and concluded that individuals were as likely to improve without treatment as with it. It appears from his work and subsequent studies that the impact obtained for individuals from professional sources was limited, variable, or even deteriorative (Carkhuff & Berensen 1967). Such changes as did take place owed more to general life expectancy than psychotherapy.

Rachman (1971) in fact takes a position for psychotherapy somewhat akin to that stated above by MacKeith for physical medicine, that treatment is about alleviation not curing. 'It may turn out, in the long run' he suggested, 'that psychotherapy does no more than provide the patient with a degree of comfort, while the disorder runs its course.'

We are in the business, then, of providing alleviation, while 'natural' remission is allowed to occur. That improvements may occur is clear, but the factors governing such improvements are not. Rachman (1971) reviewing the literature on the effects of psychotherapy almost twenty years after Eysenck's paper, concluded with a set of similarly sober reflections on the efficacy of psychotherapy, but pointed to the occurrence of fortuitous life events as critical to improvements. He also added that in spite of a vast literature devoted to outcome studies, still very little was known about the factors which could generate fortuitous improvements. Indeed Rachman stated that: 'the identification of these restorative events and study of the manner in which they affect the process of remission would be of considerable value.'

Given that understanding of factors influencing remission from behavioural disorders is so central to the provision of services, this gap in our knowledge was remarkable. Not only was little known of the process of remission, but also few attempts appear to have been made to understand it. Eysenck's concept of spontaneous remission provides one such attempt.

At least, his twin arguments on psychotherapy effects and spontaneous remission mark an attempt to identify one aspect of the broader issue of factors which influence remission.

His arguments destroyed our days of innocence; we could no longer assume that we had the power to intervene for 'another's good'. Any such intervention had in future to be justified by reference to an understanding of rates of remission.

Or rather, one would expect that to be the case, yet there is an absence of a clearly established review of the literature on remission (the exception being 'outcome studies' covered by Rachman (1971). The literature contains clues but few systematic explanations are available. Some clues will be introduced and certain problems considered in relation to the arguments in Eysenck's paper. But the papers on spontaneous remission and then on psychotherapy have to provide the starting point. This is in spite of the fact that the issue itself is over thirty years old. These arguments will be explored, following on from Rachman's (1971) observations, although the evidence of more recent researchers will be considered.

Spontaneous remission — learning components

The term 'spontaneous remission' is used to refer to improvements which occur in the absence of formal psychiatric treatment. It does not represent a belief in 'uncaused' changes. It is not argued that the mere passage of time generates such improvements but rather that fortuitous events in time are responsible.

The conditions under which events are more or less likely to occur are covered in Eysenck's early papers, by reference to conditioning studies and, more specifically, the concept of extinction, but also to his model of personality. In essence, it is held that individuals, by virtue of their personality, will vary in their responsiveness to conditioning. Thus emotional introverts will acquire behaviour readily. They will, therefore tend to develop excessive reactions (phobias etc.) in response to short-term stressful environmental events.

Added to this is the argument that appropriate behaviours of the neurotic type are, in the long term, not likely to be reinforced by the individual's environment and will disappear (extinction)

Eysenck's position therefore contains the twin pillars of personality and learning theory.

Extinction, it is agreed, is the fate of most neurotic behaviour and thereby explains the process of spontaneous remission. The concept therefore covers characteristics of the behaviour (i.e. behavioural excess), the individual (responsiveness to conditioning) and the environmental response (actual conditioning events experienced). These broadly based concepts were subsequently extended to include a more specific basis of explanation (Eysenck 1976).

Essentially, in his current model of neurosis, Eysenck rewrites the classical law of extinction and thereby provides an explanation of why some behaviours extinguish (remit), while others increase (enhance). This being the central paradox — why do not all neurotic behaviours extinguish in accordance with the classical learning predictions?

The early experiments of Pavlov (1927) in which dogs were taught to salivate in response to a tone, provided the basis for the classical view, the view that extinction is expected to occur over time. (The argument is more complicated than this, (see Lane, 1983, and Eysenck and Martin, 1987). Yet some behaviours do not extinguish. It is argued in the current theory that there are two consequences which may follow: extinction or enhancement of the response. He postulates also two types of response, those which have drive properties and those which do not. For example, if we return to Pavlov's dogs, it can be argued that the experiment only worked when the dogs were hungry. (That is, the hunger drive was present). Conditioned stimuli which do not produce drives extinguish in accordance with the classical law.

On the other hand, when some drive-producing response such as anxiety is being conditioned enhancement, not extinction, takes place. In brief then, conditioned stimuli which do not produce drives extinguish; those which do, are enhanced.

Fear/Anxiety responses are a prime example of responses which possess drive properties. The main stimuli giving rise to response might include pain, but would more commonly include frustration and conflict giving rise to frustration. The types and consequences of response therefore need to be considered. One would expect a preponderance of particular kinds of behaviour to remit and others to enhance.

However, Eysenck goes further than this and postulates conditions which favour enhancement. His argument is in line with his earlier theory that introversion/extraversion and emotionability/stability are implicated. (The other two, he maintains, are length and strength of the stimuli presentation and to this should be added timing.)

This more detailed analysis means that we would expect differences in rates of remission between behaviours and according to personality type, and thus a more elaborate spontaneous remission argument would be necessary.

Learning Patterns

However, the influence of the patterns of learning, by which the problem behaviours are originally learned, is more complicated than often appears. It is sometimes assumed that in a simplistic 'behavioural' framework, learning is simply a matter of linking any stimulus with any response to produce an association. Yet it appears (Rachlin 1976) that even in the closely controlled conditions of the laboratory, some behaviours have proved remarkably difficult to change.

In studies with animals, certain classes of behaviour — such as defence, attack and fear responses — do traditionally show such difficulty. (Azrin et Al 1966, Bolles 1970, Rachlin 1976), It is argued that innate processes are set to sensitise a person to certain types of stimuli and facilitate conditioning of response to those stimuli. In these terms, one cannot view learning as the product of environmental events, but rather as interactions with response tendencies of the species (Staddon & Simelhag 1971). Given such response tendencies, differences in patterns of remission would be expected.

More recently, the tone of Eysenck's (1987) argument has changed and while it is still asserted that principles of conditioning and extinction are basic, it is not asserted that, 'in particular cases other factors may not be of considerable importance....'. It is also not asserted that all human behaviour can be reduced to principles derived from animal behaviour, and the role of cognitions is seen as having a place in learning theory.

It should be noted additionally that learning patterns do vary. It has been argued that the types of specific learning to which an individual has been exposed make certain behaviours, once acquired, resistant to extinction (Lane 1983). To take one example, delinquency, a difference might relate to the diversity and specificity of the stimulus and reinforcement patterns encountered. Such differences in patterns may themselves explain divergence in remission.

The application of learning principles in varied situations such as schools, psychiatric hospitals and training centres for the mentally handicapped has, it is claimed (Trasler & Farrington 1979), led to some success. However, the same authors, in commenting on applications with offenders in institutions, states that there have been 'many failures and few successes'. This distinction, it is argued lies not in the failure of the principles, but rather in their inappropriate application. Adolescent delinquency, Trasler argues, is maintained by reinforcers located in the individual's environment, encountered at certain periods in life. Thus contingencies applied outside that environment, i.e. in institutions, will not influence long-term behaviour.

Descent into persistent delinquency, furthermore, is in part due to the progressive erosion of alternative sources of reinforcement imposed through court action. This question of lack of alternative is also mentioned by Cohen (1973) as part of the particular pattern of reinforcement for 'socially deviant youth'. Cohen draws a parallel with the economic system in the USA. Its strength, he argues, lies in the fact that individuals work for hope of future reward, not just for immediate gain. This pattern of occasional, rather than regular, reward, is known as 'intermittent' reinforcement. Thus, in the same way that behaviours valued in the economic system are persistent, when a schedule reinforces anti-social behaviour, it is also resistant and therefore hard to combat.

A behaviour such as burglary is on an intermittent schedule, i.e. sometimes you get something valuable, sometimes you do not; and therefore it persists. Additionally, often very ineffective punishment schedules apply (i.e. the chances of getting caught are small and punishment happens long after the offence, rather than immediately). The effect is to teach only avoidance behaviours, 'keeping out of the way of the police'. Finally, we have the lack of alternative avenues for reinforcement (where else can the individual reap similar rewards?) in those youngsters who lack necessary skills for pro-social achievement. These elements taken together, it is argued, make such anti-social behaviour difficult to change.

Studies of life in school point to a similar lack of alternative rewards and learning patterns very close to those described for delinquency (Lane 1973, Hammersley and Woods, 1984, McGuiness and Craggs, 1986). A similar explanation for persistence of difficulties for the Impossible Child may be viable.

The discussions above raised the question of the differences in reinforcement schedules applied to the behaviour. The second aspect of this is the pattern of stimuli which elicits the response. Suppose, for example, the delinquent stole from a variety of locations. The stimuli, which then became conditioned to the expectation of reward, would be equally varied and most of them completely unknown. For example, Jack may walk into a shop to buy a newspaper. The owner is in the stockroom, and Jack is slightly irritated because it means he has to wait and might miss his train. Henry might walk into the shop to buy a newspaper. The owner is in the stockroom, and Henry picks up a paper and 200 cigarettes and walks out. Both individuals were presented with the same stimulus, the empty shop, but the response was different. Both Jack and Henry entered the shop intending to buy newspapers, but for Jack its emptiness signified the need to wait, with the possible consequence of missing the train. For Henry, the emptiness signified the chance to steal, with the likely consequence of reward. Each, in Thomas' phrase (1953), 'defined the situation differently'.

Anti-social behaviours such as stealing, which develop in this fashion can lead to the accumulation of a large number of stimuli which give rise to the definition of a situation, as one in which the response of stealing is likely to lead to reward. Similarly within the school situation, the variety of contexts which might give rise to a definition of the situation as leading to the possibility of disruptive, disturbing, or challenging behaviours is very wide.

This argument leads to the idea that a difference between behaviours which remit easily and which do not, lies in the diversity of the patterns of such definitions. Contrast this with an individual whose fear of a cat was developed on the basis of classical conditioning. He will, on encountering a cat, show fear. If he runs away, the fear may reduce and he is negatively reinforced. The pattern of stimuli in this situation however, is relatively limited and the reinforcement schedule is fairly constant. Therefore, an attempt at extinction could take place with relative ease, since the factors involved are known or easily identifiable, and the correlation between them could be easily broken. Whereas the individual who steals may do so in the most diverse of situations, and the reinforcement is likely to be intermittent. It is therefore more difficult to identify the stimuli which might elicit the behaviour, and the reinforcement schedule itself has resulted in associations which are resistant to extinction.

Of course, one must look also beyond the existence of the particular pattern, to the consequences of any given response or future response and on the response of others. In particular, things which the individual has not learned as a result of the existence of the given pattern, may have to be considered in any attempt at change. That is, the individual has not only learnt to act in a given way, he has also, by doing so, failed to learn the alternative behaviour appropriate to the situation. Consequently, the alternative behaviour likely to lead to reward is not in the individual's repertoire (Lane 1974).

Spontaneous remission — personality components

Even accepting the basic value of the principles discussed above and the proposition that some behaviours are acquired more easily than others, it still remains necessary to explain why some individuals respond more readily than others to certain learning situations.

This can be partly explained in terms of past learning influencing later learning, but it is argued by Eysenck & Eysenck (1975) that individuals vary constitutionally in responsiveness to conditioning. Evidence in relation to response to counselling programmes, therapy, discipline and probation (Lane, 1974, 1976, 1978. McWilliams 1975), has indicated that certain features of temperament are of influence in governing response in groups similar to those in this present study to various learning situations. The relationship between personality and response is therefore worth exploration.

The relationship with regard to neurotic behaviours is thought to include the incubation of anxiety responses and the personality of the emotional introvert. This argument, concerned with anxiety or 'neurotic' based patterns, does not directly assist in the consideration of remission from conduct disorders. Nevertheless, the proposition of a relationship between extraversion and neuroticism and anti-social behaviour takes us some way towards an explanation. It is argued in this theory (Eysenck 1970), which links the learning theory principles discussed above and personality, that extraverts should take part in more anti-social behaviour than introverts, on the basis of their level of conditionability. The theory maintains that conditioning is the basis for the development of socialised behaviour and 'conscience'. Thus people who condition badly would be at a disadvantage in acquiring 'those conditioned socialised responses which go to make non-delinquent behaviour'. (Of course, the argument would also lead to a view that introverts brought up in a highly delinquent environment learn more such behaviour.)

Neuroticism in the theory acts as an amplifying device, by virtue of its drive properties. When it is appreciated that high E and N individuals tend to be 'impulsive, like to take chances, to get aggressive, lose their temper, crave excitement, are moody, tense and irritable', it can be understood why they might get into more trouble than individuals who display the opposite characteristics.

However, while this general theory has received some support, it has also contained obvious gaps; and it has proved difficult to translate the general point that E and N results in more anti-social behaviour into specific predictions such as the likelihood of delinquent activity. The argument that E and N are influential in conduct disorders has therefore been extended to include the concept of psychoticism or toughmindedness. Several studies reported by Eysenck & Eysenck (1975) and more recently by Eysenck & Gudjonsson (1989) do relate the concept to various specific conduct disorders, including groups sharing patterns such as drug dependency (Teasdale et.al., 1971). Allsopp and Feldman (1974) have also demonstrated that anti-social behaviour in schoolgirls was related to high levels of P, E and N, and other findings (Lane 1974, 1988) also pointed to the influence of 'P'. The concept of toughmindedness (P) was made more useful for this current study of remission because of its relationship with a poor response to therapy (Lane 1974 1976, Eysenck & Eysenck, 1975). We need now to review the 'P' factor.

The P Factor

Consistent findings have been reported linking 'P' to behaviour difficulties and to a role in therapy responses in children (Lane 1974 1976 1978). In particular, it was argued that toughminded individuals did not respond to supportive types of counselling, but rather to utilitarian reward. One characteristic of toughmindedness, a lack of empathy, means such individuals are untouched by therapies relying on sympathetic involvements. They also show a disregard for danger and consequences, tending to act on impulse and not to think about punishment and the long-term effects of their behaviour. Therefore, techniques which rely on retribution, moral inducement or concern for the other person, also do not touch them.

The 'P' factor is one which is simply untouched by traditional therapies. This finding is supported by the Eysencks' (1975) conclusion to their vast review of the literature on 'P', indicating that P+ scores are found in abundance in psychopaths and criminals. Additionally, among neurotics, P+ scores are characterised by a poor response to various forms of psychotherapy.

The differences in patterns of score in criminal populations, it is also argued, can be differentiated in terms of personality and type of offence. The view is proposed that crimes involving aggressive behaviour would carry implications of high 'P' (Eysenck & Eysenck 1976). Marriage (1975) has found similar relationships between high 'P' and crimes of violence. The 'P' factor does therefore appear to be a promising candidate for a predictive role in both disorder and remission.

The E Factor

Extraversion has proved a difficult and inconsistent factor in a number of studies. While the general association of E and lack of conditionality has found some support, prediction of high levels in problem groups has been less successful. It has perhaps now been recognised that such groups will vary on this dimension and that Eysenck's own studies now incorporate such variations. For example, they have been able to differentiate types of crime by level of Extraversion. Gang activity and 'con' tricks seem to go with high E. Those involved in violence also feature in this category, whereas social inadequates are more likely to be introverts. An interesting result in a study of recidivism in Borstal boys did show that only E significantly predicted reconviction at three years follow-up. Pierson (1969), using the Cattell Personality Model, also found that delinquents who did not respond to programmes tended to be 'adventurously extravert'. McWilliams (1975) found (although only in association with low N) that the extraverts had higher rates of reconviction. A study of response to discipline in school children (Lane 1978) paralleled McWilliams' findings.

Some effect from E is therefore to be expected and it must be included in any hypothesis of behaviour change.

The N Factor

Neuroticism is seen as crucial in Eysenck's model, as a drive component in the genesis of anxiety responses and also in that of anti-social behaviour. It is seen as strengthening any tendency which exists. Thus, the easily conditioned introvert who is high in N will acquire more fear and anxiety responses, whereas the poorly conditioned extravert, deficient in social behaviour, will similarly find the N factor acting as a drive component.

However, this component has proved difficult to interpret, for it could also be argued that the lack of drive in low N extraverts would even further reduce their likelihood of acquiring anti-social behaviour and hence increase persistence of anti-social acts. Similarly difficulties are reported in studies of anxiety in test-taking situations (Sarason 1972).

There is considerable dispute in the experimental literature on the question of the influence of anxiety on response. Anxiety is not synonymous with emotional stability (N), as used here, but there are generally high correlations between measures of neuroticism and anxiety. As Wine (1971) and Sarason (1958, 1972) and Sarason & Johnson (1976) indicate, it is necessary to avoid a simplistic approach. Emotional stability (neuroticism) as measured by Eysenck is theoretically separable into two components: arousal (the automatic component) and worry (the cognitive component). The two in fact correlate highly — those who are easily aroused tend to worry more, but they are in principle capable of separation. That separation was undertaken (Lane 1976) for pupils who persistently failed to respond to therapy, and it was found that while the persistently failing showed the arousal levels of a control group, they worried significantly (.05) less about, for example, what other people thought of them.

They did not worry enough for such an opinion to have an effect, so too low a level can be a component of continuation of failure.

Wine (1971), working on the problem of anxiety in test-taking situations, has also demonstrated that these two components need to be considered, but argues that it is too much worry which is debilitating to performance. So, at either extreme, the worry factor can be related to failure, but obviously for different reasons.

Sarason (1972) has argued on the basis of considerable evidence, that highly test-anxious individuals are badly affected by achievement or evaluation instructions, and the knowledge that their failure will be reported. On the other hand, under neutral conditions, they do somewhat better, and under reassuring or task-oriented conditions, they may perform in a superior fashion to those with low levels of test anxiety.

Sarason & Johnson (1976) have shown that combined impact of life changes (stress) and the individual's position on the anxiety dimension have to be taken into account. How the individual's views change, negatively or positively, affects response to it . A jump from test anxiety to emotional instability cannot be directly made, but the results of the data are similar and make it necessary to consider the individual's basic (trait) level of emotional responsiveness, the particular (state) situations the individual is likely to encounter and their evaluation (definition) of the situation.

The L factor

The L (lie score) is not a personality dimension and its influence remains to be clarified. Low lie scores are consistently found in groups showing certain types of behaviour problems (conduct disorders) and high scores in other groups (the psychotic).

The personality components have proved controversial but are central to Eysenck's theory. They are fortunately easy to measure and therefore can be incorporated into research on remission.

Spontaneous Remission — conclusion

In spite of all the arguments over Eysenck's concept of spontaneous remission, it is now generally accepted that the effect (but by no means the explanation or the precise level) is genuine and, as Malan et.al., (1968) point out, the case for a high rate of spontaneous remission in neurotic disorders is proved, '..... and that is the end of it' (see Rachman and Wilson, 1980, for a more recent review). A crucial point is then established in understanding remission. But there are unfortunately limits to the value of this view for our present endeavour.

The spontaneous remission argument was concerned with 'neurotic' disorders. It had lacked extension into factors affecting remission in a wide range of other disorders. However, Topping (1983) has looked at the argument and extended it into the field of disruptive behaviour in school. He examined twenty one systems for dealing with disruptive behaviour. He has made the case for differential effect between behaviours, but still considers it appropriate to apply the concept, certainly in respect of outcome studies. The variety in findings in the literature on children continues to present difficulties, as a very recent review indicates (Callias 1990). The validity of the concept has also, sometimes unnecessarily, been tied in with the particular Eysenckian personality and conditioning conception of behaviour which, as Berger (1977) remarks, 'has given rise to some dispute'. The independence of the personality and conditioning theories can be maintained although they are twin pillars of Eysenck's position.

CHAPTER FOUR

The effectiveness of psychotherapy

Introduction

This chapter considers the debate on psychotherapy. The major difficulties with the conventional outcome literature resulted in a move in the earlier Impossible Child studies (Lane 1978) towards considering process for individuals, rather than between therapies. Alternative approaches such as this have subsequently been recommended by other researchers. (Rachman & Wilson 1980)

The ineffectiveness of psychotherapy?

In a number of papers from 1952 onwards, Eysenck examined evidence related to the effectiveness of psychotherapy. He underlined the difficulties inherent in such a task and cautioned against evaluations being regarded as precise comparisons. Nevertheless his conclusions, although widely debated, attacked or dismissed, have in large measure been supported by subsequent experimental findings, although it is now accepted that his argument needs modification, as outlined above.

In a review of counselling and psychotherapy, Colby (1964) concluded that 'chaos prevails', a remark paralleled by Rogers (1963) in his observation that the field was 'in a mess', and underpinning Eysenck's assault on psychotherapies. Carkhuff and Berenson (1967) took the argument further and exposed a whole series of 'myths' surrounding therapy, the chief one being that therapy was 'most likely' to rehabilitate the troubled person. Rather, they likened therapy to a life-saving game in which the life-savers (therapists) had not learnt to swim, in spite of elaborate training and techniques; thus they could not help because they could not, in similar circumstances, help themselves. This attack on the 'technique of therapy' was echoed by Goldstein (1971) in a major review of psychotherapeutic attraction.

> In our view, psychotherapy as generally practised has long included major efficiency-reducing trappings, that is procedures and conceptualisations embedded in clinical lore, which are largely or totally irrelevant to patient change. This belief is fostered by remarkable similarities in reported improvement rates across therapeutic approaches — approaches differing widely in purported techniques. (Goldstein 1971)

Rachman's (1971) review of the evidence on the effectiveness of psychotherapy concluded that, in general, it was not effective: since that date numerous reviews have appeared, many partial, poorly controlled, or simply irrelevant. Unfortunately, the vested interests of opposing groups have led, not to careful evaluation, but rather to 'evaluation war'.

The most influential major review (Smith & Glass 1977) is superior to most but not without its faults. It covers 375 studies and demonstrates that about 10% of the variance in outcome is due to allocation to treatment or non-treatment groups. Given the costs involved in therapy, this seems a disappointingly low figure. It also suggests a slight advantage to behavioural methods. However, the divisions between verbal and behavioural therapies covered by the authors is crude. Thus, eclectic, rational-emotive and psychoanalytic methods are grouped as verbal. Yet, almost by definition, eclectic therapists use some behavioural methods, as do rational-emotive therapists. (See for example, Carkhuff & Berenson 1967, and Ellis & Greiger 1977). The average follow-up for the 375 studies was three and a half months. The lack of adequate long-term studies makes any conclusion on remission dubious, but widespread and substantial effectiveness is not established. It does however, in line with other studies, indicate a small beneficial effect from treatment (Ellis & Greiger 1977), at least in the short term.

There has been sustained criticism of the Smith and Glass study, for example by Rachman and Wilson (1980), but their more positive view on therapy effectiveness is also echoed in the Rachman and Wilson review. Research with children's problems has also begun to point to beneficial effects. A major report by a Newcastle team (Kolvin et.al., 1981) demonstrated effects over and above 'spontaneous remission' for some therapies. In a forthcoming chapter, Callias (1990) presents a picture which is also more positive than could have been possible a decade earlier. Topping's (1983) review in particular provided evidence that some things do work. However, it was to support systems which operate on school change and not just individual change that he awarded top marks.

The extreme pessimism of Eysenck's original study is gradually giving way. That this has taken so long is remarkable.

The cry for more detailed research extends from Eysenck (1952) through the hypothesis above and into Shapiro's (1980) plea for more precise and sophisticated research strategies ... to identify the therapeutic ingredients of the psychotherapies (*deja vu?*). To the practitioner seeking guidance by reading the research, the disputes between verbal and behavioural therapies (Shapiro 1980) and within behaviour therapy (Marzillier 1980) must make it appear that "chaos still rules".

The limitations in the outcome studies which perpetuate the idea that only one thing works or nothing works have given rise to the idea that specific therapies be applied to specific needs. This view is not without its advocates, perhaps motivated by a 'natural' tendency to wish that the conflict between the schools be resolved by 'taking the best of each'! The major attempts at such an accommodation are to be found in the eclectic schools (Truax & Carkhuff 1966 and Carkhuff & Berenson 1967) and the burgeoning of alternative multi-modal or eclectic theories. The recent excellent series of texts on different methods of psychotherapy practised in Britain (Open University Press) are testament to this. In the barrage of ideas, Shapiro's (1980) plea for 'precise specification of interventions singly or in combination, maximally effective for given populations', should not be lost. However, while the idea of matching need with therapy is appealing, it is necessary for the advocate to demonstrate certain points.

1. **That such specific needs exist** — there is no point in establishing elaborate matching programmes if no specific gain beyond the 'general therapeutic effect' of any therapy is apparent.

2. **That it is possible to determine specific clinical needs** — the realistic consideration of which client groups may benefit from a given therapy is confused by disputes over the whole basis of problem classification itself (Krasner & Ullman 1973).

3. **That is possible to match need and technique** — few attempts, rather than 'assertions', at such an approach are available, although elaborate matching studies have appeared. Goldstein (1971) and his associates have demonstrated the effectiveness of a range of procedures for therapist/client matching, which are successful with student counselling populations, but not in clinical settings. However, as Meyer and Turkat (1980) argue, the literature is devoid of any clarity on methods of choosing a match between client and techniques. A serious attempt to take account of individual differences was advocated by Eysenck and Gudjonsson (1989), but they can point to little research to support such a position.

4.   **That multimodal approaches to therapy are more effective** — Rachlin (1977) and Greenspoon and Lamel (1978) have argued that the superiority of behavioural methods make additions unnecessary. Marzillier (1980) takes a less dogmatic view but, in commenting on disputes about the addition of cognitive methods of behaviour therapy, questions whether or not there is any good evidence for or against. He concludes that....'there quite simply isn't any'. Marzillier's view has not prevented a flood of interest in cognitive-behavioural approaches, but recent reviewers still make the same plea for a determination of which methods work best with which clients under what conditions (Dryden and Golden, 1986).

To the point made by Dryden and Golden could be added the issue of differences in rates of remission by type of problem. That psychotherapies vary in effectiveness with different problem areas, has been a consistent finding since the early therapy studies.

Distinctions between behaviours in rates of remission

There is considerable dispute over the validity of diagnostic grouping for childhood, an issue taken up previously. Discussion of difference in rates of response is somewhat confounded by differences in diagnosis between studies. The broad distinction between neurotic and conduct disorders is widely, although not universally, accepted. Studies using such categories have, however, produced consistent findings.

Something of the same heated criticism which attached to Eysenck's accounts of psychotherapy with adults greeted the publication by Levitt (1963) of results obtained for psychotherapy on approximately 8000 children. The same conclusion applied: that those children who received psychotherapy did no better than those who did not, and that about 70%, with or without treatment, remitted in about two years. Criticism of the work followed (see Rachman 1971). This was duly answered and subsequent replication by other workers substantially supported Levitt's conclusions. A later paper, however, provides analysis of outcome within diagnostic categories. Levitt (1983) concluded that the improvement rate with therapy was lowest for cases of delinquency and anti-social acting out, and highest for cases of behavioural symptoms, such as enuresis and school phobia.

Similar findings have been reported by other workers. For example, Hare (1966) found that the neurotic did best, while those with conduct disorders had an unfavourable outcome. Warren (1965) ranked outcomes in order, from neurotic, mixed disorders, conduct disorders, to the psychotic. David et al (1968) conclude their follow-up study by confirming that the main factor determining outcome is not the specific therapy used but rather the behaviour to be treated. A variety of other views and studies provide further general agreement on this point (e.g. Robbins 1966, Gossett et al 1973, Kolvin 1981, Topping 1983).

In the very important and classic thirty year follow up of children who received child guidance, Robbins (1966) demonstrated not only a clearly different outcome for children originally referred for anxiety-type reactions to those referred for anti-social disorders, but also that anti-social behaviour in childhood was predictive of disorders in adult life. Further support for Robbin's conclusions comes from a study by Dowling (1978) of transfer from junior to secondary schools. He found that anti-social behaviours were more persistent than neurotic types.

The strength of such associations has given rise to the idea that 'nothing predicts behaviour like behaviour'. A number of studies which have looked at this concept, have generally supported it, but with reservations. (Dowling 1978). This aspect will be considered in more detail later.

The clear differences which emerge from the types of disorders give some support to the possible explanation that certain behaviours themselves might be more difficult to change. This might interact with response to conditioning (the issue raised by Eysenck). It would therefore be argued that neurotics and neurotic behaviour condition more readily. This would help explain high spontaneous remission rates for neurotic disorders. It would be difficult to explain the variation simply as lack of conditionability, since even with emotional disorders interactive effects will occur. For example, in emotional disorders will be found anxiety states with a high level of conditionability and also conditions with a strong historical component, in which conditionability was lower. It is necessary then to consider conditionability, as argued previously, but also to go beyond this and look for clues to other features which may later be important in remission.

Predictions from behaviour — specific or general

One study only will be considered in this section, since its findings reflect the literature fairly well and, as it does represent a follow-up study of children, is directly relevant to the present endeavour.

Dowling(1978), in a study of 400+ children followed from primary to secondary school, set out to determine how accurately one could predict which children would have adjustment problems after transfer. Information from tests, questions and rating were compared with outcome variables of behaviour, attitudes to school and attendance. The data were analysed in terms of each of nine predictor variables, in forecasting each of the criterion variables. The efficiency of the predictors in combination was evaluated. It was found that predictive accuracy was generally low. Of the four criteria, attendance was predicted most accurately, with 49% of the variance accounted for. Least accurately predicted was attitude to school. The inclusion of more than one prediction variable did little to improve the accuracy of the predictions. Behaviour in the primary school was the best single predictor of teachers' ratings of behaviour after transfer. Sex (male) and primary school attendance were the best predictors of attitude to school and secondary attendance respectively.

In their study Pumfey and Ward (quoted in Dowling 1978) found that an initial measure of behaviour was the best predictor and little was gained by including more than a few variables. He also provided definite support for Robbins (1966) regarding the differential prognosis of neurotic and anti-social behaviour: anti-social behaviours were more persistent than neurotic types. Some support was found for Clarizio's (1968) view that only profound disorders predict later dysfunction reasonably well, in that all children with severe problems had difficulty following transfer. West (1977) has also found that combining predictions added very little, with behaviour being the best single predictor of later outcome.

Dowling concludes that the accuracy of prediction is too low to identify 'at risk' groups, but it does suggest that more diligent monitoring by secondary teachers would be useful. Some schools do pick up those needing support, but others do not. He suggests that simple screening devices added to teacher monitoring would assist the process.

Conclusion

An overwhelmingly large literature on the effects of psychotherapy has emerged as a result of Eysenck's original paper. Depressingly, many of the same arguments which featured in the response to its publication remain to be fought over, nearly forty years later.

Certainly there have been modifications and progress, but the current range of critiques of the Smith and Glass study leaves little reason for optimism. Individual therapy, it appears, still contributes relatively little to change but some modest progress has been made. Difficulties of conduct remain as highly resistant to therapeutic endeavours. Fortunately, our children do not have to wait for another decade of therapy research for, as has been increasingly demonstrated in the interim, schools matter and policy matters (Rutter et.al.,1979).

Perhaps the position for behaviour is as it was for medicine and it is to public/policy effects and not individual therapies that we must look. But for the individual the key to change may still lie in those fortuitous events which stimulate 'spontaneous' remission. Understanding them in conjunction with change events in schools may provide the most powerful structure for change for the Impossible Child. Recent detailed studies of patterns of learning have emerged and, particularly in the last ten years, have lost the sense of tiredness which accompanied their previous status of 'received' wisdom (Martin 1988).

Learning theory has begun to open up and expand. Skinner is questioned and, as Rachlin (1976) points out, the 'organism' at the centre of the experiment has been rediscovered. A change in view is perhaps reflected in the recommended description of individuals taking part in research as participants, not as subjects. (British Psychological Society, 1989) The person at the centre of the endeavour is beginning to be seen.

Personality trait theories and their relationship to behaviour also seem to have re-emerged as a viable area of study, after some years in the wilderness, as Marriage (1981) has remarked and Ajzen (1988) has more recently confirmed. But it is a less dogmatic theory and one which incorporates the social with the individual. The role of personality in disorder and remission was featured in the data laid down for the follow-up studies of the Impossible Child even though at that time personality theory had wilted under the assault of situation-specific, behavioural studies.

Nevertheless, in spite of the more positive and broadly based debate which shows signs of emerging, no really substantial answers have been offered towards answering Rachman's (1971) plea for the 'identification of restorative events and the manner in which they affect the process of remission'. The concept remains a live issue, despite its age.

All the studies we have looked at on spontaneous remission and psychotherapies represent a direct outcome of the dispute, but a number of by-products have also been stimulated by the discussion. One of these, and by far the most direct product of the dispute, is the concept that the behaviour itself is the most predictive indication of the outcome. A second area, less directly related, concerns the concept of multiple stress. The debate over psychotherapy certainly exposed the difficulties inherent in single causal explanations and multiple stress theories have recently emerged from the general vague label of 'multi-causal' into more precise concepts, such as Stott's 'multiple congenital impairment'.

The next chapter looks at these somewhat overlapping by-products.

CHAPTER FIVE

Multiple environmental stress in the study of failure

Discord and disturbance?

It is claimed that there is evidence for the validity of broad categories of disorders in children (Rutter, 1977). A brief look at some of these categories of disorders suggests that there may be different correlations for the disorders and thus it may not simply be the diagnosis which is relevant to outcome, but also features associated with it. Just one example of this is that, for children, family discord and disruption have been found to be associated with disturbances of conduct (Rutter & Madge 1976), while they are not particularly associated with emotional disturbances (Bennett 1960, Wardle 1961, Rutter 1971). Other examples are available for other conditions: see for example studies reviewed in Rutter and Hersov (1977), Hersov, Berger and Shaffer (1978), Wall (1979), and Trasler and Farrington (1979).

Rutter (1977) argues that: although there is a far from one-to-one association between family background and type of child psychiatric disorders, family features do differentiate significantly between emotional disturbances, hyperkineses and conduct disorders (which are rather similar to background) infantile autism and schizophrenia.

It appears then that, since disorders which differ in rates of remission may also have different correlates, the study of such correlates may be of help in explaining the difference in rates. An earlier review of the literature (Lane 1983), certainly supported Rutter's perspective.

Two issues arise from this factor, relevant to the issue of remission.

1) If certain behaviours (i.e. conduct disorders) are predictive of later disorder, how specific is that prediction? This was the issue raised in the previous chapter.

2) If, as Rutter (1977) suggests, certain environmental correlates separate disorders, would specific correlates be found more often in disorders having low rates of remission?

The task in both cases is complicated by the fact that, although the literature on correlation of disorder is vast, far fewer long-term studies have been undertaken which help to unravel the conflicting components. Additionally, definitions of disorders vary from study to study, and there is certainly not total agreement on the importance of a given factor. Nevertheless, the pattern of correlates for disorders is certainly worth further study.

Environmental correlates of failure

Certain demographic factors consistently appear in the literature across a range of disorders. Characteristics such as age, sex, social class, family community and school are frequently mentioned as cause and effect (Wall 1979). The actual role of these elements however, is a matter of some dispute, and traditionally respected notions of the relationship of, say, failure and social class are now under attack (Stott et.al.,1975). Aspects were taken up at different points above, and were reviewed elsewhere (Lane 1978). Some preliminary conclusions are in order.

Age — There are considerable deviations in patterns across age groups for certain behaviours. Some are time-located, while others occur and recur at different points. This makes any comparisons and predictions difficult. However, since some behaviours may be more persistent than others (Stott 1971), an understanding of such variations is necessary.

Sex — Gender differences in behaviour are among the most consistent in the literature. Throughout a range of problems, physical, learning and behaviour, gender rates differ. Of particular note is the tendency of boys to predominate in certain categories such as conduct disorders, particularly aggressive behaviours. (Roland 1988). The few girls who also exhibit such patterns are therefore of particular interest.

Social class — Until recently, it was generally assumed that social class was significantly associated with specific patterns of disorder. While such correlations exist, doubt has been cast increasingly on the explanations offered (Rutter et al 1970). Additionally, the social class differences discovered in some studies are small, in terms of their relationship to severe disorder, not significant (Stott 1971). Particular care in the interpretation of social class variables is therefore necessary.

Family — Differences in family interaction has long been argued as an important factor in disorder. The issue is complicated, however, by the differences in such effects between boys and girls: boys seem to be more affected. No simple relationships therefore exist. A persistent finding is correlation between size of family, school failure and behaviour problems; although again, this is partly confounded by differences between the sexes.

Community — A variety of community studies have in the past stressed the relationship between neighbourhood and conduct. More recently, the broad assumptions of 'contagion' effects within particular areas have been questioned.

School — The role of the school in preventing or creating failure has belatedly taken its place as an area of study, and few could now deny it a central role.

Many of the assumptions generally held on the relationship between disorder and demographic factors are now being questioned. Even those that remain are confounded by other variables. Nevertheless, studies within these areas give rise to a major alternative theoretical position on disorder and remission, and that it is the concept of multiple stress impairment. Stott (1975), Wall (1979), Rutter (1978) and Brown and Madge (1982) in different ways and from a different base, all propose similar explanations.

The concept of multiple stress

If one general conclusion is possible it is that disorders that have a poor long-term outcome relate to a variety of stresses rather than to any single cause (Wall 1979). Yet even this comprehensive and consequently not very enlightening finding is in large measure an assumption, since the data is very limited. For although we have some idea of the factors which correlate with disorders of poor outcome, we have less idea of maintaining elements; and we have virtually no idea at all of the events which can redirect the 'star-crossed' child from his fate. Nevertheless, the idea of 'multiple stressors' which in different ways they all present, represents a key concept as a potential explanation of remission or its lack. One would presumably argue that individuals facing multiple stresses were not only more likely than those with single stresses to have disorders, but also were less likely to recover from them.

Stott's large-scale study of conduct disorders produced evidence for his concept of multiple impairment. Because of the importance of this concept, these conclusions are quoted in some detail. Stott and his associates, using the BSAG, studied approximately 2500 school pupils across the age and cultural range. The conclusions of the study are as follows:

1. **Sex** — Maladjustment was preponderant amongst males but this was restricted entirely to the overactive form, the score being twice that for girls. Underactive disorders were also more common in boys, although not significantly so. This difference cannot be explained simply in cultural terms, since although it is assumed that aggressive behaviour is permitted or encouraged in boys, the same cannot be said of withdrawal, which was also twice as common.

43

2. **Age** — No trend in under-reactive disorders by age were noted. The behaviours indicating under-reactive maladjustment were remarkably consistent, irrespective of age. Over-reactive behaviours also changed much less than many would expect. The expectations were that older pupils would tend to get on with age peers and gain more control of aggressive responses to frustration, but also to become more hostile and domineering.

3. **Social class** — A trend was noted for disturbance to be at higher rates, the lower the social class of the individual. This only barely reached significance when the highest and lowest class category were compared and was most particularly marked in the 5-8 year group among girls and confined to the severest category. Thus, no general social class maladjustment tendency as a cultural artifact was apparent; a congenital adverse post natal environment seems a more realistic explanation.

4. **Urban/rural** — Rural children were better adjusted than urban children, although this only reached significance for over-reactivity amongst boys. This could not be accounted for by social class difference since rural incomes were generally lower.

5. **Ill-health** — A pronounced tendency was found for maladjustment and ill-health to go together. This, together with other data, demonstrated an interrelationship of disease, mental retardation and temperamental impairment. The most feasible explanation for this is that behavioural and somatic impairment share a common congenital origin with a determinant for each of the main forms of maladjustment.

6. **Motor impairment** — A consistent relationship was found between motor impairment and maladjustment (particularly inconsequence).

7. **Delinquency** — Similarities in degree of maladjustment, irrespective of social class among delinquents, casts doubts on the cultural theory of delinquency.

On the basis of this considerable data, Stott argues for the impact of multiple congenital impairment in behaviour problems. This is supported by the fact that the least healthy show between two and four times as much maladjustment. The common origin of the physical and the psychological is seen as one of neurological dysfunction.

Rutter (1978) has summarised various environmental influences in the genesis of conduct disorder. From his series of epidemeological studies, he concluded that environmental factors are multiple and interact with such features as genetic vulnerability and personality characteristics of the child. Single chronic stresses are seen as unimportant, the damage coming from multiple stress interacting with constitutional features to potentiate each other's influence. Thus, the reasons why some children improve and others do not would seem to lie in the balance of good and bad influences experienced by the child in the process of development. Wall (1979), reviewing a wider basis of evidence in several areas of handicap, makes a similar observation.

Any attempt to relate these concepts in a follow-up study of behaviour disorder raises certain concerns. Firstly, many disorders are defined solely as behaviour present beyond the developmentally normal time. Secondly, the same behaviour may take on a different prognosis at different stages; some learning problems will have a good prognosis in young children but not in adolescence. Thirdly, the same behaviour is defined differently by age. For example, stealing is non-criminal in young children. These discrepancies would make it difficult to identify factors of influence independent of diagnosis.

Perhaps one can put the case no more strongly than this: certain areas, additional to the traditional concerns of family, community and school, appear to be candidates for a role in remission from disorder. Within a framework of a theory of multiple impairment and stress the main candidates are:

genetic vulnerability, brain damage/neurological signs, multiple congenital impairments, temperamental problems early in childhood, conduct disorders at school, learning difficulties at school, family discord, a specific disorder and criminality in the parents, poor peer relationships, and pattern of onset (Lane, 1983).

These features may have been correlated with the occurrence of disorders in a number of studies but their exact role is uncertain. They may act as predisposing factors making acquisition more likely. Whether they additionally have a role in the maintenance of these behaviours is less clear, given Yule's (1978), point that factors involved in maintenance and in acquisition may be quite distinct. It is nevertheless valid to argue that multiple environmental stresses do provide a potential explanation for why some children improve and others do not. That explanation lies in the concept of balance of good and bad influences, (Rutter 1978). One can conclude with Wall (1979), that there are few cases where one cause predominates: much more common is a combination of small impediments acting like 'straws on the proverbial camel's back'. Wall adds an important observation which serves to question premature attempts to link specific predispositions with outcome. It is, he states,

.... one of the most striking facts to come from the research — that almost any combination of adverse factors may be associated with failure, or be found in success: indeed, the only difference which can be fully established is that failing children have in the background, on the average, more adverse factors than do successful children.

Difficulties remain, but at this stage it is clear that the multiple stresses encountered by the child must be considered, as must the relationship between the behaviour seen and later outcome. The problem lies in interpreting the interplay of these features, so that some movement can be made towards meeting Rachman's plea for understanding of life-events and the process of remission. Some preliminary points are now considered.

Fortuitous life events and the process of remission

During the life history of an individual, change often takes place in small ways at given, possibly critical, moments. The literature on such critical moments is notable by its absence. It seems reasonable to argue, as does Wall (1979), that a balance of good and bad influences may be at work, but a clear picture of such influences is missing.

We are in a situation where the pressure of deficits of an environment may or may not be matched by the resources that the individual can mobilise for himself, i.e. his assets, like general level of ability, or by resources that can be mobilised for him by those who make up his human environment. If the threshold of difficulty is low and the resources reasonably high, then the balance will move to success: if the threshold of difficulty is high and the resources are low, then failure will accumulate. (Wall 1979)

A research model in which tests are administered at given intervals fails to identify these fortuitous events. It will only point to general correlations (Davis et.al.,1972, Rutter et.al.,1970, Osborn and West 1979). Similarly, while clinical case studies can often elicit factors of influence at a given moment, the follow-up period is usually so short and objective evaluation so limited, that the wider range factors impinging on the client is lost. The understanding of fortuitous events requires the combination of an intimate knowledge of the case study and the time-scale and objective test of longitudinal research. Outside of a vastly financed national project, such understanding is probably only possible on the basis of the cumulative record of practitioners who maintain contacts with their clients over many years. Such records are few.

Interest in this type of research has increased, although it remains a relatively unpopular area of study. The potential that might be discovered in such cumulative records makes it a valuable endeavour. The key to understanding critical moments in the life history of an individual and relating that experience to the broader question of remission, may lie in the use of such records to test theoretical models. Thus concepts of personality and multiple stress could be examined in the light of a life history. For example, the question could be asked as to whether changes in the level of stress experienced led to any change in behaviour. By asking such questions repeatedly, over a series of cases, clues as to the impact of fortuitous events might emerge.

The life histories of individuals also serve to remind us that, in the maze of concepts presented, the central figure of the child in need remains.

The problem, as far as this study is concerned, is to link case-study material and experimental test. It is attempted by specifying points of change and any corresponding life events. But before getting there we must chart the more familiar waters of inferential statistics.

Conclusion

This section of the book originally posed a question: 'What do we need to consider if the process by which some children who present behavioural problems improve and other do not, is to be understood ?'

There appear to be three main areas of interest.

1. The influence of predisposing factors: these include arguments on the influence of personality and the role of multiple stress.

2. Certain behaviours seem more resistant to change: the fact that behaviours do vary indicates that some seem more prone to spontaneous remission.

3. Subsequent events influence progress: the concept of fortuitous events does appear worth exploration, although therapy appears to be of variable influence.

Certain themes emerge to provide potential theoretical models of remission, These will have to form the initial core of the research data for the Impossible Child. These themes are:

4. the view that behaviour is its own best predictor of future events.

5. the existence of various environmental correlates of disorder, giving rise to the concept of multiple stress.

6. the idea that there are differences in conditionability to which specific personality features contribute.

Each of these areas is explored in the next section. Those which stand up are further examined using follow-up data. Finally, fortuitous moments in time are explored, drawing together ideas on labelling and belief systems with the experimental data. A model is thus built of the Impossible Child's impossibility and from that, a model for working with the child can be developed, presented, demonstrated and evaluated.

There are then a range of factors which need to be addressed if we are to understand the Impossible Child. But it must never be forgotten that the participants in this study are all individual children, with individual perspectives. As Wall (1979) remarks, 'Some children seem hopelessly star-crossed from the start.'

Yet, in spite of this, some children make it. Why? It is hoped that, at least in the limited case of the children in this study, this question can here be unravelled. But, we should remember that without waiting around for us, many of the children did break the label and undermine the myth.

CHAPTER SIX

Predicting the behaviour of the impossible child

'What does an Impossible Child do exactly?'

The Impossible Child has been defined according to research-based criteria but, as the teacher quoted in the heading points out, this does not give an impression of the behaviour. Unfortunately, doing so is difficult. Patterns of behaviour which were described by teachers as examples of the difficulties they faced and listing them might provoke some sympathy for the teachers but it would not take us very far. Nevertheless, it may be useful to create some sense of the pattern, before presenting a more considered view.

This will be provided in three ways. The behaviours exhibited by groups of children will be discussed, the concept of the 'game' will be introduced and the idea of philosophical boundaries (sore spots) will be explored.

Patterns of behaviour in problem groups.

Defining a child's behaviour according to the norms of a test is convenient for a research study. The teacher, however, is not dealing with norms but with behaviours which make the running of the daily business of the classroom more difficult. So what we need is a picture of some of these behaviours.

We begin by reviewing the referral forms for three groups of children (25 per group), in order to look at the behaviour categories for which they were referred.

Group A consisted of pupils presenting difficulties sufficient for the Educational Psychologist for the school to be asked to give an opinion.

Group B consisted of those referred for assistance to the Islington Educational Guidance Centre for conduct problems.

Group C consisted of pupils referred to the Centre who carried the additional label Impossible.

(Some of the pupils in Group A were subsequently referred to the Centre but not under a conduct problem label.)

The behaviours for all groups were very varied but could be grouped into those behaviours concerned with work difficulties, such as concentration problems, behaviour problems which were described as disruptive, those related to emotional or medical problems, non attendance/lateness, fighting/bullying, and compliance problems (abuse, rudeness, anti-authority responses or failure to comply with teacher requests).

The number in the referral lists for each behaviour was calculated.

Number of behaviours in each category for pupils referred

Group	A	B	C
Work difficulties	28	21	26
Disruptive	22	40	20
Emotional/Medical	14	3	0
Non attendance	13	5	5
Fighting/Bullying	4	8	15
Compliance problems	2	16	30
totals	**83**	**93**	**96**
Mean	3.3	3.7	3.8

In terms of average number of behaviours per child referred there is very little to choose between them. In terms of pattern, however, those who were seen but not referred to the centre had work difficulties plus disruption as the largest grouping. Those referred but not regarded as impossible, were presenting work difficulties and higher levels of disruptive behaviours. Those in the impossible group were presenting work difficulties and disruption but compliance problems represented the largest grouping.

It would appear that failure to comply is the distinguishing feature of the impossible group. The overall level of difficulty is little different from the other pupils referred.

Disaffection, disruption, disorganisation and the 'Game'.

In an earlier study (Lane, 1973) of children presenting problems in school, the motivation for behaving in accordance with school rules was considered. It was argued that some children would need little reinforcement for conforming to school rules since they would have internalised the value system of the school. They would believe in it. For others, disaffected with their life in school, there would be little to be gained from conformity with the social order. They might be persuaded to conform if it was 'made worth their while' but otherwise disaffection would lead to disruption or withdrawal.

However, disruption is not too much of a problem: you can predict, within reasonable limits, its occurrence in the school system. Since you can predict it, you can create rules to manage it. Schools will vary on the type of rules they impose and the sanctions possible, but as long as the behaviour is predictable, it should be containable within that framework (Lane, 1980, 1989).

What happens if the behaviour falls outside of the rules? If the rules provide for a general purpose response they might be used. But if the behaviour displayed is simply beyond the teacher's experience and yet is not so bizarre as to attract a 'medical' label, how might the teacher respond?

To clarify this, let us look at two examples that caused teachers concern.

Winston aged 13, was referred by his school for violent and impulsive outbursts towards teachers and peers. He would run around the classroom, refuse to carry out instructions, not complete set work, and fight with other pupils. This obviously presented problems for the school but the behaviour was at least covered by the rules. He did other things which were less extreme but presented more of a problem. He would dance on the tables in lessons in which he was bored, much to the amusement of other pupils. (He was a talented dancer.) He would refuse to go to the school's punishment class when asked, but would go there when not asked. Thus a teacher seeking to discipline him in accordance with the rules would find the procedure hindered by the fact that he was pleading to be punished.

Peter, aged 15, had a very high IQ score, certainly above that of all but a few of his teachers. He was also very disruptive in class. According to practice in the school, a pupil could only maintain a place in the top set if both work and behaviour were satisfactory. Peter had gradually sunk to the lower sets. He had caused some difficulty by wearing earrings to school. (This was before the days when it was fashionable.) He had been suspended for doing so, but successfully appealed on the grounds that no school rule existed forbidding boys to wear earrings. The school solved the problem another way but he regarded it as a victory.

A more difficult problem was presented by Peter's use of reinforcement principles to shape teachers' behaviour. He had picked up the idea that if you consistently smile or show an interest in what someone is doing in response to specific behaviours, you will shape these behaviours. He used this idea to persuade a group of pupils to show an interest in the work of a student teacher only when he was standing in a particular place in the room. Very quickly they discovered that they could determine in advance where they would get the teacher to stand. They also discovered that the effect was not restricted to student teachers. How do you punish children for smiling and taking an interest in the work?

The pupils were not being disruptive exactly but they were causing substantial disorganisation. These represent just two examples in a long list of behaviours which, although not extreme, had a profoundly disorganising effect on teacher morale and the classroom.

How might the effect of such a pattern be explained?

The sociologist Cohen (1959) has referred to the fact that a sociology of social disorganisation may be independent of a sociology of deviance. A behaviour may be deviant (as in the disruptive behaviours of the groups above) but that does not necessarily mean that disorganisation of the classroom will result. Cohen provides the example of a game. It has rules, and those rules define the game. Things happen in accordance with the rules. Nevertheless, the rules will specify what happens if someone breaks the rules. There might be a penalty or, in extreme cases, someone might be sent off. But, since these acts of deviance are in fact predicted by the rules, they are themselves game events and do not cause the game to be disorganised. But if someone walks off with the ball, the only ball, the game is disorganised. The rules do not provide for a situation in which the game might be played without the ball.

Disorganisation in this sense can occur in any social setting including the classroom. The conditions most likely to give rise to disorganisation occur when the '... situations the participants confront cannot be defined as system events or when there is no clear definition of the constitutive possibilities of action' (Cohen, 1959). They also occur when the participants are not motivated to play the game.

It is those behaviours which have the potential for disorganisation which are seen as most irritating to teachers. 'It may not seem very much but it is driving me up the wall!' The accumulation of those events likely to lead to disorganisation is perhaps the defining feature of the 'compliance' pattern for the groups described above.

Putting your finger on the sore spots.

There is another, equally difficult aspect of the concept of disorganisation which might be relevant to the Impossible Child.

What happens when the game players no longer know what to do or the umpires cannot agree? The game breaks down in a mess. In working with many of the pupils referred, one theme which emerged was the difficulty presented by those pupils who created conflict between staff. It was usually obvious. A staff member would refer to a child as a 'perfect example of what happens when ...'. It would not be until you spoke to another member of staff that you realised that the 'perfect example' in fact referred to that member's philosophy of teaching. What was being witnessed was a conflict played out between staff through the particular child. 'Putting a finger on the sore spots' at the boundaries of system behaviours and philosophies, seemed to be something the Impossible Child was very good at.

Getting a sense of 'what exactly' it is that the Impossible Child did is not easy. Explaining it is even less easy, but when it confronted you in your classroom, you certainly knew it was there.

Inadequate through they might be, the more traditional classifications of the behaviours also require scrutiny.

Provisional findings for the Impossible Child

Over a period of years a data pool of pupils, parents and teachers was constructed, based on samples of children from schools in different areas both urban and rural. This data pool, which eventually reached over 3,000, provided the source for a number of studies for the provisional research on the Impossible Child. Details of these groups are contained in earlier research reports (Lane, 1976, 1978, 1983).

The research review raised questions about the level/type of behaviour difficulty, its duration, the children's views of themselves and their response to therapy. Each is described below.

1. Level of difficulty on the Bristol Social Adjustment Guide (BSAG)

The definition of the Impossible Child originally used included the score obtained by the pupil on BSAG. Of course, before using those criteria, the pattern of scoring actually found in pupils labelled as impossible had to be established. Therefore, a sample of sixty pupils defined by their teachers as having various levels of difficulty, was tested on the basis of BSAG scores provided by teachers who knew the pupils well but were not involved in the research project.

The initial findings indicated that on over-reactive behaviours on BSAG, the group of impossible children did score higher than any other group, including pupils seen as having severe but not impossible problems. However, this finding was limited to secondary age boys.

On under-reactive problems they did not score higher than the other groups, and this was true for both boys and girls.

When the syndrome scores were compared, the impossible pupils, both boys and girls, were found to score consistently higher on hostility but not on other dimensions.

It appeared that the Impossible Child was not only more badly behaved but also showed more hostility to adults. It seems that children who are hostile to adults consider them untrustworthy, and that children who have lost faith in their loyalty are more likely to be rated as impossible than other difficult children.

2. Duration of difficulty

Within the initial sample group, only the pupils labelled as impossible could meet the criteria of two years duration for problems plus at least one year of intervention. The case histories of the pupils are particularly revealing.

The impossible group — The majority first presented problems in primary education (40% in infants, 40% in juniors and 20% in secondary). They averaged 4.2 separate professional agency interventions, child guidance and social work being the most common.

The severe group — The majority (70%) of this group first presented problems at secondary school, 30% also causing difficulties in juniors. However, careful review of the school records did reveal that most had some difficulties at an earlier age, but these had not resulted in outside intervention. They averaged 1.3. professional interventions.

The impossible group therefore had problems of longer duration and were presenting (at least the secondary aged boys) higher levels of difficulty, particularly of the hostile type.

Careful study of the case histories, however, does raise some questions. Difficulties were apparent for both severe and impossible groups earlier, but the form of intervention varied. Only some received an outside referral. Did that fact rather than the difficulty impact on how they were later seen?

3. The child's view of his own behaviour

Several preliminary studies of child self-report had been used to explore ways of comparing the teacher's and the child's picture of the events in the classroom. A self report BSAG proved the most effective. The development of the idea is traced in two earlier papers (EGC, 1975, 1984). The possible value of the information can be gauged by taking an example of one child's self-report.

Eric is always ready to answer and willing, but constantly seeks help when he could manage by himself. He is sometimes in a bad mood and avoids the teacher but talks to other children. He likes sympathy but is reluctant to ask, openly does things which he knows are wrong in front of the teacher, but becomes antagonistic in response to correction ... He can stand up for himself, flies into a temper if provoked, gets up to dangerous and foolish pranks when with a gang, but can behave in a well-disciplined manner... He is not as attractive as most, stutters, has headaches...

This abstract from Eric's self-report is notable for a number of features. It does identify difficult behaviours, but it also points to appropriate behaviours. It refers to learning, behaviour and health issues. The picture certainly provides a basis for comparison with the teacher's view, because what is listed is actual examples of behaviour, not generalities. This is in contrast to a number of available measures of children's behaviour problems, which list only negatives and do not provide an opportunity for the child to present an overall picture. The emphasis on behaviours seen rather than on ratings of severity is also helpful.

Discussion with the pupils about these types of reports revealed the fact that they liked them because they were able to list positive aspects and because they could point to examples of what they did. They also frequently added items to the list.

(I have to add that several of our pupils complained about the use of Eric as an example. They did not consider him bad enough, so thought it would give the wrong impression of them.)

An initial comparison of pupil and teacher BSAGs did indicate a reasonable level of agreement and therefore further studies were undertaken by Hymans and Lane (1981, Lane 1984). One of these studies is discussed here.

A sample of 52 pupils (26 boys and 26 girls aged 11 to 15) assessed their own behaviour in the classrooms of specific teachers. Those teachers also assessed the pupils. Correlations (r) were obtained for both over and under-reactive scores. The value for over-reactive scores was significant but not those for under-reaction.

It appears that a reasonable level of agreement between pupils and teachers applies to the more obvious over-reactive types of behaviour, but not for under-active behaviours such as withdrawal and depression. A comparison of the scores for the sub-groupings (syndromes) indicated that both inconsequence and hostility produced significant correlations. Thus the pupils and teachers agree on the levels of impulsive hostile behaviour. The scores on all under-reactive syndromes, unforthcomingness (timidity etc.) withdrawal and depression failed to show a relationship.

This finding has a number of implications for any attempt to develop definitions of a pupil's behaviour based only on teacher report. The idea of looking at possible discrepancy is strengthened. It would be valuable to identity those behaviours which a teacher may not see but which are important to the child, such as depression. It may be very hard for a teacher to recognise that the child who is actively disrupting their class might also be depressed.

Differences in outcome prediction by behaviour

The discussion of the literature had raised a number of questions concerning the extent to which behaviour problems could predict later difficulties, such as delinquency. This possibility has to be explored. It was also previously argued that differences in outcome (remission) would occur by type of behaviour and sex, and this, too, is examined. (For a detailed examination, see Lane, 1983).

Behaviour problems in school and later delinquency.

A sample of 100 pupils (50 boys and 50 girls) from one secondary school were followed over a period of five years. An additional group of fifty pupils identified as being troublesome in school were also followed. Any delinquency notified in a sample of school, welfare and criminal records was recorded. A rate of delinquency of 4% was found in the random group compared with 26% in the problem group. The difference on Chi Square reached significance at the .001 level.

Rates of delinquency by gender.

A random sample of 50 boys and 50 girls from one school (as above) were followed over a five year period and delinquency data collected. The delinquency rate for girls was found to be 4% and for boys 20%. The difference is again significant (Chi Square at .05 level.)

Differential outcome for anxiety and behaviour problems.

The school records of a sample of children were examined for evidence of any record of conduct or anxiety-related problems. It must be noted that no formal diagnosis was made. Specific comments on the behaviour of the children were used to classify them. Thus a child described as becoming panic-stricken when left alone in a room, or as having an abnormal dread of water, even in a sink or laboratory, would be identified as having an anxiety problem. A comment simply referring to an 'anxious child' would not be classified. Similarly, specifically identified behaviour problems led to a classification of 'conduct-disordered'. After a five year period, the records were checked and any repeating comments noted. In 69 cases, records could be used to reclassify the pupils. A recovery rate for anxiety and conduct groups was calculated. The recovery rate for the anxious group was found to be 65% and for the conduct group 31%. (Chi Square at .02)

This finding supports the conclusions of other researchers that conduct disorders show a lower rate of recovery than anxiety problems.

Change in response to therapy

The pattern of change in behaviour problems in relation to therapy was examined in two samples.

Two groups (each of 20 pupils) who had received a three month programme of intervention for behaviour problems were measured on BSAG, prior to therapy, three months later, and again three years later, to see if any improvement continued. All measures were independent of the therapy programme. Of interest to our study is the question of differences in change for the varied syndromes: did some behaviours change more than others?

When improvement occurred it did so across all the syndromes, and where it did not failure was equally global. However, the calculation of a change ratio for each individual item of behaviour on the BSAG revealed that some behaviours showed little evidence of change in response to therapy while others improved substantially. It appeared that when children made progress it tended to result in a global improvement. Nevertheless some behaviours were more resistant or responsive to change than others.

Conclusion

These preliminary studies lend support to a number of previous findings in the literature. The idea that behaviour predicts behaviour receives some support. The specific predictions are more difficult to make, although individual analysis of behaviours may merit further study. The findings on pupil self-report are both useful and confusing. It appears that teachers and pupils can agree about some behaviours but not on others. It is probably safer, therefore, to keep these measures separate for the experimental data, but their role in case-study analysis is likely to prove of considerable interest. A study of remission for the Impossible Child would benefit from the inclusion of varied measures of behaviour problems. Such an approach will be adopted in the later studies.

CHAPTER SEVEN

Multiple stress and the balance of resources

Multiple stress: a preliminary exploration

A variety of theories exist which relate specific factors to disorder. Social class, health, family problems etc. have all found support as exploratory concepts. Multiple stress theories, as we have indicated, have increasingly become preferred to these single factor explanations. Furthermore, the child disadvantaged by a number of individual factors may be more likely to experience particular environmental disadvantages. According to this framework an interactive effect operates: the child least able to cope with stress experiences more of it.

If these concepts are to be of value in understanding the Impossible Child, it is necessary to establish that they are likely to discriminate between those children who present and those who do not present difficulties in school. However, if this is to be of more than academic interest, the factors need to be measured in a way which would be available to teachers and other professionals. It might then be possible to include them in case-study attempts at change. Attempting to construct measures based on available data is never completely satisfactory, but as long as the limitations of the data are respected and extrapolations to other groups are not made, a reasonable test of the multiple stress concept is possible.

This study looks at these explanations in two ways. Firstly, as factors which distinguish groups with, from those without conduct disorders and secondly, as factors which discriminate between those individuals with disorders who improve and those who do not (measured over a ten year period). The sample used was taken from one school, and the pupils cannot be viewed as representing the Impossible Child, but they do represent groups seen as difficult by their school. This will provide the framework for the later study of the Impossible Child.

A sample of factors linked to multiple stress

As Wall (1979) has remarked, the voluminous literature on handicap and disorders of conduct is marked chiefly by the fact that everything has been correlated with everything else. Most theories receive some support and equally, fail to meet someone else's replication criteria. In the field of conduct disorders, two specific factors are fairly consistently reported: gender (boys being more prone to disorder than girls) and behaviour patterns (children with difficulties are more likely to have later difficulties). These two factors were considered in the previous chapter; now we explore selected factors that have generally received support in the literature (Wall's comment notwithstanding).

The areas to be explored include:

Health — based on Stott's (1975) work, it is argued that individuals with conduct disorders tend to have multiple congenital impairments and so would have higher levels of health, sensory or neurological signs of impairment than other children.

Personality — Thomas (et.al., 1968) among others, has pointed out that early indications of temperamental difficulties are associated with disorder.

Social class — this is a frequently cited factor although, as Rutter (et.al., 1970) points out, its role is not as clear-cut as often assumed.

Family factors — Osborn & West (1978) provide clear evidence for the importance of family factors in disorder.

Peer relationships — poor peer relationships have been noted as discriminatory factors marking those with more serious difficulties. (Ullman & Giovanni 1964, Lane 1978).

Siblings — both number of siblings and position in the family are specific features of family factors identified as relating to behaviour.

Each of these factors will be considered:

- to establish whether the single factor is important.
- to see if several factors together relate to disorder.
- to look at the interaction of these factors with certain specific events.
- to look at the factors as a means of discriminating between groups with and without problems.
- to look at the role of the factors in the process of change.

The school sample for multiple stress

The children in this study were all drawn from one school. The sample was in two parts and consisted of:

Sample 1: A random sample of 100 pupils, boys and girls. They were obtained by using a frame of pupils in a school 'house' (that is, a proportional cross-section of the school) from which pupils receiving specialist help for any difficulty had been removed. Thus, the groups contained individuals with difficulties, but not those in special treatment. The group was reduced by random number allocation.

Sample 2: A sample of pupils selected from the same school, consisting of pupils receiving help for any type of conduct disorder. The group consisted of 64 pupils, but the data on three were incomplete and one was randomly excluded to produce a sample of 60. A separate study for those with learning difficulties and remission patterns is in progress. Sample 1 was entitled *random* Sample 2 was entitled *mixed* (conduct).

Collecting data for the samples on the factors listed proved a complicated task. The main problem was the variety of reports available. In particular, the mixed problem group, not unsurprisingly, was more thoroughly reported than the random group. This produced an obvious bias in information load. To overcome this, it was decided to use as a source of information only data contained on standard school files, not the special additional files on some pupils. This had the effect of underestimating difficulties. The other difficulty was the sheer volume of information to sift. Missing data of a factual nature (i.e. number of siblings) was tracked down, but no missing opinions were sought.

It was decided to use a single secondary school for this study since the type of data collected might be highly variable between schools and limit the conclusions possible. Since a random group of pupils was to be used, certain difficulties were likely. The pupils were not necessarily presenting any difficulties and therefore the amount of information contained in the files would be sparse. Comparing sparse files across schools seemed a problematic procedure. Containing the study in one school at least assured the likelihood that recording methods would be consistent. Using one school also ensured that only a limited number of referring primary school files would need to be traced. This would be more economical but also more effective since the school would follow a single procedure for using information from primary records.

The pupils were therefore selected from one secondary school but all transferred files from the primary schools were also included so that contemporary records of the pupils' behaviour were available. The pupils considered included a sample across the school and a sample with difficulties. This enabled consideration to be given to differences between pupils with and without problems, also (more important for this present research) to differences within the problem group itself. (A more detailed account of the method used is contained in Lane, 1983). Thus, groups are both assessed 'as seen' by school

61

files. Nothing more is being made of the data than that it documents how children were seen by their school. All the records were searched on the child from age five and data up to fifteen years of age included. The specific items of data were assessed as follows:

Health — Any notes on the school files of specific health or sensory difficulties were recorded and counted. Also noted were, any comments specifically about a child's clumsiness or lack of co-ordination. The final figure given for this factor was the score of individual items noted, no weight was assigned to particular features. The special files on the children were not included, although these indicated that the data underestimates the role of the health factor.

Personality — Personality cannot be measured directly from school files but comments can. In order to make the varied data more specific, it was decided to count only the references to a child in which the child 'as a person' was referred to, rather than items of behaviour or work. Items such as, 'The child is a bad influence', 'He is an unpleasant demanding child', were counted, emphasising how the teacher saw the personality of the child. Where a clear distinction was possible the items were separated into negative and positive comments, and ambiguous items were discarded. Repeated items were ignored: if two teachers recorded the child as 'demanding', it would only count as one item.

Two items are therefore recorded in the data, namely: Persneg — Personality negative — comments. Perspos — Personality positive — comments.

Social class — This item was measured by using the Registrar General Scale 1-5. The occupation of the father or, if absent, the mother was noted. In fact, occupations changed over the ten year period, so only the occupation recorded at the point of secondary school transfer was used.

Family factors — As discussed above, difficulties occur when recording information on family patterns from files. To try to provide a framework for such recording, specific items of fact or information were noted and counted. For example: Fact — single parent family, in financial difficulties. Information — Mother has been up to the school several times to discuss Jason's work, is always helpful in discussing difficulties.

The facts and information were grouped into positive or negative items and counted, again discounting ambiguous items. For example: 'Parent is always up at the school' could be positive or negative.

The items are recorded in the data, as namely: Famneg — family fact/information viewed negatively. Fampos — family fact/information viewed positively.

It should be noted that for all family and personality items, how the child/family was viewed is being assessed, not the child or family directly.

Interestingly, little hard data was contained in the files. In many cases, the family received little if any mention. This was partly due to the fact that this study ignored additional files that contained more information.

Peer relationships — comments on the child's relationship with peers were graded on a scale of 1-3 based on teacher comments, 1 being positive to 3 negative.

Siblings — Number of siblings (at age 11 years) were counted, and sibling position (at age 11 years) also noted and graded as 1 (oldest), 2 (intermediate), and 3 (youngest).

Outcome measures for the school sample

The aim now was to consider a variety of measures of behaviour problems and changes in patterns of behaviour. Change events in the family and the school were also noted.

The multiple-stress factors above were then correlated with the variety of outcome measures, and the random and mixed groups considered together, and the mixed groups separately. By considering them together, differences between random and mixed groups should emerge, and by considering mixed groups separately, the strength of any factor within the group should be highlighted.

The outcomes noted were as follows:

1. **Specific behaviour problems (SPB).**
Any specific difficulty was noted and counted. Repeat items were only counted once. For example, a child whose behaviour was described as 'never sits still', by several teachers was counted once only. If additionally a teacher stated that 'he runs around the classroom, and never sits in his seat for long', the first part of the comment would be added, but not the second. All the records over a ten year period were searched.

2. **Time scale for behaviour difficulties (TIM SPB).**
The period of years over which continuing behaviour problems were noted was recorded. Where a child started having problems at seven and stopped at nine the score was given as 2. Unfortunately, a child who had difficulties at five and again at thirteen, but not in between, is also scored 2 in this system. So only the years in which a problem was recorded are measured and the pattern of behaviour is not reflected.

3. **Initial comment on behaviour (ICB).**
The comments on the child's behaviour as recorded in the infant school were graded 1-3 (good-bad). This provided some measure of the initial difficulties faced by the child.

63

4. **Time scale for comments on positive behaviour (TIM ICB).**
As a method of tracing the pattern of subsequent comments, also recorded were number of years in which the initial comment in infant school was repeated by subsequent teachers, thus providing a measure of consistency of positive report.

5. **Change in behaviour (CHB).**
Patterns of change in the child's behaviour were graded 1-3. Any substantial change in the behaviour recorded on the files was noted and graded in this way. Only substantial changes were noted, since minor 'ups and downs' were frequent: the comment had to state that the child was much, considerably, greatly, etc., improved or deteriorated in order to be counted. Minor changes or no change were graded at the mid-point, score 2. Given the variety of comments on file, it was felt that any finer grading would be spurious.

6. **Individual precipitation at change (PREC).**
As one method of looking at the interaction of factors with environmental events, it was decided to record any correspondence between noted change in behaviour (in point 5 above) and comments on changed circumstances in the child or family. Such changes were again graded 1-3, with the mid-point 2 indicting no noticeable change. Factors such as death of parent were included as negative, but where possible the child's view of the event provided the grading guide.

7. **Structural precipitation in school at change (STRCH).**
Following on from point 6, changes noted in correspondence with major differences of school situation were noted. These included a change of year, school organisation, curriculum, etc. They were graded 1-3 on the basis of the way they were viewed by the school, rather than by the child. For example, moving the child into a new teaching group to encourage him would be seen as good, whereas demoting him as a punishment would be seen as bad. Points 6 and 7 represent an attempt to tie together data and historical case material. If events at specific points do correspond with changes in behaviour, some movement towards understanding the relationship between fortuitous and other factors is possible.

The samples considered included a combined sample, (random plus problem groups) the random sample, and the mixed problem group sample.

The findings for the school sample
The combined sample — The results for the combined table (N=160) separates neatly into two sets of outcomes.

1. Items related to the occurrence of problems.

All the items except for sibling position produce significant results. Thus, for the number of specific problem behaviours (SPB) and the time scale for these behaviours (TIMSPB) those pupils showing the most difficulty are marked by:

a) more health problems
b) high negative personality reports and lower numbers of positive reports.
c) lower social class membership
d) high levels of negative family reports and lower levels of positive reports
e) poor relationships with peers.
f) membership of larger families.

Clearly a multiple grouping of difficulties is in evidence. The pupils are characterised not by any specific disadvantage but by several together. The strength of the associations vary however, with a negative view of the child's personality receiving the strongest coefficient. The initial comments on behaviour (ICB) and the time scale for positive reports (TIMICB) show a parallel set of relationships indicating that positive reports are associated with the opposite characteristic to negative ones. This strengthens the position for the multiple viewpoint.

2. Items related to change.

The pattern of items related to change (CHB) is quite different from that related to the occurrence of the disorder. Only one item: 'Positive Personality', is linked to change (in a positive direction). Again, only the item: 'Positive Family', is linked to change (in a positive direction), in terms of individual precipitation (PREC). No items show any relationship with structural changes in school (STRCH).

Across the sample as a whole, therefore, while all the accepted items correlated with the occurrence of disorder, only positive personality and family correlated with positive change.

The random sample —The results for the random group alone (N=100) indicate a similar pattern, but only the strongest items still retain their significance.

1. Items related to the occurrence of problems.

Health, personality positive and negative, family negative and peer relationships show a consistent result, with social class linked to time-scale for problems.

2.   Items related to change.

No factors link with change and only positive family with precipitation. In terms of structural factors, oddly the less healthy and those from larger families do better. This latter result requires investigation. It may be that such children were offered positive advantages by way of compensation by their teachers, although such advantages are not translated into actual behaviour change. However, such speculation would require case-study analysis to substantiate or refute it, and cannot be taken into account here.

The mixed problem sample — If the pattern of results within the problem group is considered (N=60), the picture is somewhat different. Again it is useful to consider the results in terms of items related to occurrence and change separately.

1.   Items related to the occurrence of problems.

All pupils in this group presented problems. Consequently, what is being measured is not the existence of problems but, rather, discrimination in terms of level of problems.

In this group, some of the items which produced strong results previously lose their impact (Health, Social Class, Family Positive). Others vary in their impact, notably 'family negative' which retains its power to discriminate time scale for positive comments (i.e. negative family is associated with absence of such comments) and sibling position. Sibling position, it might be remembered, failed to discriminate between the groups but in this case it is associated with time scale. The last-born child seems to have a shorter time scale for problems and longer time-scale for positive reports. The items which retain their ability to discriminate even within the problem group are personality negative and positive, poor peer relationships and being a member of a large family. As before, personality negative produces the strongest result.

2.   Items related to change.

Within the problem group, several items relate to change in behaviour (CHB). Those most likely to change appear to be:

a)   Healthier.
b)   Have more positive and fewer negative personality features.
c)   Come from higher social class.
d)   Have more positive family features.
e)   Have better peer relationships.
f)   Come from smaller families.

Once more the personality items featured most strongly.

In relation to individual precipitation, those with positive personality characteristics and from higher social classes seem to have more positive experiences. Similarly, fewer negative personality characteristics, higher social class and a more positive, smaller family are associated with positive structural changes within the school.

Conclusions

These features of change, together with the results for occurrence of problems, suggest not only a multiple stress factor in the occurrence of problems, but also an interactive effect on the process of change. The suggestion of this (albeit limited) study is that pupils presenting conduct disorders in school are more likely to suffer multiple problems than other pupils. Recovery from their disorders is also reflected in the multiple patterns they present. Pupils who develop conduct difficulties but recover from them, are more likely to have positive compensatory features and also to be the recipients of positive individual or structural assistance in their lives. Conversely, those least able to deal with multiple stresses are more likely to receive them.

Although this study was conducted before publication of the major review of evidence on deprivation by Brown and Madge (1982), our small scale research reflects their findings in many respects. They argue that there is now plenty of evidence that life cycle disadvantage can be both exacerbated and reduced by experiences. The point made by Wall (1979) stills holds: there are a wide variety of life stressors which may link with health/handicap and adjustment problems. A more recent review of the literature on life events as stressors in children (Johnson, 1986) closely reflects Wall's view. Johnson argues that the literature provides considerable support for the idea that there is a relationship between cumulative negative life changes and adjustment problems but that no simple problem/life stress-relationship can be assumed. Despite all the odds, some children overcome the disadvantages stacked against them. The research from both the UK and USA, all points to the crucial role of education. If pupils and parents can be encouraged and supported then even the most severely disadvantaged participate actively in their own progress. (Widlake, 1990)

The findings in this present study also point to such conclusions. Additionally, the role of personal factors is raised. 'Personality' comments are not the same as personality measures but they indicate that a factor taken into account was how the child was viewed. Brown and Madge contend that ability and temperamental characteristics such as 'drive' influence the advantage likely to be taken of opportunities but that they also impact on the way stresses are managed. Personality factors will therefore be considered in more detail.

Examining multiple stress factors in the lives of the Impossible Child may, therefore, be worthwhile. This is particularly important if, as is suggested here, those with most difficulties are least likely to receive compensating help. What might turn out to be crucial in the attempt to promote change is working with a concept of balance of positive and negative resources being available to the child within the same school. If our Impossible Children turn out to be those who have the most problems and receive the least help, we would be much nearer to explaining the persistence of their problems and hence impossibility.

CHAPTER EIGHT

Personality and the impossible child

She doesn't understand the way I dance!

That personality is a factor in understanding the Impossible Child is evident from this comment by one of the pupils. The difficulty he had in getting his teacher to see that his style was an important part of him as a person caused many communication breakdowns. In their views of pupil/teacher interaction the children clearly see personality differences as part of the picture.

The literature review pointed to the role of arousal and personality. The debate about the role of personality in anti-social behaviour may be old but it is still lively. The part played by the Eysenck and Eysenck (1976) personality model was discussed in Chapter Three. Briefly, they present a bio-social model in which social factors interact with biological features. In relation to anti-social behaviour the theory predicts that extraversion (E), neuroticism or emotional stability (N) and psychoticism or toughmindedness (P), are all positively related to anti-social behaviour.

The argument is one which postulates a predisposition (not a predestination) for certain personality types to react anti-socially to environmental stress. Thus environment and personality are seen as equally important.

It has been argued that introverted individuals condition more readily than the extraverted, that is, that they learn a new response in fewer experiences of it. It is suggested that the extraverted person would therefore be likely to have a deficit of conditioned socialised responses. It should be noted that, by the same token, the introverted child praised for anti-social conduct and punished for socialised behaviour, would be more likely to show anti-social behaviour (Raine and Venables, 1981).

It is also argued that high levels of N will act as an amplifying device on whatever tendency was present. Thus anti-social children would be seen as both high E and N. An alternative position, supported by Pierson (1969), sees delinquent youths as individuals who are resistant to normal pressures to change because they lack anxiety. This position receives support from Lane (1974), who has argued that it is the extraverted stable individuals who are likely to have socialised behaviour difficulties, whereas Allsopp and Feldman (1974) have demonstrated that anti-social schoolgirls showed both high E and N.

Eysenck and Eysenck (1976) have also pointed to the impact of psychoticism (P) or toughmindedness, as it is called in children. High levels of P are linked to a range of more serious disorders such as persistent criminality and psychopathy. Lane (1974) has argued that children seen as especially difficult to handle by their teachers would exhibit high levels of P, being seen as bad people, not simply as badly behaved. The importance of this argument is that they would be more likely to be the subject of a punitive response by their teachers and less likely to receive pro-social reinforcement. This argument received some support in earlier studies (Lane, 1974, 1976, 1978). Eysenck and Eysenck (1975) have developed a 'criminality' scale which looked at the combined effect of high P, E and N and demonstrated that this scale was predictive of anti-social behaviour in the classroom. Lane and Hymans (1982) evaluated that scale and found that it correlated with a measure of teacher-assessed behaviour and discriminated between children convicted as delinquents. The early studies conducted at the Islington Centre therefore alternatively supported the position taken by Eysenck and Eysenck or the contradictory position of Pierson.

Some reconciliation might be possible in that Eysenck and Gudjonsson (1989) have recently modified their position and argued that extraversion is more important with youth and neuroticism with age. Thus a variable role for N would be expected. More importantly, it has been argued that different types of anti-social behaviour in children may reflect varying components of P, E, and N. If an interactive view on the relationship between personality and behaviour is to be taken seriously, then such variations would be expected.

Provisional consideration of the role played by personality is necessary, to decide if it should be included in the measurement of the Impossible Child in the later studies.

Preliminary studies of personality components and behaviour difficulties

Since most of the preliminary studies undertaken as part of this research series have been widely published, full details are not included (Lane, 1983, 1987). Only the key themes are here explored.

In an attempt to explore the contribution of personality to behaviour problems and to resolve the contradictions in earlier papers (Lane, 1974), a series of studies were undertaken.

An earlier study (Lane, 1978), had looked at a group of 40 secondary pupils matched by age, sex and class, who were classified as presenting: no problems in school, some behaviour problems in school, behaviour problems severe

70

enough to require expert help, and those who had failed to respond to expert help and were regarded as 'impossible'. The results indicated a strong tendency for P scores to increase with level of difficulty, and similarly for E scores. Scores on both N and the Lie scale of the Eysenck Personality Questionnaire, showed a variable pattern, but for the most severe group low scores were noted.

An attempt to link the personality scoring with behaviour difficulties as measured by the Bristol Social Adjustment Guide in a group of 20 secondary pupils did indicate a specific pattern. The toughminded P child was found to be more likely to show Hostility on BSAG (Rank Correlation, 0.79). Both E and N failed to show any relationship, but high E plus N scores did correlate with Inconsequence (at 0.41). Inconsequence is marked by impulsivity, anxiety, etc. This result suggested that more specific predictions for the relationship between personality and behaviour were necessary than just a general disorder/extraversion link.

Two further studies looked at P, E, and N scores for a small follow-up sample of pupils who became involved in drug use, but whose scores were measured prior to use. This indicated that high P and high N were factors. As a consequence, a series of programmes using contracts, social and cognitive skills training, anxiety management and token economy was developed as a preventive response to drug use (Lane, 1976). The importance of considering individual differences in the design of such programmes was stressed. For example, you do not use anxiety management with those scoring very low on N.

Further studies looked at the attitude of teachers to certain pupils and indicated a tendency for some groups of badly behaved pupils to be seen less favourably than others who were similarly badly behaved. The attitude of teachers clearly varied. Some children, although difficult, were more popular with teachers. High P scores were implicated in the less popular group.

On the basis of these studies, it was apparent that the EPQ was measuring something useful but the scoring pattern did not fit the Eysenckian predictions. However, the samples used, while independent, were small and so a further series of studies were undertaken.

A group of 120 pupils from a number of schools were classified on the basis of existing school records into: no problem, some problem or severe problem groupings. EPQ's were administered and an analysis of variance in the scoring undertaken. Significant differences were found for all personality factors and the Lie Score. The psychoticism and extraversion factors did appear to support the Eysenckian model but the scores on neuroticism did not, supporting rather the alternative position of Pierson.

An earlier study (Lane and Hymans, 1982), had established a relationship between the EPQ 'Criminality' scale and convictions. This scale includes P, E, and N factors. A further study, considered groups of children who had been originally tested on the EPQ and had demonstrated the presence of delinquency in a five year follow-up. A sample of 120 pupils with or without convictions, matched for age, sex and class, was available. The findings indicated that P predicted delinquency, number of convictions, persistence of delinquency and violent offences. A low Lie score also predicted delinquency, number of convictions and violent offences. Extraversion failed on all measures and a low level of neuroticism showed a tendency to be associated with delinquency and violent offences.

The most consistent pattern is that found between toughmindedness P, and difficulties, but E and N show inconsistent results. This creates difficulties for the conditioning model of delinquency proposed by the Eysencks.

Personality and outcome measures

An additional area of interest is the prediction that personality might relate to different outcome measures (Lane, 1974).

This study examined the possible role of personality in predicting response to discipline in schools, using a sample of 40 secondary children. They were split, based on a blind rating of school records, into groups who responded to discipline, who responded then lapsed, or who never responded to discipline. A set of categories based on levels of extraversion and emotional stability were then devised. A pattern emerged which suggested that Stable Extraverts were the least likely to respond and Emotional Introverts the most likely to respond, with Stable Introverts not far behind. The group most likely to respond but then lapse were the Emotional Extraverts.

The relationship between personality and response to therapy in children with learning difficulties was explored for a group of 17 secondary pupils. High scores on P were found to relate to failure and low scores on N and L were similarly associated. This suggested -surprisingly- that children responding to therapy for learning difficulties were more emotionally unstable than those who did not.

Similar themes emerged in a study of the use of counselling with children with reading difficulties by Lawrence (1971). The use of supportive counselling was advocated but he discovered that those responding to the programmes tended to have high levels of guilt proneness as measured on the Cattell and Cattell (1969) personality model. Lane (1976) investigated this finding, using both the Cattells' and Eysencks' models, and found a significant relationship between poor response and high P, low N, low anxiety and low guilt proneness.

This led to the suggestion that an approach to therapy which took account of individual response style would be more effective. Thus, a learning theory approach or supportive counselling might be used depending on the personality features of the children. A study which looked at outcome for four groups of children with learning problems (Lane, 1976) lent some support to the idea. Introverted, tenderminded (low P) pupils preferred counselling and extraverted pupils preferred a token economy system with clearly established rewards.

Similar recommendations have emerged from studies by Rahman and Eysenck (1978) of adult neurotic patients and of delinquency by Eysenck and Gudjonsson (1989). The latter have argued that low-arousal groups (extraverts) respond better to high-profile management based on rewards, whereas low-arousal groups (introverts) respond better to low-profile counselling or punishment.

Conclusions and contradictions

A number of contradictory findings emerged from these preliminary studies. In some cases but not in others the personality factors were found to lie in the predicted directions. To some extent the confusion in the results of other researchers referred to by both Eysenck and Eysenck (1976) and West and Farrington (1973) is reflected in this data.

The consistent theme is found in the role played by psychoticism. Toughminded (high P) children are more likely to present behaviour problems in school, become delinquent, stay delinquent longer, commit violent offences and not respond to attempts at change.

Extraversion, for so long the central feature of the theory of conditionability and conduct disorder/criminality, fails to hold up consistently. It does discriminate both type and level of conduct disorder, but played little role in delinquency and therapy outcome. It is apparent that some revision of the concept is necessary: its effect is most noticeable in combination with other factors.

The impact of neuroticism in these studies, where effects are apparent, lies more consistently in the direction of low N as a component of the persistent presentation of difficulties of conduct. Although, as some of the data indicated, some groups fit the pattern of high N scores.

The role of the Lie scale is also significant. Eysenck and Eysenck (1976) suggest that over and above the detection of faking, the scale measures a trait of conformity. Thus more conformist individuals obtain higher Lie scores than the less conformist . To the extent that such a view is correct, it would support the expectation that the pupils in this study who were less conformist (conduct difficulties, delinquent, resistant to therapy) would be expected to have low Lie scores.

A way of resolving these variations may be to take the argument outside the narrower conditioning model and place it within a broader multifactorial and interactive conception which links individual differences with behavioural and sociological analyses. Thus personality components would be seen to interact in defined ways with the outcome being determined by the setting. This position has been argued elsewhere (Lane, 1983) and enables specific predictions to be made of the type of behaviour likely in a given setting and the impact of any proposed intervention.

It is clear that individual differences have to be taken into account. They will have to be included in the examination of the Impossible Child, but the pattern may prove more complex than is implied by a conditioning model of behaviour.

CHAPTER NINE

Remission from difficulties for the impossible child

An integrated approach to understanding the Impossible Child

So far the data obtained has indicated that at least three explanatory concepts have a value in the process of remission for children presenting difficulties in school.

The action style of the pupil (personality) certainly seems to play a part. The more extravert pupils are more likely to present conduct difficulties. Tough-minded (high scores on Psychoticism) children are more often involved in both difficulties in school and later criminality. Being viewed as a bad person by your teacher also predicted how you would be seen at later stages of your school career. This explanation must be included in any attempt to look at the pattern for the Impossible Child.

The concept of multiple factors being present in the occurrence of difficulties received some support in the earlier data. The idea of a balance of resources playing a part in remission also seems worthy of further examination. Further exploration of the effect of such features would be useful, in particular, to uncover how they might relate to change. How does the child with multiple disadvantages recover from that situation?

A number of previous studies have demonstrated that the best predictor of future behaviour is present behaviour. This consistency argument was supported in the preliminary studies undertaken here. It was found, however, that pupils could change and that when they did, change was maintained over extended periods. Some behaviours did appear more resistant to change than others, and so a finer analysis than 'conduct disorder' may be needed. More specific predictions of outcome might improve understanding of remission, as 'troublesome behaviour' in school may prove too imprecise a category. Nevertheless, as the follow-up data on delinquency showed, even a general category predicted later delinquency.

However, these different theories, even if they are predictive, leave a number of questions unanswered. Are the different concepts interrelated in some way? Which concept is more important in explaining remission? This chapter starts to answer these questions, exploring the pattern of explanation for a group of children seen as impossible by their schools.

A factor analysis of explanations for the Impossible Child

Previous studies had produced an array of correlation coefficients for a set of variables which suggested some underlying patterns. Since the present study is likely to produce a similar array, it needs to reduce the data to see if there was some underlying pattern of relationships. If the data can be reduced to a smaller set of factors which account for any observed interrelations in the data, it enables a better understanding of remission for the Impossible Child. The relative strengths of the different explanations could then be judged.

The contributions of the three theories is assessed:

1. **The behaviour itself.**
2. **Personality.**
3. **Multiple stress.**
   a) Predisposing (family etc.).
   b) Precipitating (fortuitous events).

Their contribution, singly or in combination, is unravelled.

Factor analysis provides a procedure for such data reduction. The procedure chosen was principal — component analysis, producing orthogonal factors. This reduces data to the smallest combination of variables, which would account for the maximum variance in the data. The analysis was undertaken with the SPSS (Nie et al 1970) procedure using varimax rotation. (Full data sheets are published separately, Lane, 1983.)

The experimental study of the Impossible Child.

The provisional conclusions above demonstrate potential explanations for an understanding of remission. The data clearly illustrate that children more likely to exhibit disorders of behaviour are also likely to experience a range of other variables in their lives, along predicted dimensions. The data also indicate that some variables which correlate with disorder also discriminate between those with higher levels of a more persistent disorder. The question remains, however, of the relative strength of the factors.

So far each of the three theoretical positions has been considered separately. What particularly requires clarification is the role of the theoretical positions in understanding remission in groups of individuals with severe problems. If all that can be demonstrated is that individuals with minor difficulties show higher levels of improvement than those with major difficulties, or that those with major difficulties are shown to experience more stress than those with minor difficulties, then little is achieved. It is more important to understand how much of the variation for individuals can be explained by reference to any given variable. In that way, the issues raised in the original literature review can be addressed.

For example, is the behaviour sufficiently predictive beyond the knowledge that other variables would impart? Does it assist understanding to be aware of the conditionability of individuals in addition to the level of difficulty they present? Does it matter what subsequent life-events are experienced, or will the weight of multiple family difficulties balance these out?

To assess some of these issues, we need to consider the fate of our Impossible Children who are seen as presenting severe difficulties. We can do so by taking measures of their position at different times and then incorporating life-events with socio-economic and psychological variables. That task is attempted through a factor analytic study of 100 pupils with severe problems, using the variables established in the previous studies. With that data available, some answers may emerge.

The Sample

The sample for the study consisted of 100 pupils classified as severe problems. The criteria for such a classification were:

The pupils had to be presenting difficulties of conduct in school sufficient to require additional specialist help. These difficulties had to be of at least two years' standing. Specialist help having been provided, the behaviour had not improved sufficiently for the child's school to be prepared to rate the behaviour as improved.

This classification is essentially administrative and therefore does not pre-judge the type of conduct difficulty to be included in the sample. Once a sufficient number of pupils fitting these criteria had been established, two sub-frames were created:

1. Pupils who, subsequent to therapy, received further help and who were then judged by their school as much improved six months after the end of a given period of therapy.

2. Pupils who, subsequent to therapy, received further help, and who were judged by their school as not improved six months after the end of a given period of therapy.

Deciding what constituted a given period of therapy was simple — in theory: it was the time from its commencement to its termination. But in practice this was seldom clear-cut: case-study analysis revealed that individuals supposedly completing a therapy would move back in and out of therapeutic support, and that some of those 'in therapy' were found to have terminated.

The number and multiplicity of support agency contacts with the pupils/families was very large. It was not unusual for a child to experience four or more therapies. A child might progress through a nurture group at infant school, a tutorial class in primary school, remedial help in early secondary career, a period of pychotherapy and then, finally, behaviour therapy, or an off-site unit towards the end of secondary life. Meanwhile, one or other parent might be receiving psychiatric treatment and siblings might also be receiving special education.

Consequently, only if a judgement was made by the given agency that a programme had been completed, successfully or otherwise, was a 'given period' deemed to have taken place, with obvious limitations for this study.

A sample of pupils was established by randomly selecting pupils from the frame, until fifty names were obtained for each of the sub-frames. The distribution of boys and girls in the main frame was biased in favour of boys. This fact, that boys presented more difficulties than girls had already been established. Previous studies had overcome the shortage of girls in the samples by selecting specified numbers of each sex. In the present study, it was felt that the impact of gender itself as a determining factor in outcome needed to be established. So the cards with the names of all the boys and girls in the sample were randomly distributed throughout the main frame. Consequently, the appearance of more boys or girls in either of the two sub-frames should reflect a real difference in this classification.

Data was collected on each of the pupils in the sample using only information in the contemporary record. The data was obviously collected at different times and the follow-up period varied from a few months in the case of the therapy ratings, to fifteen years in the case of infant behaviour/criminal convictions comparisons. The follow-up specifications are therefore provided separately for each variable, rather than by reference to an average and misleading figure (see below). The data obtained for the sample of 100 pupils was subjected to a factor analysis.

The method of therapy requires some comment. All the pupils selected had received previous periods of help from a variety of theoretical positions. For example, Tutorial groups often work from a pychotherapeutic perspective, and Nurture groups from a developmental position. The pupils in this sample had been through such processes. They then came within the framework of a behaviourally-oriented therapy. The fact that some of them improved is not evidence of the superiority of a behavioural position, nor was this the purpose of the study. Our concern was with remission and not with the strength of respective therapies. We were investigating the factors that correlated with the differences between pupils who, in spite of a variety of provisions, had failed to improve.

All the pupils in the sample came within the auspices of the Islington Educational Guidance Centre. So they were all subject to an analysis of their problems using the procedure outlined in Lane (1978) and an intervention designed in accordance with that methodology. The context for the intervention would have varied and so would the personnel carrying out the programme, but all programmes would have been monitored by Centre staff. This raises the question of whether different staff could effect outcome. This was considered earlier (1976) and when two groups of pupils were monitored with different staff, no effect was apparent. A controlled study was undertaken in a centre other than the author's, using essentially the same model and working in a similar area. They considered outcomes across pupils for twelve different therapists. Coulby (personal communication) reported that assignment to a particular therapist had no apparent effect on outcome. (see also Coulby and Harper, 1983)

The study therefore compares 50 pupils who had not responded to a variety of therapies and 50 pupils who, while previously non-responsive, finally did so. We now consider factors correlating with that remission.

Method

General descriptions of the methods (and problems) used in collating information were provided previously. The areas included in the current study are outlined, but relate to the earlier descriptions. New measures are described more fully.

Initial rating of success in therapy

At the completion of a 'given period' of therapy, the pupils' schools were asked to rate the child's behaviour in school. The teacher responsible for the overall monitoring of progress was usually the person who made the judgement based on reports obtained from other teachers. In some cases, this task was delegated by the senior teacher to other staff members. The rating was as follows:

a) To count as improved, the child had to be exhibiting much less difficulty than previously and at a level sufficient for the child to be contained in school without further specialist support

This definition does not require the total absence of difficulties but follows the administrative basis for their original classification. On this basis, they would no longer be considered a 'severe problem'.

b) To count as not improved, the child had to be exhibiting similar (that is, only slightly better, the same, or worse) levels of difficulty as previously, such that specialist help was still required.

This definition places the child as remaining within the category of a 'severe problem'.

Various rating systems were used experimentally in the early stages of the research as alternative measures of change, but it was found that the factor which most effectively differentiated pupils was the issue of whether or not the child could now be contained in school without further specialist help.

Subsequent rating of success in therapy
Six months after the completion of therapy, teachers in school were asked to repeat the assessment above. The maintenance of any gains made were thereby established.

Intelligence
This section included only IQ scores obtained from individually administered tests. In most cases, this is based on a 'WISC' full-scale score. However, in some cases other comparable tests were used, such as the 'Stanford Binet'. The scores were extracted from records; judgements as to the appropriate measures were clinical. Some caution is necessary in the interpretation of this data, as control of how and when the data was obtained was not available. In all cases, the data was recorded prior to the given therapy, consequently follow-up periods of two years and above are possible for the subsequent measures of change and conviction.

The following factors were measured as previously described:

a) Number of siblings.
b) Social class.
c) Personality (Teacher comments).
d) Family factors.
e) Health.
f) Peer relationships.
g) Sibling position.
h) Initial comment on a behaviour.

    i)   Individual precipitation in school.

    j)   Structural precipitation in school.

Data on conviction obtained, as described previously, was included but only two measures were used:

    a)   Total number of convictions.

    b)   Time scale for convictions.

Change in behaviour

This factor was measured as before. However, a fixed point was assessed, that is, the end of school career (two to five year follow-up).

Personality

The Eysenck Personality Questionnaire (as previously) was used. However, in relation to the present study, all questionnaires were individually administered. The follow-up periods available vary, depending on the comparisons, from a few months to more than five years. Data on the three factors of Psychoticism, Extraversion, and Neuroticism are included together with the Lie scale score.

Behaviour

The Bristol Social Adjustment Guide was completed on all pupils in the sample by a teacher, prior to the 'given period' of therapy and after the six month follow-up. This assessment parallels the rating for therapy outcome, but provides a breakdown by type of behaviour. In this way, particular patterns (syndromes) of behaviour varying in outcome might be assessed.

Since the total score for 'Over-reaction' is a composite of the syndrome scores, it was excluded from the analysis in favour of the more precise syndrome scores. The total score for under-reaction was included, but consequently the under-reactive syndrome scores were excluded. This procedure was necessary because of the very low level of scoring on under-reaction, necessitating a combined score.

The total score for over-reaction on BSAG for both groups prior to therapy is included below. This indicates that they fit the additional criteria of the original study in terms of level of BSAG score. It is of interest that the average score is not as high as that reported in previous studies. The Impossible Child is not seen as Impossible simply because of a high score for difficulties.

Total overreaction score on BSAG

	Mean	SD
Improved	19.23	10.82
Not improved	19.69	8.75

N= 100

The table indicates that prior to therapy the two groups did not differ in mean level of total behaviour problems recorded by the schools. In terms of the total level of behaviour problems, the two groups are therefore initially comparable.

Data Analysis: Results

A Principal factor analysis was undertaken on the thirty three variables listed. The effect of this procedure was to reduce the data to two main factors. These factors link together the variables. Each factor is then given a name which tries to express its meaning. The labels chosen here are mine; on reading the components you may choose a different label; what is important is to try to get a picture of what this grouping of variables might mean.

Factor 1: Behaviour towards others. This factor is marked most strongly by items relating to the way the child's behaviour and personality is seen by the teacher. However, it is not a general behavioural component, since certain items (Inconsequence for example) are not strongly associated with this factor. It does, nevertheless, indicate a continuity of assessment from infant school behaviour (ICB) to final secondary assessment (CHB) and subsequent delinquency (Con). It represents then the child's behaviour towards others and the way the child is seen by others, so is labelled, 'Behaviour towards others'.

The main contributions to this factor are as follows:

.67 — Personality negative (as seen by teacher).
.65 — Change — CHB — (final rating by teacher).
.64 — Peer maladaptiveness (final rating on BSAG).
.60 — Therapy success (low rating on follow-up).
.57 — Poor peer relations (teacher assessment).
.55 — Positive personality (low rating by teacher).
.54 — Convictions.
.53 — Initial rating by teachers (ICB).
.53 — Hostility (initial rating on BSAG).
.52 — Peer maladaptiveness (initial rating on BSAG).
.51 — Hostility (final rating on BSAG).
.50 — Time scale for convictions.

82

The specificity of these correlations is noteworthy:
Hostility, initial and final.
Peer maladaptiveness, initial and final, and poor peer relations.
Initial (infant) and final (secondary) comment on behaviour.

Inconsequence, however, does not form part of this factor. It is suggestive of a pattern in which the child, initially labelled as someone hostile to adults and having poor relationships with other children, is consistently seen in such a light. The absence of inconsequence does strengthen the view that it is behaviour directed towards others, rather than more general behaviour difficulties, which are the critical components of this factor.

Factor 2: Reactivity The remaining over-reactive behavioural variable of inconsequence dominates this factor but includes the personality component of extraversion. It is suggestive of a general 'reactivity' factor. Inexplicably, the variable under-reaction (initial, but not final) also features strongly. It is suggestive of the general level of reactivity in behaviour, so I have called it Reactivity'.

The main contributions are:
.87 — Inconsequence (final rating on BSAG).
.85 — Inconsequence (initial rating on BSAG).
.73 — Under-reaction (initial rating on BSAG),
.73 — Hostility (final rating on BSAG).
.59 — Extraversion (on EPQ).

Stott has suggested that, over time, the inconsequential child may suffer rejection from adults. The appearance of hostility at final stages may indicate such a pattern.

The two factors identified here are useful, but still represent a relatively crude grouping of variables. It is possible to refine the analysis, using the procedure of Varimax Rotation to produce a psychologically more meaningful pattern. As a result of such a procedure, ten factors were extracted, with a new order being created. The naming of the factors takes place in the same way as before. You look at the pattern and try to express it as meaningfully as possible.

Factor 1 : Reactivity
.97 — Inconsequence (BSAG follow up).
.91 — Hostility (BSAG follow up).
.83 — Inconsequence (BSAG initial).
.75 — Under-reaction (BSAG initial).
.71 — Extraversion (EPQ).
.53 — Hostility (BSAG) initial.

This factor is something of an enigma. Certain of its variables provide a clear picture related to the activity of the pupil.

Inconsequence, initial and follow-up, indicates over-reactive behaviours, marked particularly by elements such as impulsivity and distractibility. These fit well with Extraversion to indicate a general level of reactivity and potentially low level of conditionability. The strong role played by hostility, that is: a loss of faith or rejection by, adults, also provides an element of interest. It may be that pupils who exhibit high reactivity/low conditionability may also be rejecting of, or rejected by adults. The specificity of the behaviour is apparent in this factor: items related to defiance of social and peer norms (also measured on BSAG) are not strongly featured.

As in the previous data, the extraversion factor is found to be related to one area of behaviour difficulty but not to others.

The stronger relationship with hostility at follow-up rather than initial stage, does suggest that hostility may be an outcome, that is: the child's impulsive behaviour leads to rejection by adults.

However, Under-reaction (on BSAG) also forms a strong component in this factor. This is exceptionally difficult to encompass in the explanation above. Had the value for under-reaction been negative, a simple reactivity dimension could have been postulated. But it is not. And there is yet another difficulty: unlike the over-reaction scores which correlate at both initial and follow-up stages under-reaction disappears from the correlation at follow-up. It contributes to the factor only at the initial stage.

So individuals are marked by impulsive, over-reactive behaviours (initial and long term) and extraversion, but they are marked also by initially, but not subsequently, under-reactive behaviours.

Speculatively, it might be possible to reconcile these components by postulating (as does Stott) a situation in which the highly inconsequential child gradually experiences more rejection from adults over time and becomes hostile as a result.

Similarly, we might postulate a situation in which the inconsequential child faces adult rejection and responds initially in a variety of ways that might include hostility to adults (over-reaction) but also withdrawal from, and unresponsiveness to, them (under-reaction). In the long run however, the general over-reactivity of the child results in the under-reactive responses extinguishing in favour of an over-reactive extravert response system.

Although the distribution of scores for under-reaction is such that they do contribute to the factor, the level of scoring is low. (The combined, not syndrome scores were included for this reason). This fact possibly lends support to the idea that, in the long run, the general reactivity level of the child comes to dominate the pattern. The child thereby also comes to be further rejected by adults and the level of hostility increases.

An alternative way to describe this would be to say that the child gradually resolves his underlying conflict with adults in terms of one symptom structure. This is, however, speculative. The more stable elements of this factor point to a general behavioural predisposition to over-reactive extraversion.

The enigma of the under-reactive findings becomes even more curious, since Coulby and Harper (1983) have reported a similar pattern based on their entirely independent data. They found the most difficult pupils to work with to be those who scored on both over- and under-reactive behaviours.

It seems as if the child who is both over-reactive and somewhat distant from people (withdrawn/depressed/unforthcoming) is less easy to get along with. There are perhaps hints here of the pattern described by Ullman and Krasner (1975) in their picture of severe behaviour problems.

Factor 2: Fortuitous events

This factor is difficult to label, but it comes closest to Rachman's 'fortuitous' events. One might also call it the 'painful' factor, thereby expressing the sense of everything in life going wrong, or the absence of positive endings (see Factor 5).

The main contributors are:

.73 — Precipitation (that is, individual negative life events).
.64 — C H B (poor final rating in school).
.62 — Structural (that is, negative changes in school).
.49 — Psychoticism (EPQ).
.41 — Therapy response (low rating for change on follow-up).
.35 — Personality seen negatively.

The pattern suggests, in part, one of the child being seen as a negative person, the psychoticism dimension probably contributing, and not in the long term responding, to therapy. But most strongly, the pattern is one of the child experiencing negative life events, both individually and in terms of school. The child is the subject of events which lead to a deterioration in his (or her) chances of progress.

It is particularly interesting to compare this factor with Factor 1, suggesting that the negative view and actions taken by the school are independent of the child's behaviour. Rather, they may be linked to the child's personality (seen negatively) or a failure to deal with the individual crises the child experiences outside school.

The appearance of individual and structural negative variables in this factor point to the role of fortuitous life-events as crucial to an understanding of remission.

Neuroticism also takes an interesting role, being moderately correlated (in a negative, i.e. low N direction) with both Factors 1 and 2. The correlations are .29 and .32 respectively.

Factor 3: Norm Violation
The main contributors are:
.74 — Non syndromic (BSAG follow-up).
.69 — Non syndromic (BSAG initial).
.67 — Peer maladaptiveness (BSAG initial).
.41 — Peer maladaptiveness (BSAG follow-up).

The non syndromic items on BSAG consist mostly of behaviours indicating violations of social norms, defiance etc.

Its independence as a factor is of interest, suggesting that the occurrence of these types of behaviour disorder are not specifically predicted by reference to the other variables. Stott, in fact, argues that norm-violating behaviours are culturally based, suggested by whatever patterns are reinforced by the groups of which the child is a member.

Factor 4 : Delinquency
The main contributors are:
.92 — Time scale for convictions.
.83 — Convictions.

This factor, like Factor 3, produces two strongly related variables which point to an independent dimension.

Interestingly, Factors 3 and 4 both represent anti-social behaviours which are independent, yet each contributes similarly to the explanation.

Factor 5 : Absence of positive beginnings
This factor (like Factor 2) is somewhat difficult to name, and the difficulty reflects something of its essence. It represents, perhaps, poor beginnings, as Factor 2 represented poor endings.
Its main contributors are:
.58 — Poor peer relationships (as seen by teacher).
.57 — Positive family features (i.e. absence of).
.54 — Positive personality features (i.e. absence of).
.43 — Poor initial comments at school.
.42 — Poor initial response to therapy.

The variables included in this factor do seem to stress the absence of positive factors. However, negative personality features as seen by the school also feature in the factor (.40), as they similarly feature in Factor 6 (.47).

Factor 6 : Poor family background

This factor was relatively easy to label, representing a traditional combination of family adversities.

The main contributors are:

.74 — Negative family features.

.48 — Low social class.

.47 — Large family.

.47 — Negative personality features.

Like Factor 5, some moderate relationships with an initial poor start to school is noted (.31), although less strongly. The emergence of two separate factors of family background — the absence of compensatory features (Factor 5) and the presence of negative features (Factor 6) — is interesting. It is often assumed that the mere presence of adversity is sufficient to merit concern. Factors 5 and 6 suggest that the presence or absence of compensatory features must also be considered.

Factor 7: Therapy responsiveness

The main contributors are:

.66 — peer maladaptiveness (BSAG follow-up).

.61 — Therapy response (long term).

.48 — Change long term.

.40 — Therapy response (initial).

The various measures of change assessed by the school are all grouped together in this one factor. This suggests a general similarity of rating across time and situation of the individual as non-responsive. It has been called a therapy-responsiveness factor, although the presence of long-term peer maladaptiveness as a component might indicate a more general lack of responsiveness to relationships.

Factor 8: Lie score

The one strong factor here is the Lie scale score of the EPQ, although some tendency is apparent for this to relate to levels of Psychoticism and low social class.

The scores are:

.71 - Lie score.

.42 - Low social class.

.42 - Psychoticism.

Factor 9: Sex, and youngest

The late emergence of gender amongst the minor factors is of interest, given its very strong showing in the earlier data. Its role within a group with severe multiple problems is perhaps not as great as in a less difficult group.

Even here it is not the main contributory variable, the scores being as follows:
.60 — Sibling position (youngest).
.45 — Initial difficulties at school.
.43 — Sex (female).

Being the youngest in the family, and female, is moderately related to initial difficulties in school.

Factor 10: Under-reaction

The only strong component of Factor 10 is the long-term measure of under-reaction on BSAG. The short-term measure of this variable proved difficult to interpret as a component of Factor 1.

In this instance, it stands virtually alone. The scores are:
.92 — Under-reaction (BSAG follow-up).
.24 — Under-reaction (BSAG initial).
.26 — Therapy success (follow-up).

Some comment on the failure of gender or IQ to emerge as key factors is necessary. Earlier studies had indicated that gender should play a role, and research referred to previously had pointed to ability as a factor. The effect of sex differences for these very difficult groups is not as powerful as other factors such as personality and life changes. This nevertheless hides differences in the results. For example, the patterns of convictions varied by gender and case study data often gave the impression that teachers were prepared to tolerate higher levels of difficulty in very bright pupils. Some of our, 'Impossible Children' had IQs of 130+, 140+, and a couple of over 150. Schools were reluctant to suspend these pupils. Yet in relation to outcome, ability does not appear to be crucial. This finding was also noted in a previous study of learning problems (Lane, 1976).

Conclusion

The intention of this study was to look at the interrelationships of variables for children with severe disorder of conduct. The data from the principal factor analysis strongly support the concept that behaviour is predictive of itself. However, this conclusion does not justify an assumption that any general rating of conduct disorder is predictive of particular later difficulties. It is clear that specific patterns exist. That pattern, relating to the general reactivity level of the child represents one factor; general relationships with others represent another factor.

The rotation of the data provides a clue to the interrelationships of the variables. The general level of reactivity retains its position as a main component. The factor called 'fortuitous events' emerges as the second component. Anti-social/Norm violation behaviours then emerge. Groups of factors indicating the lack of positive and the presence of negative family features then link with initial school difficulties.

The patterns of behaviour and the events which subsequently impinge upon the child therefore emerge as the main contributors to final outcome or remission. The patterns are not so strong or unequivocal as to determine an absolute process along these lines, but the suggestion of the study for this group of children with severe difficulties is that general patterns of family background and adversity do relate to initial difficulties in school. Later outcome is largely dependent on what subsequently happens to the child. A major portion of these subsequent events were within the control of the school, and those that were not were, nevertheless, known to professionals associated with the child.

It is, however, to the actual behaviour of the child that the main effect lies.

We can now look in more detail at those subsequent events and the patterns of behaviour shown by the child in response to them. We are moving closer to a partial, but useful, picture of the Impossible Child.

A comment from one of the pupils

Carole asked a good many questions about this process of factor analysis. She thought it sounded like using the computer to find whatever pattern you liked. Being able to name things as you pleased did not seem right to her. When the pattern of rotation was explained, she was even more dubious, and the idea that you could pick the method used to rotate the data and that might produce yet more different patterns, left her feeling that the whole process was meaningless. (In fact, a rotation using a different method produced similar results in this case.) Gould (1981), in discussing the 'Mismeasure of Man' and the way factor analysis has been used, would share some of her doubts.

Factor analysis is an attempt to extract meaning from a diverse set of features. It does have a place, but the existence of a complex set of figures does not guarantee meaningful results.

In looking at the data, the reader, like Carole, must retain a degree of doubt, and ask the question:

'Does it make sense to me?'

CHAPTER TEN

Fortuitous events: key events, key people and key moments

Issues worth exploring

The last chapter concluded by citing a number of areas worth further exploration if the pattern of factors which enhance the prospects of remission are to be understood. Unlike that chapter, which provided clear statistical arguments, the findings in this section can be expected to be messier. It is in the nature of the subject that we are dealing with less precise concepts, as we explore the sense of the experience for the child and the teacher.

Briefly to restate the key conclusions from the last chapter, it was argued that behaviour itself is the key predictor, but that events in the child's environment were also critical in respect of long term outcome. It was apparent that simply changing behaviour was not enough; you also had to act to change the way the child was viewed. Intervention was necessary to change the significant negative life experiences faced by the child. Attempts to promote remission therefore require a multimodal input, focusing on the behaviour and the significant agents and events in the child's life. Effective short-term therapy needs to be supported by longer-term action in the community of which the child is a member. The primary focus for this was seen to be the school.

That is what the pattern looks like. We have yet to explore in detail the specific events in the child's life featured in the previous statistical data. We know that events in school and outside are important but not how they cause an effect. That task is now attempted.

The examination of case study data is seldom easy. A rich source of information is available. The starting points for the examination have already been highlighted: they are the points of change in behaviour marked by individual events in the child's life and structural changes in the school.

Whereas in the previous study correlations between events were noted, here the events themselves are explored.

The case studies of the group of one hundred pupils provide the basic data for our discussion here. Much of the material will eventually be published in additional briefing papers.

Key people, key points and key events do change the balance.

As established in the earlier data, key changes in the child's life corresponded directly with changes in behaviour. If, say, major overcrowding at home which caused the child problems with hygiene, lateness, never having the right books, etc, was resolved through rehousing, this child's behaviour did change. Change was linked to the behaviour. Moving house would not be relevant unless there was a specific connection with behaviour difficulties. Rehousing, undertaken as part of a planned programme of removal of an abusing parent, for example, could result in changed behaviour. Reducing specific stress clearly mattered. In a number of cases, the involvement of a new key person had an impact. The appointment of a social worker, or a different social worker, was an important component of change in some cases, where that appointment was marked by action to change the life space of the child or family. Changes which had been requested by the school but blocked by one social worker were enacted with the appointment of a new worker, with beneficial results. Alternatively, a new social worker was able to block a referral for residential placement requested by the school, whereas the previous worker had been prepared to collude with the request even though disagreeing with it.

The patterns of changes were variable, allowing for no clear conclusions, only that change in life space did correlate with change in behaviour. Of course not every change helped every time, but enough did so to show that appropriate action could result in a specific improvement. In some cases where several positive changes occurred in the child's life, change was noted even when they were not specifically related to the problem area. This usually took the form of a comment that the child seemed happier. If this observation was picked up and action then taken in the school to use the opportunity for positive change, improvement could result and this in fact happened in a few cases. In some cases the teachers and social workers maintained a sufficiently good relationship to cue each other specifically about the change needed. A teacher would, for instance, alert the social worker that this was a good moment to call at the home to review progress on their jointly-agreed programme because things were going well in school. This meant meeting the family, which the social worker regularly had to visit with bad news, at a time when they were feeling positive. There were several examples of such cooperation between agents but no pattern, in terms of theoretical model or specific actions or workers involved, was identified. The catalyst was as likely to be a youth worker as a social worker, a counsellor, or even a councillor. The Head of Year or of House in the school, however, frequently had a significant role in change processes of this kind.

Changes in school and the role of the Year Head.

Accordingly, attention was paid to the key role of Head of Year/House in the secondary school. For primary school pupils, the key role could as easily be occupied by a class teacher, deputy head, head, special-post holder, or sometimes a welfare assistant, dinner lady, school secretary.

Discussions had previously been undertaken with all the heads of year involved and their views on pupils and on factors relevant to change, and their style of working had been noted. This information was not analysed or made known to staff working with pupils, but it was recovered after the data on change had been assembled. This was linked to other data on patterns of interaction. From a research perspective this information is less satisfactory than the earlier findings but it is certainly richly illuminating.

Long term progress was related to changes in school. These included a change of year, a different curriculum, a new reward system (positive reporting systems as opposed to a negative report card) and so forth.

Children also made progress and were helped by many different teachers and heads of year, who varied in style and beliefs. In general you did not have to be a particular type of teacher to establish a working relationship. Nevertheless, for the most difficult of the pupils, some found themselves allies in their head of year and some found indifference or contestants.

The teachers differed and the pattern identified by Hargreaves, (et.al.,1975) reflects the style of the differences. I cannot improve on his account, so repeat to some extent part of it here.

'The deviance-provocative teacher believes that the pupils he defines as deviant do not want to work in school and will do anything to avoid it. He thinks it is impossible to provide conditions under which they will work; if they are ever to work then the pupils must change. In disciplinary matters he sees his interaction with these pupils as a contest or battle — and one that he must win ...they cannot be trusted ... they are resistant, hostile and committed to their deviance. He refuses to believe that any signs of improvement are authentic.'

'The deviance-insulative teacher believes that these pupils like all pupils really want to work. If pupils do not work the conditions are believed to be at fault. He believes that these conditions can be changed and that it is his responsibility to initiate that change... he rarely makes negative evaluative comments on pupils who misbehave... he encourages signs of improvement... he enjoys meeting them outside of the classroom, where he can joke with them and take an interest in their personal problems. He trusts them.'

Although the positive flavour to some extent was reflected in the Year Heads who had most success with the pupils, it is not quite that simple. Some teachers who would certainly fit the insulative description turned out to be very destructive in their dealings with the pupils when faced with continuing disorder from the child in spite of the teachers' efforts. Positive teachers could find themselves being destroyed by the pupils. Being positive was not enough.

The comments of the pupils about the teachers is illuminating:

'He stands up for you.' 'He always sticks to what he says, that's bad sometimes.' 'My mum says he is the only teacher who ever takes any trouble with her.' 'You know where you stand.' 'When Mr. XXX tried to get me kicked out, she was in there arguing.' 'Strict, but you can have a laugh as well.' 'He told me he takes no shit but he don't give it either.' 'She changed the lessons round and when my mum was ill, fixed it for me to get my mark late.' 'A tough bastard but you can have a real laugh sometimes.' 'No one will cross him, but he never hits anyone and seems quiet, it's funny.' 'She really wants you to do well and really works for you if you don't mess up too much. You can't get away with anything, she always checks.' 'I didn't like her at first but she does try to help, she wrote some nice letters to my social worker, she is fair.' 'When I was in Court he worked really hard so I didn't get sent away.' 'The only person I would ever go back to for help when I left school.' 'If you make a deal you have to stick to it, but if you don't he finds out what was wrong and works out what you can do.'

This is only a small sample of opinions but they reveal a pattern that is worth thinking about. I read them as reflecting:

1) Willingness to support the child/take an interest in child and family.

2) Firm but fair/a model who is powerful but not abusing.

3) Someone who sticks to agreements and expects the child to also, but who will help the child to do so rather than blame him (or her) if he does not.

4) A fixer, someone who makes things happen.

5) Flexible and with a sense of proportion - and humour.

This is only an impression; it is most useful to look at what the teachers actually did. This allows some of these impressions to be directly tested. Some attempts to do so are discussed below, but first we explore more impressions from the data. Some were shared by teachers, social workers and other professionals involved with the child or family. The ten most consistent patterns from the case material that emerged were as follows:

1. The types of changes that teachers/social workers encouraged in the life space of the child varied. The more successful pupils were involved with

professionals who were prepared to make more system changes, and who expected individual change in return.

2. Some teachers who would otherwise be seen as negative worked very hard to generate change. In all these cases, the teacher took a 'special needs' view of the child as deserving of help, and tried to provide it.

3. None of the most effective practitioners were very tolerant of theory. They were pragmatists, who wanted to see things work. The least successful tended to hold fixed views about what children should or should not do, and what types of support should be offered. Others among the less successful practitioners adhered to particular theories of practice to guide their work or, at least, to influence their attributions of cause, which they were not prepared to alter in the face of contradictory evidence.

4. In some cases, seeing the child as with special needs had a positive effect; sometimes it did not. But all the teachers and some of the other professionals, who were successful recognised that these were especially difficult children. Consequently, they did not get too upset with failure. They referred to individual differences and frequently mentioned the need to be flexible with the child.

5. They were also more prepared to recognise differences in the child's behaviour across situations and time. In initial referrals they were less likely to say that the child was difficult with everyone. They were prepared to identify change points in previous years, terms or between classes. When they did not themselves know of such examples, they were willing to learn from accounts of such events. The response was in terms of: 'what can be learned' rather than 'the record must be wrong'. They used the impossible label less or stopped using it sooner.

But they also recognised the difficulties that the child presented for colleagues, and did not try to ignore problems. Colleagues and pupils were supported. They recognised that the going would be hard, identified that fact for colleagues, accepted the risk, and managed the consequences in a systematic way.

6. They deliberately set out to reduce stress on a temporary basis. They changed the balance of resources even if it meant a temporary system adjustment. They were also prepared to argue for long term adjustments to help other children, based on what they have learned from working with Impossible Children.

7. They placed strong emphasis on teaching the child skills, social and academic. There was a commitment to the pastoral curriculum, not just pastoral work.

8. There was an emphasis on performance. They did not accept low standards.

9. They made a purposeful attempt to manage the micro-politics in the school. They were aware of those who were likely to prevent change and tried to involve them or, if that failed, to neutralise their impact. They knew about the 'sore spots' and were careful not to press them. But they would take on responsibility if necessary, in the sense of putting their own competence on the line for their belief that change was possible. They recognised the game of disorder and insulated other teachers from the worst effects of the child's attempts to play it.

10. They maintained a long term involvement with the child. The child called back from time to time. They were more often involved with effective social work practice. Where actual events improved... family rehoused, abusing parent moved, mother stopped drinking etc, they tried to link their work to the effective action achieved by the social workers. Most particularly they and the social workers fostered and supported the children who made a positive commitment to change, either through changing the balance of resources to facilitate the clients' skill development or teaching the clients the skills to manage by themselves. These patterns of support, when shared by professionals who had community involvement with the child (social/youth work etc.), were further enhanced.

The pattern that emerged from the case-study material raises questions about the findings in the previous chapter, where it was argued that changes in the child's life space, in structural changes in the school, through the curriculum, change of year etc, were key components in change. The patterns above do not undermine the importance of those key changes, but they suggest that something more was involved. They were not just fortuitous, but planned (sometimes in a rough and ready way) and intentional. Even those that were not planned (e.g. a death) were used in some way to enhance change. So there are key events but there are also key people who effectively turned the event into a key moment for change. They were active 'fixers'.

Is it possible that the underlying theme was the belief of the key agents involved? A belief that change was possible, combined with the attempt to resolve situations so that change was effected.

It is the patterns of belief that we considered now.

Belief in change

Behavioural consistency provided the starting point for this analysis. Olweus, (1979) has traced the high level of consistency that applies to behaviour in childhood. Therefore inconsistencies are of interest.

Accordingly the first strategy was to examine the histories of the pupils for periods of inconsistency. We sought to identify points at which a different pattern of behaviour emerged in a particular year or class.

Firstly any inconsistency was traced and differences in the child's life-space identified. Where case-study material was available, the attitudes and ideas of the pupils and families was established.

So we have, as a starting point, records on 100 pupils over a ten year period.

How much inconsistency was there? A surprising amount. Few of the pupils' records showed consistency each year and term. This is, of course, misleading because most of them were being rated as consistently badly behaved. Over 60% first presented problems in the Primary school. But differences in the way they were rated by teachers each year, and each term (if records were available) were the norm. They were not uniformly difficult, although they were rated so.

This inconsistency was even more noticeable in the report books the pupils used as part of their work at the Islington Centre. A review of 100 such books (not a completely overlapping group with the one above) was most revealing. The book traces the response of teachers, in the form of a comment, to the pupils at the end of every lesson for one school term. In reality many teachers failed to make regular comments and pupils forgot to collect them, but a substantial number were available (around 10,000). Patterns of behaviour measured by these comments were found to vary widely. A child could be rated as excellent in one class and receive no positive comment in the next. A maths lesson on Monday with one teacher could receive a positive comment, yet maths on Thursday, with a different teacher, might not. These very great differences indicated that so called 'impossible' children did in fact receive a high level of positive comments in some circumstances.

The explanations offered by the pupils and teachers for these differences are many and varied. For example, a pupil would say that the bad comment in maths was because he was no good at maths, but explain the good comment in terms of the teacher being okay.

To some extent these differences in patterns could be explained in terms of the attributions made. Thus if the teacher attributed positive behaviour to the pupil's actions, then the child expressed positive views towards that teacher. The attributions affected the balance of the learning experiences. Where a previous negative history existed between pupil and teacher, the balance could still be changed provided that both child and change agents came to construe the situation as one in which change was possible. When they saw the pupil

97

making an effort, teachers kept saying that they now believed it was worth trying, since some change was apparent. Curiously, the pupils tended to say much the same!

In fact, it did not matter how this was rationalised (a whole variety of 'explanations' appeared in the case material). If a change in behaviour took place, a change in attitude followed some of the time.

The beliefs of the children were particularly interesting. As reported elsewhere (Lane, 1984), there was a relationship between personality characteristics and self-report data on behaviour. Some pupils were more consistently prepared than others to report themselves as bad. Some had an investment in being bad. Yet the work the child and parent contributed to change, if and when they saw a way forward, was remarkable. (... can we agree ... can we find a way out ... forget about blame ... can it be done ...?) They became dissatisfied when what was offered was not useful to them; they became disaffected when they could see no way forward.

While these general conclusions from the data are interesting, they offer little of assistance in any specific case. Many of the things that were being said at the Islington Centre in the 1970s are now being said by many others (and more eloquently). It is true that getting the organisation of the school right makes a substantial difference. The conclusions of the Elton Report (1989) make a great deal of sense. But to understand what is happening for the individual child requires a detailed investigation of the events happening moment by moment for that child.

Such data was obtained on several thousand separate occasions, through individual observations by teachers, pupils, staff at the Islington Centre and others. What it indicates is the need for fine-grained analysis if you are to understand what is happening for the child.

There are vast pools of data available from the studies (some of which will appear in other studies in due course), but they indicate that while a very wide range of situations can give rise to conflict, the same situations were seen by others as satisfactory. It depends not so much on external judgements of the situation but on the question 'What meaning do the participants attach to the situation?'

For example:

One of the most widely-used techniques at the Islington Centre was to provide a positive report book which the child gave to the teacher at the end of every lesson. For some of those pupils (in the early days of the Centre), there was a high external value in using the books, since they were linked to reward.

Two things could be measured: the frequency with which the child presented the book and the level of checking by the teacher. However, the degree of presentation for checking reflected the confidence of the child that the book would be checked ... a prediction was involved.

The answers children gave when asked why they did not present their books for comment, reflected their belief in the extent to which it was worth doing. 'He never gives positive reports so it's not worth asking', was a typical answer. Could a child be persuaded to change that belief?

To change the prediction you had to increase the pupil's sense of control over what to do if a teacher did not offer a positive comment.

Unfortunately, the prior behaviour (history) between the pupil and teacher was a good predictor of response ... if circumstances remained unchanged. Creating a belief in the possibility of change was the main problem. Effective change agents (teachers, pupils, parents or advisers) enhanced the belief but also delivered on their promises. The hostility noted in pupils, in the previous data, was due to failed promises in the past. A similar point could be made in reverse for teachers.

Thus the likelihood of change depends upon certain beliefs and values held by the child, namely:

a)   The value placed on the behaviour: is it worth my while?

b)   The value placed on the change agent: ... is s/he worth trusting/important?

c)   The belief that change (my attempts) will be supported (or checked).

d)   The belief that it can be achieved: ... the steps are small and manageable ... I have the knowledge and skills necessary ... or will be helped to acquire them.

To some extent there is a 'theory of planned action' in use by the pupils here (Ajzen, 1988). Children did try to maximise gains/minimise losses if they could see a way to do so. The problem for the Impossible Child was their difficulty in seeing a way, for certain reasons:

1.   They had a preference for novelty, and the most effective action might be boring. The use of a scripted approach to group therapy (Lane, 1975) revealed this very clearly. Based on work by Sarason (1972), pupils were provided with examples of alternative ways to handle problem situations. The novel, exciting way appealed most but often proved ineffective. The pupils were much more enthusiastic about giving examples of things going wrong than going right, which they found boring. They had to work hard to see the issue of consequence (Yes, but what outcome do you want when you talk to Police Officers ... to get arrested or not?)

2.   Communication is a co-operative enterprise in which certain assumptions apply (Howitt, et.al., 1989). The pupils had less sense of these rules as they applied to authority figures.

3. Low conditionability was a factor. It was possible to observe a more rapid response to scripted work in pupils who were introverted. They were the ones who quickly learned and used the techniques. Most of the pupils were low on conditionability and needed external reinforcement initially. (This was indicated by token use for the programmes.)

4. They had a less organised experience of rule learning.

5. Less reinforcement was available to the Impossible Child ... less preferred child: the things he valued were not reinforced in school.

6. They had less experience of co-operative learning.

7. The approach to rules and their observance was based on the attitude: 'What's in it for me?'

Compliance had some limited value in set circumstances, but the Impossible Child sets greater value on non-compliance. How then do we increase the value seen in compliance? This was particularly a problem in dealing with the tough-minded child. Given the additional problem of fewer opportunities, this led to a balance of negative and positive resources that was inappropriate and unhelpful.

The answer was not in excusing such children from compliance and the requirements to use rules. If they did not learn how to comply at school, their opportunities were even further reduced and long term delinquency became one of few options open.

The answer? There was no single answer, but a range of approaches, some of which were being followed by some of the change agents. These included:

Increasing opportunities ... reinstituting co-operative learning ... reinforcing and maintaining change ... and teaching survival skills which enabled the child to gain reinforcement from the natural environment.

Some change agents were doing this.

The actions of the change agents

A number of situations were reported where the child intended to do well in a class but did not. A study of these provides us with useful insights. The Head of Year (or House) responsible for the programme looked at the explanations offered. One common example of a child's response was along the lines of:

'The teacher started shouting at me as I walked in and I forgot what I was supposed to do'.

How were such responses handled? Year heads and social workers who, although varying in style, theory, etc, were effective, tended to use a problem solving approach to the child. They tended to examine intentions and actions, not to judge. The questions they asked the child were:

- What did you want to happen (intend)?
- What happened?
- What caused it to happen in that way?
- What could you do next time?
- What happened when you tried it? (They checked the truth of the response, as the child knew they would.)

These Heads of Year were providing a problem-solving model, which they had the power to make happen for the child ... they were not averse to some backdoor encouragement or arm-twisting of staff, to make sure they responded to the child's next attempt to improve behaviour.

So the child was taught a model for solving conflict and reinforced for using it.

This is what tended to happen naturally, so the obvious step was to try to teach it directly to pupils and to those teachers who were not using it.

For pupils in particular, it was taught through the use of contracts, the report book, specific cueing techniques. For teachers, there was reinforcement for adopting the approach, and many came on training courses or took part in school-focused training events, run from 1975 onwards. Some were better than others at learning this approach and the difference was based in part on:

a)   The type of attributions they made.

b)   Their power position in school... whether or not they felt confident enough to challenge and able to handle failure if a programme did not work. They needed to learn not make failure a personal matter

c)   The extent to which they generally favoured a reward orientation.

d)   The extent to which they took a long-term interest in the child, so that even when they not directly involved, they would maintain a benevolent concern.

Much else was done, so many things that it is difficult to list them. Data reported later indicated an average of around eight intervention techniques per child. What they had in common was that they were based on individual analysis of need and on flexible programmes. You had to do what worked, within the context of the values you and the child held. Being hidebound by pet theories was not helpful.

Conclusions

The findings above support the idea of an active change process, in which the participants are negotiating shared understandings and developing planned actions based on an exploration of what is actually happening in the context in which the problem is defined. Key moments, people and events were identified, and the following emphasised:

- the behaviour of those who are change agents, and on building a shared concern, a contract in which each party has a stake in success.

- exploration of individual differences, beliefs, structural changes, history etc..

- clear shared understandings of cause and on what needs to be done.

- a clear plan: what, how, when, who etc.

- checking, that is, clear performance targets, which are evaluated and then supported in the long term.

It is these patterns which, in a variety of ways and with each teacher, pupil and parent doing it differently, mark out those who changed from those who did not.

A further comment by the pupils.

The Impossible Child intervened at this point to argue that this picture does not accurately reflect the impact of teachers and the school. By concentrating on positive change, they say, that I fail to give weight to the stress caused by bad teachers and practice.

'We may be b*******, but so are some teachers.'

The point is well taken. Lawrence, (1973) made the point that you do have to take account of the fact that there are some teachers with exceptionally low professional standards. Inadequate curriculum and support, teachers who leave just too many promises unfilled and low morale, all contribute to a loss of trust by pupils in the possibility of change. We are not very good as a profession at giving pupils a legitimate outlet for their complaints against staff. Some teachers are bad for all children but especially for those with difficulties. We tolerate the pain they cause to our shame.

Our pupils agree with her. The case files support her. In a number of cases, children's lives were wasted by the actions of a small number of teachers determined that the child would not succeed or be given credit for anything. They wanted the child out of the school and they made sure that it happened.

'The grim fact that must never be forgotten is that each child goes this way but once, and every day one child is cramped and hampered and fails to grow, takes its toll not only on him but on the future of the city and the nation.' (Herrick, 1971)

But most of our teachers, if they could see a way forward, would try it, and not a few worked furiously to make sure positive change was achieved.

CHAPTER ELEVEN

A framework for understanding the impossible child

The central question

This chapter will attempt to draw together some of the major points raised in the literature review and the explanatory theories proposed. The extent to which the data obtained in this study assists in understanding the points raised will be explored . It must be stated again as it was initially, that the study addresses itself only to certain issues in understanding remission, and applies only to those studied. In Chapter 3, the central question of the study was posed:

> 'What do we need to consider if we are to understand the process by which some children who present behaviour problems improve (remit) and others do not?'

The question itself poses further questions: nevertheless, a start has been made.

What is remission?

Remission is, at least, simple to define. It is a process by which individuals identified as having difficulties considered noteworthy, by someone in a position of power, later come to be considered as no longer a cause for concern.

Although the definition is simple, the process itself is not. We have seen that remission is from something i.e. 'noteworthy difficulties', but how those difficulties might be classified is less straightforward. There is no widespread agreement on the basis of classification, although various systems receive differing degrees of support. We have indicated some of these issues in relation to clinical classification, and mentioned also the question of labelling raised in sociological findings. We saw that how the child was classified and the provision available, were intimately linked.

This link becomes even more critical given the new criteria for classification or a 'statement of needs' set out in the 1981 Education Act. While not having the categorised basis of earlier systems, the Act nevertheless still locates the statement of need essentially as the child's. It does not address itself to questions about the role of the school or other professionals in creating difficulties, even though such questions are asked in the research literature. In relation to the new Act, Warnock (1983), stressed that an Act aimed at integration cannot work without a more imaginative approach from teachers, and of this she sees little evidence. However, moves towards school-based work are encouraging. The impact of the Education Reform Act (1988) shifts the argument from an educational to a market philosophy. Its impact on partnership with pupils, parents and the provision of support programmes remains to be evaluated. (Widlake, 1990)

Remission depends on the available resources and the response of the school. According to this view however, it is also important to remember that the concept of remission is more than the presence and continuance of disorder. The concern is with change. Establishing that a difficulty exists, or even correlates, between disorder and other variables does not, of itself, assist in understanding remission. Factors related to the process of change must be elicited. As Yule (1978) argued, factors related to the occurrence of a disorder are not necessarily involved in its maintenance. Consequently, not only must the fate of the behaviour be considered, but also of the label attached to the child. Any difference between these two is of interest. The role of any factor in relation to disorder must be separately considered as a possible component in remission. These different aspects of remission therefore require examination.

What factors correlate with the occurrence of difficulties ?

Three propositions were given particular attention:

1. **That personality features made conduct difficulties more likely to occur.**

It was argued that conditionability (high Extraversion) influenced the likelihood of conduct difficulties developing. Furthermore, high drive levels (high Neuroticism) were also implicated. Psychoticism was also seen as a crucial component.

The data, in relation to general conduct disorder in school, supported the position for E & P, but not N. However, when translated into a prediction for criminality, only P emerged.

Conditionability (in so far as it is reflected in E) is therefore seen to play a role, but the nature of its influence in respect of particular patterns of behaviour needed further clarification.

The later study with the Impossible Child did provided such clarification, in that it formed part of a factor associated with hyperactive/distractible behaviour

(Inconsequence on BSAG). It was not linked with norm-violating or peer-maladaptive behaviour. It was also linked more strongly with hostility to adults in the long term, rather than short term, suggesting that hostility emerges as an outcome of the pattern of difficulties over time.

In relation to the occurrence of disorder, P is found to be associated with general conduct and criminality. E is found to be related to general conduct disorder, but it is probably through its association with specific hyperactive types of behaviour that its effect is greatest.

2. That those suffering multiple stresses are more likely to develop conduct disorders.

This position was strongly supported. Across a wide range of measures, it was found that the level of disorder related to the level of adversity and the absence of positive compensating features.

3. That the occurrence of behaviour difficulties at one stage are predictive of difficulties at a later stage.

Again this position was strongly supported. Even a broadly drawn category of conduct disorder was predictive of later delinquency.

To sum up, it is apparent that all three theoretical positions receive some support, and play a role in the occurrence of conduct difficulties.

What factors correlate with remission from difficulties?

The study of multiple components provided some evidence that continuation of disorder was more likely in individuals suffering more, rather than less, adversity. Even within that general conclusion, certain features, notably teacher-assessed personality, emerged more strongly than others.

Although valid, this general level of adversity argument takes us only so far. A more subtle examination is necessary. The study of the group of children presenting severe conduct disorders (our Impossible Children) provided some of the answers. Two general factors were apparent, dominated by variables indicating behavioural features. That two such features should emerge serves to emphasise that a general category of 'conduct disorder' is too imprecise, The continuity of negative behaviour rating by teachers from the first to the final years of secondary school is particularly noteworthy. That certain children are seen not only as badly behaved but as 'bad' people, who are themselves at loggerheads with adults and peers, raises important questions as to the sources of support available to such pupils. Their subsequent delinquent career extends their conflict with others, from a period stretching in some cases from five to twenty years of age.

The second main factor suggests that certain children are temperamentally (extravertly) inclined to consistent difficulties of conduct marked by inconsequential (impulsive) behaviours. Such children and such behaviours cannot be lumped together in a general anti-authority grouping even though they may come eventually to be in direct conflict with adults. Thus, the behaviour itself, in relation to specific items rather than generalised categories, must be the focus of attention. The results also raised the distinction between a rating as improved (remission) and behavioural evidence of change. The two might not be the same thing.

Beyond the focus on the behaviour itself, other features emerge. The most important of these corresponds, in part, to the concept of 'fortuitous events' influencing outcome. It is apparent that pupils showing less teacher-related change long term are also the subject of negative life experiences, both as individuals and in terms of their school careers.

The detailed material from the case study data pointed to a range of factors of importance. The view held by the child and key others, particularly teachers, had a major impact. The beliefs about change generated (or failed to generate) change. The extent to which professionals, teachers and social workers, for example, were able to assist children and parents to act effectively on their environment significantly affected outcomes. The Impossible Child generated particular stress at 'sore spots' in the system. The wide range of behaviours exhibited and the equally wide range of techniques used to work with the pupils indicates that individual analysis is necessary. A packaged set of approaches is unlikely to meet the complexity of each situation.

The personality feature of Psychoticism also appears and suggests a pattern in which the high P child is more likely to be the recipient of punishing, rather than reinforcing life events (in part independently of the behaviour). Therefore we must look not simply at the child's behaviour, but also to the events experienced, for an explanation of remission.

Two further elements of interest are the absence of positive family and other features and a preponderance of negative features, which appear also to play a role in the initial occurrence of problems. Thus, the child who starts life in a difficult situation is more likely to develop behaviour problems, but it is to subsequent events that one must look for evidence of maintaining factors.

What then is the pattern of remission?

It is apparent that the process of remission involves more than a change in behaviour. To some extent, it appears that the behaviour of the child and a rating as improved are independent variables. In reality the belief system of the key change agents (primarily teachers) is part of the overall pattern. If they do not believe in the possibility of change, they will not see it even when the behavioural evidence exists. As argued elsewhere, perhaps we can only see what we believe (Lane, 1989). The relationship between final ratings, life events and personality features points to some children being less likely then others to be given whatever help is available.

A general factor of 'behaviour towards others' appears to suggest that certain behaviours, namely those directed towards adults or peers, are more strongly featured, positively or negatively, in a rating of change by teachers than more impulsive behaviours.

Understanding remission requires a detailed knowledge of the behaviour itself and the way it is viewed by key agents. It requires also a consideration of the events that happen in the life of the child.

Knowing that the child has suffered multiple adversities tends to strengthen any prediction of later difficulties, as does the absence of positive compensating features. However, remission relates very strongly to the subsequent events in the child's life, rather than to the general presence or absence of adversity. The expectation remains that those suffering greater adversity will develop more problems of conduct over a longer time scale, but it is only a partial explanation.

Certain patterns of conduct, namely impulsive behaviours (inconsequence) are seen to be related to general impulsivity or personality (extraversion). It seems that the extravert child who develops or shows conduct difficulties of an impulsive type will be less likely to change and will also develop further difficulties in time, in response to the actions of others (hostility).

Understanding remission, therefore, involves all three of the explanatory propositions originally stated. They are not mutually exclusive but interact in defined ways. As to which explanation carries the strongest prediction, it appears to be 'Behaviour predicting subsequent behaviour of a similar type'. The strength of the other factors discovered does nevertheless underline the need to take account of their role. It is apparent that simply changing behaviour is not enough; one must act also to change the way the child is viewed, and to deal with the significant negative life-events the child experiences. To this extent, professional attempts to promote remission require a multi-model input, focusing on the behaviour and the significant agents and events in the child's life. An effective short-term therapeutic intervention would need to be supported by longer term action in the Child's community. The primary focus would seem to be the school.

Promoting remission

To achieve change we must:

- Act to change the behaviour itself, a task made particularly difficult by the low levels of conditionability of the pupil.

- Act to change the action of the school itself towards the child.

- Assist the child through individual crisis periods, rather than rejecting him (or her) because of his difficult nature.

The child most difficult to like is also the most in need of support.

Such action must involve the school in providing ongoing support, and also the range of other agencies and professionals involved at different stages in the life of the child and family.

The traditionally established variables of multiple adversity draw attention once again to the need for support for families at risk. However, there has also been a traditional tendency to place all behavioural disorder at the door of the poor family. Such a position is not tenable for these pupils.

The school itself, in the way children are labelled and the response offered, is part of the situation of concern. Ongoing action within the community of the child, and principally the school, is needed.

This is not an easy task, but it does point to the need to include five key elements in any change process.

1. How is the behaviour to be defined? The definition phase.

It is clear that the behaviour of the child must be carefully defined in the context in which it occurs. That change in behaviour may not be recognised raises important questions about the objectives of those involved. A variety of people are making the decisions, including the child. Each person able to influence the outcome may have to be included in the definition of the problem. Discrepancies between their views may be the appropriate point to start a change process. Given this interactive labelling process, any approach may require a social exchange of meaning/value. A contract for change may be necessary to enhance that process. The role each party is to play in the change process may have to be defined as part of the contract.

A definition phase based on social exchange concepts would represent the obvious starting point for a change process.

2. What factors must be taken into account? The exploration phase.

The data suggests the existence of constitutional and historical factors which have shaped the behaviour of the child. These predisposing factors are part of the child's past. There is little to be gained by considering them unless they impact on the present — and there is a suggestion that they might. For example, if there has been a history of problems between a child and a teacher, the beliefs that they hold, based on that history, influence the present. Knowing the history can help to construct a framework for change. The child's personal style of action (personality) will influence preferred behavioural styles for responding to events. Knowing those patterns has the potential to improve programme design.

Individual differences will, therefore, have to be taken into account in any change programme.

The patterns of support within the school and the community/family were found to be implicated, so may have to be included. So some predisposing events will need to be explored if their impact in the present can be demonstrated.

It was, however, current events that were found to alter the balance for the child, the reinforcement available for change and the beliefs of the participants. The data indicated that the day-to-day learning experiences of the child in school were important and could be altered, resulting in powerful beneficial effects.

Events which precipitate and maintain current behaviours must feature strongly in any analysis. Although group comparisons have been drawn, the particular combinations of events for each child, happening day by day, will be unique. Global change packages are unlikely to be helpful. What is needed is a careful formulation of the key factors for each child.

3. What is it like for me? A personal formulation phase.

Each child's, teacher's, school's, family's unique view of the events which matter must be understood. This must be backed by careful experimental data collected in the context in which the problem is defined. Thus, for each event, a formulation which explains what factors control the occurrence of the behaviour in context must be provided. If what is happening is understood, changing what is happening becomes possible.

4. What must we do to change? A planned intervention phase.

If it is to take account of key factors and potentially involve several change agents, the change process is going to be complex. Without a step by step plan, the process is going to become muddled. No one will be accountable, and the child will lose. Each person's responsibility for the change will have to be determined. The detail of what each is expected to do will have to be known. The outcome (performance) against which success is going to be measured must be specified. In this way the complexity might be successfully managed. However, the data suggests that long term change might have to be managed, in addition to short term interventions. An evaluation and follow-up process, to ensure that gains are not lost and new problems are tackled, will have to be included.

5. What must we do to ensure continued success? An evaluation phase.

We know that long term outcome depends on the events that happen subsequently to the child. We also know that change in behaviour may not be related to an evaluation of change by key agents. An agreed basis must be established to measure change for each programme. Once a predetermined performance target has been reached, the new situation must be addressed. It was established that, faced with success, new demands may emerge which are difficult for the child to manage. A long term support strategy may be needed until the child has developed the skills to meet new challenges, and not just to solve the existing difficulties. A careful evaluation and follow-up process is required.

Where next?

This is what the process looks like from the perspective of a research model. How might it be put into practice? How will the process of analysis be carried out? What will the intervention process look like? Will it work in practice? What outcome can we expect from undertaking what looks like a great deal of work? Part two of this study attempts to answer these questions.

A postscript

Peter, one of the most impossible of the impossible children, was delighted with the complexity of the material. He was pleased that it proved so hard to unravel even part of the picture. But he was even more pleased to discover that his scores on most of the measures were more extreme than anybody else's. 'Is that some sort of record?', he wanted to know. He also echoed the views of teachers when they laid down the challenge that the ideas would never work with their particular monster. 'I want to see if you get anywhere with me.', he stated at the beginning of his programme. Of course, we could not get anywhere if he wanted to prove his superiority by beating us. The challenge for us was not to beat him but to get him on board and to use his considerable power to improve his life chances rather than to perpetuate his impossibility

PART TWO

WORKING WITH THE IMPOSSIBLE CHILD

CHAPTER TWELVE

An introduction to school-focused analysis

Origins — The model discussed here evolved over a period of several years. It is very much based on the idea of behaviour as an experiment and is derived from the research data. It was first published in 1974 although it drew on earlier papers. It was revised in 1978 and almost immediately restructured for teaching purposes in 1979. Further revisions took place in 1983/1984. The current version is less complicated, but the underlying theoretical framework remains the same.

The original paper (Lane, 1974), was extensively used for training workshops, prior to the publication of the training manual in 1978. It has been applied in a wide variety of settings. Thus analysis of individual problems, by teachers and by psychologists in school settings, has featured alongside group work, whole school programmes and training analysis. Under a different title, 'Context-focused Analysis', it has been used in clinical, family and social work settings. It has also formed a framework for management analysis in public and private sector organisations, and as a structure for counselling. The detail varies in these different contexts but the basic outline remains. A number of other practitioners have used, adapted and evolved their own versions of this approach and have in turn influenced the thinking here (see for example those practitioners represented in Lane and Tattum, 1987,1990, Green and Bayley, 1987, Bayley, 1990, Coulby, 1981, Coulby and Harper, 1983, and Lane and Van Oudtshoorn, 1990.)

Some assumptions — We have already established that an individual is not a static element who can be precisely defined by a score on a test or other unit of measurement. Behaviour is characterised by change as well as considerable continuity. A person's behaviour does not exist in isolation from the context in which it occurs. It is part of a complex web of events that include biological states and social/political influences. One cannot always know the full picture, so any system of analysis will proceed by segmenting the full pattern into units which can be discovered, without losing sight of the influence of other areas. One strives towards an ecological picture, but may settle for less.

To observe any behaviour requires some idea of the reasons (objectives) for the behaviour. So inferences about the intention (meaning) of the behaviour form part of even the most objective system. The difference in an experimental approach is that the intention or meaning is not assumed from a theoretical conception but is tested and defined in such a way that an independent observer without access to the theoretical model could agree that the event took place. The actors themselves will also be able to reach such an agreement, without one, usually the client, having to rely on the others, usually the teacher/therapists, to interpret the meaning of the event. It has to become a partnership of exploration which seriously addresses the issue of power and the wider concerns which each party brings to the process.

Practicality —There are always limitations on the time and other resources that can be brought to a situation. These limitations must be recognised and used creatively. Fortunately, the underlying principle of the approach makes that possible. It is assumed that, at each stage, a working hypothesis is being used. There is never a certainty, only a best estimate given the available data. The process is exploratory and individuals are not assigned to categories and hence to treatment modalities. Thus, where a child has a so-called intellectual deficit, it is not the score that is of interest, but rather the style of the performance and the teaching to which the child has been exposed. The child who disrupts the class is not assigned to a maladjusted category; rather the factors in that class influencing the pupils and teachers behaviour are examined for potential for change in the situation. The change process is itself a working hypothesis to be further refined through the experience of the learning taking place for each party. Analysing the needs and generating that change will depend on the realities of that situation. It cannot be approached in a grandiose way which requires busy teachers to spend months collecting data and then waiting months for any effect. In many cases, any change would be immediate or at least within a week. At the end of the analysis the parties will understand the factors controlling the behaviour as it is at that moment. Therefore it might be possible to change part of it from that moment. Yes, even with an Impossible Child!

Age restrictions — The emphasis on a shared process has sometimes given rise to doubts about the age range for which the approach is applicable, particularly where open files were used, as was the practice of the Islington Centre. The problem really is one of balance. Very young children may take a less direct role than older children. That assumption must always be tested, for some amazing ideas have been produced by five and six years olds, which led on to effective intervention programmes . On occasions a teacher/psychologist/social worker/ manager would use the model to analyse difficulties without involving the client at all. Such a process is about management control and if the individual has thought the process through and can justify it in the particular circumstances, then it may be acceptable. Nevertheless, the programmes or their variants have been used extensively at Islington and elsewhere with several thousand children right across the age range. Even in work with Nursery-aged children such as a three year old described as 'catastrophic', a level of involvement is maintained. The youngest child ever called impossible (although it was the effect on staff that was being described), was nine months old. I admit that his views were not sought.

Constraints on the model — The reader should not confuse the educational analysis described here with diagnostic processes used by psychologists and psychiatrists. Those are the province of the specialists. This approach is intended to be:

a). Acceptable in the school situation, using readily available techniques. b). Educational in the sense of facilitating new learning. c). Derived from and responsive to the previous research findings.

To provide an overview, on page 116 is an outline of the process.

The structure of the process — The idea of performance discrepancy, introduced in the research data, forms the basis of the way the model is used in working with clients. Clients will each have their own way of working through a problem-solving process, and the aim is to assist with that working through. Each person will go through these steps. The one hundred or so pupils and a similar number of teachers on whom the research into how people learned to change was initially based, (Lane, 1976), were using similar models when they had made a commitment to another to work on change. The model, in its several variants, was subsequently used by several thousand individuals in a variety of contexts. This is not to say that they did not sometimes sabotage the work or go off at a tangent but, when faced with a shared concern leading to a need to work on a problem individuals tend to ask fundamentally similar questions about the situation:

1. What is wrong? ... This is what's wrong.
2. Why is it wrong ..?
3. This is why it's wrong ...
4. What can I do about it? ... This is what I can do about it
5. I've done it. ... What can I do next?

CHART ONE

AN OUTLINE OF SCHOOL-FOCUSED ANALYSIS

Someone tries to correct their performance or solve a problem

He/she may go through a series of steps or phases:

The five phases of school (context) focused analysis

DEFINE: the problem or objective

EXPLORE: the factors of influence

FORMULATE: an explanation of the factors of influence

INTERVENE: using an action plan based on the formulation

EVALUATE: the outcome of the plan based on the formulation

These steps may be repeated several times in a variety of ways, using the framework of their own style of learning

D   E   F   I   N   E

Our framework makes use of this pattern to derive a problem-solving approach that feels okay to those using it.

Individuals would often miss out steps or undertake them in a different sequence or wrap the elements up together, or get a sudden sense of the solution while still searching for the problem, but even then, expressing the process in this way helped. The most common jump was from step 1 to step 3. Interestingly, such a jump is featured in a number of texts on how to solve problems. Individuals are advised to define the problem, define a range of solutions and then evaluate the solutions before deciding which to choose. It seems to me that this misses out two steps which feel important to people, to do with knowing why something is wrong. It is certainly possible to say, 'never mind the reasons, just give me the solution', but the ability of individuals to solve other problems next time round is enhanced if they have acquired knowledge of a process, rather than simply a cookbook of solutions. Where the parameters of a problem are known, the step from problem to generation of options to action on a chosen option is viable. When the parameters are not known such an approach often leads to a whole series of ineffective solutions being tried and abandoned. A problem-solving approach which explores the unknown world of the possible is necessary when clear solutions are not available. (Lane, 1990) The model of analysis provides a format for this way of solving problems. (see pages 118-119) The chapters which follow introduce the model.

Too much should not be made of this model. It is one way of working, not the only way of working. It reflects, with varying degrees of accuracy, the learning process. It does however, provide a framework for working with the Impossible Child. It is to the details that we must now turn.

CHART TWO

A SUMMARY OF THE PHASES OF SCHOOL-FOCUSED ANALYSIS

Phase 1. Definition

Someone becomes aware that a problem exists. This may be a vague sense of something not feeling right, or something definitely going wrong. It may come from feedback from others or from themselves, but they do need a sense of performance error (discrepancy). This is not how it should: be, feel, act, taste, look, work, etc.. In order to understand it they will have to specify the components of the behaviour in question, that is,the vague sense will gradually give way to a (fairly) precise definition of the problem which can be shared with others, "a shared concern".
The process is one of growing awareness.

Phase 2. Exploration

They seek information about the problem. This information may be sought from others, particularly when the feedback originated with someone else. It might come through monitoring their own performance, 'What's going on here?'. They may try to reconstruct the error, but they will gradually gather data on the factors which are influencing their behaviour. They may need to redefine their own view or seek to change the views of others. If they do gain some understanding of the factors involved, they will try to develop some sense of what is appropriate behaviour.
The process is one of observation.

Phase 3. Formulation

They will test the validity of any explanations. They will use behaviour as an experiment. They may check out the validity of their own standards of performance with others. They may try out different actions or explanations to see what feedback they get. Eventually they will get a sense that they understand the situation.....'That's it !'.
The process is one of hypothesis testing (the pragmatic scientist).

Phase 4. Intervention

They will develop a plan of action. Based on their understanding of what is the problem and what factors influence it, and the course of action necessary for change, they will design a specific plan. It will ideally specify the 'what, how, who and when' necessary for behaviour change.

The process is one of structured practice.

Phase 5. Evaluation

They will evaluate their new performance against the standards. They will monitor themselves, seek feedback, and (if they have learnt the lessons of this process) they will praise themselves for their success, not blame themselves for failure, but regard it as evidence that they need to re-assess the situation. They will, if successful, seek evidence of new areas which might arise, maintain their gains and set new objectives.

The process is one of monitored achievement.

An individual's success at this process depends upon obtaining accurate information, getting a valid explanation, choosing an appropriate plan of action and monitoring and receiving positive feedback on their efforts.....

WITHIN A SUPPORTIVE ENVIRONMENT.

CHAPTER THIRTEEN

Defining the problem

PHASE ONE: DEFINITION

The process for defining the problem is the first phase of the work. It has three steps which represent main tasks which are likely to have to be completed. The process will be considered in relation to a case from 1975 (first published in 1978). This pupil is not an impossible child (although easily could have become one) but the example is useful as a starting point and an elaboration of some of the earlier material is included to illustrate some of the pitfalls. Some more complex case studies follow, which illustrate some of the major problems that can arise.

In order to make sense of the process you need to think of yourself as one of the characters. You might be a Headteacher, a Special Needs Advisor within the School, a Head of Year/House in a Secondary School, a Parent, one of the Children involved, a Psychologist or someone from a Behaviour Support Team, or you could be me in 1975, struggling with one of my first referrals and keen not to antagonise the school. In placing yourself in one of these roles, consider the advantages and disadvantages of the process from the perspective employed. There are always victims and beneficiaries of any process.

WHERE DO YOU START?

Someone, somewhere, has identified a behaviour(s) to be changed — the problem. In the case of children, the problem as identified usually exists as a statement of intent or an initial referral statement. A start has to be made with that statement, however vague it might be.

For example:

Jack is a mean vicious boy to Mary and we or somebody ought to do something about him.

Contained within such statements and most referrals are three elements:

a) The problem

b) The objective of the referring agent

c) A preliminary ascription of role.

Jack is the problem ... maybe it is his behaviour but maybe it is him the person ... mean and vicious.

Something must be done, a vague objective so far.

By us or ... somebody, that is not just the classroom teacher but somebody else must help.

It is very important to be aware that there are three elements, all of them important. Originally we paid attention to the first two but only minor attention to the third. Now we examine each in turn.

THE PROBLEM : DESCRIPTIONS OF BEHAVIOUR

It is important to remember that behaviour is both complex and dynamic. (Our thanks to Bayley, 1990, and the Southwark Team, for clarification of these two issues. What follows draws on their manual.)

(i) Behaviour is complex

During a day we engage in a wide range of behaviours. We are better at some things than others; we perform better in some settings than others. Anyone who has followed a whole class or an individual child around the different lessons and breaks of a day at secondary school will testify to the wide range of behaviours shown. This observation is important to us for several reasons. Firstly, any global description of an individual's behaviour is bound to be a generalisation, often coloured with strong emotive feelings. In fact, the difference between 'acceptable' or 'unacceptable' behaviour can often boil down to a number of key points. Student and teacher alike both benefit from having a precise idea of what needs changing in a situation.

Secondly, it is important to break a problem down into its discrete parts so that we can estimate whether or not the problem is within our competence. We cannot effect complete personality changes (even if we wanted to) but we can assist in making changes in particular aspects of a situation. This is very important in dynamic institutions like schools. We intervene in the life of the child and a complex organisation for relatively brief periods; we are bound to get bogged down unless we have a clear and limited idea of our objectives, and that starts with clear problem definition.

(ii) Behaviour is dynamic.

We know from the literature review and data in part one, that as much as 70% of 'emotional and behavioural difficulties' experienced by children naturally remit, usually within about a year. We also know that people's behaviour changes through time. This is particularly so with growing children. Teachers know that many children 'grow through a problem'.

This point is particularly important when it comes to focusing on 'difficult' children. Close observation often shows that the behaviour last year is different from this year. The child that used to fight a lot and not concentrate in lessons may this year be truculent and in fact get quite an amount of work done. But last year's reputation hangs on. Or the behaviour may have changed completely. A referred student may come with a bulging folder tracing her history through difficulties with a severe speech impediment in her youth, her behaviour involving doing very little work, sometimes hitting other children and ignoring teachers when spoken to. These were recognisably real problems, but the school's perception of her behaviour was coloured by the 'abnormal' classification that came with the bulky file.

Once we start work with a student or group of students, behaviour will go on changing. We will not be able to know the effect of our intervention unless we have a clear definition of the problem to compare with the later situation. In this way we, and the student and the school, can assess the effect of our intervention.

PHASE 1. Step 1. We need an initial statement of problem

The first step is to get an accurate description of the problem. But from what perspective?

We have seen from the research that a variety of perspectives will be involved. So the first question becomes:

"Who are the significant agents in this process?"

The child and teacher must be involved, but also involved may be parents, other teachers, pupils, helpers, etc... Any person who is identified as someone able significantly to influence the outcome of the change process must be identified and a statement of the problem, as seen by them, obtained.

There are four important parts to the 'significant agents' question.

- **Who is the client ?**
John Few, (1978) in his work with the Islington Centre, identified this issue as critical in support work.

- **Who should be involved ?**
Anyone who has a stake might have to be included.

- **Who are the gatekeepers and bankers ?**
This question arises from our experience establishing the support service. (Lane, 1987, Lane and Tattum, 1990) Some people will be critical because they can open or close gates leading to information and solutions, and some

people hold the resources necessary to a change process. The micropolitics of the situation is important. (Hoyle, 1986)

- **Who benefits from the referral and who does not ?**

This issue can sometimes be critical. Recently an alternative way to obtain 'root definitions of the system' has appeared. Although not, as yet, used by us it provides an elegant set of questions. (Checkland, 1989)

C.. Customer — who are the victims and beneficiaries?
A.. Actors — who will have to take necessary action?
T.. Transformation process — how will inputs be transformed into outputs?
W.. Worldview — what view of the world is implied?
O.. Owner — who has the power to say no?
E.. Environmental constraints — what constraints are present in the system?
This range of issues are all present within the apparently simple task of defining the problem.

WE START WITH THE STATEMENTS OF THE REFERRING AGENT. These statements will be muddled or concise, describe the behaviour or not, but they are an important starting-point in understanding the meaning that each party sees in the behaviour.

Consider the statement, 'Sarah is a disturbed child. She has always been a problem and causes a great deal of disruption in school'. This statement involves a number of elements. There is an interpretive element — 'Sarah is a disturbed child'. There is an historical statement — 'She has always been a problem'. There is a very general statement — 'causes a great deal of disruption in school'. All this information will be of use and can give us an idea of the perceptions held of the problem by the significant agents. But it does not tell us what Sarah does.

A more useful statement might be — 'Sarah frequently cries at the beginning of lessons. She sometimes has temper fits and throws things at other children'.

This statement gives us something to observe. To put it another way, an independent observer could judge whether or not such a set of behaviours exist.

As the end product of a process of defining a problem, then, a more precise statement may be obtained. If that statement can become an agreed definition which represents the shared concern of those involved, much would have been achieved. It is the process of moving towards a shared concern which constitutes the work of the first phase of the process.

The idea of a performance-discrepancy provides the linking mechanism to achieve that shared concern. There is little point in defining what the child should not do unless what the child should do is defined as an alternative. The use of a term like 'should' of course, implies a value judgement. Those value judgements are part of the reality of the system. However, muddled definitions are all part of the system as well. Very often, clients have to start with something vague, a feeling, belief, issue. Working through that to a shared concern is part of the process. It is a mistake (one I made frequently in the early days) simply to push the client to define more precisely. It is possible to start form a general statement and gradually work towards a sense of a shared concern which can then be defined in specific terms. Without that process of working for a shared concern, conflict will simply be perpetuated.

The child will have a view, as will the other parties. They work towards a definition of the behaviour of concern by reference to its alternatives. The discrepancy between performance now and performance as intended becomes the shared concern. Once a shared concern is possible, shared objectives become possible.

Some of the mechanisms for achieving that shared concern are now discussed.

Strategies for defining a problem

If a clear definition of the problem is not possible at the outset, there are a number of strategies we can adopt.

(a) *Collect anecdotal material* — school files, referral sheets, reports and records all contain useful material. It will contain a mixture of assumptions and observations but can be a useful starting point.

(b) *Provide a checklist* — make up a simple list of behaviours and ask teacher(s) and student(s) to tick appropriate ones. It may be useful to ask the teacher to rate the frequency and severity of behaviour compared with that of other pupils.

(c) *Collect test data* — Teacher(s)and student(s) can be asked to complete test forms such as BSAG and to write in comments. These forms provide clear initial data.

(d) *Incidents* — It can be useful to get reports of several recent 'incidents'. It is important to get as much fact and as little interpretation as possible.

(e) *Interviews and observation* — Discussing the definition with the referring teacher or the student or observing the student (in a lesson for example) is an effective way to define a problem. It is quite expensive in time.

(f) *Be inventive* — people vary greatly in how they express concerns. Over the years this has included references to literature, songs, a passage of music, a dance movement, an image, a sculpture, a drawing, etc. Be welcoming of this variety, as it does provide a way in to understanding what the concern means to that individual. It is important to remember that these processes provide a starting point which are later refined to become a shared concern.

That later concern will be expressed in a form which makes the testing of hypotheses possible.

Points which need to be considered before proceeding.
* Check whether or not the problem has been defined by reference to an alternative behaviour. (performance discrepancy)

After we have used some or all the above methods to collect information, we can ask the question:
* Does the data obtained make it possible to define the problem so that an analysis of it can proceed? We cannot move on until we clearly understand the presenting problem.

Initial Statement of the Problem

The process of working towards an initial statement of the problem may sometimes be time-consuming, but it is worth the effort. If you can obtain a shared concern, frequently the rest of the process works very quickly because the parties have a commitment to change. Now we can create an initial statement of the problem. This statement should be free of assumptions as to causes. It should not be assumed that the child is the cause of the problem, or that it is the child who must change. All the participating agents are involved and all may need to modify their behaviour.

It may be useful to divide the problem or problems into specific and general features. There may be quite precise points regarding particular types of incidents or circumstances and some observations on more general patterns of behaviour. For example;

'Robert does not work when he is asked to'. (Specific)

'Robert punches and kicks other children when he is teased'. (Specific)

'Robert spends very little time in the company of other children'. (General)

These, of course, are the teachers' definitions. Robert might be saying that his concern is:

'Not getting help with work.'

'Being teased.'

'The children don't like me.'

There is clearly a difference in emphasis, but the possibility of expressing a shared concern exists if both parties can agree to suspend judgements about the 'cause' of the problem and instead redefine their concerns in such a way that they can share them. Once the problem is defined, the objectives of those involved can be discussed. In practice, the discussion of objectives may precede

126

the statement of the problem. This is usually less satisfactory, but may be necessary if tempers run very high. If those involved can agree on the objectives, then the more detailed discussion necessary to understand the problem becomes easier.

PHASE 1. Step 2. The Initial Definition of the Objectives

Next we have to clarify and integrate the objectives of the main participants. What do they want to happen and how far do their objectives match?

The first difficulty that arises is: who should be included in this discussion? Should it be just the referring agents (the school usually), or should it include the student(s) concerned, and the parents? This is a matter for professional discretion. However it is best to include the views of the student(s) and parents or guardians, as they are likely to influence the outcome. Those who have a stake in the outcome are ignored at one's peril. The aim here is to obtain at least an initial agreement on objectives.

Usually the problems and the objectives will coincide. For example, if a student is getting involved in lots of fights, the objective will probably be to stop that happening. However, the problem and the objective do not always coincide. For example, the problem may be fighting in school and the school's objective may be to get the child removed, but the child's objective may be to stop people teasing him. Or there may be several problems, such as lateness and getting into fights, and the school and parents may disagree on the relative importance of the different problems.

Usually it is possible with further discussion to get some agreement on objectives. If not, we can still proceed to analyse the problem but keeping the different objectives and priorities of the parties clearly distinct. Each set of problem definitions and objectives can be analysed, treating each as valid. The task of reaching agreement will then await further information.

Other issues arise that must be included in these initial discussions.

(i) **Participants' expectations.**
The participants will have some expectations about what help is to be offered. These should be fully discussed both in order that the participants' expectations can be clarified and, where possible, taken into account, in order that any misconceptions concerning future interventions can be discussed.

(ii) **Acceptable methods of work**
Even at an early stage it will be necessary to make clear what options are possible for working with a problem — these may range from partial withdrawal to a unit, individual support work, counselling, modified curriculum and so on. Reaching agreement is not attempted at this stage, but the range of options and

what is or is not acceptable must be borne in mind. It represents part of the reality base the parties operate.

One of the major complaints from parents about assessment processes was that they were not fully informed of the implications of their agreement. Much misunderstanding can be avoided, and trust can be built, if time is taken with this issue. The professional(s) involved may find it difficult but it is essential.

(iii) **Feasibility**

It is useful to make sure that the objectives being sought are realistic, given the available resources. The anxiety and hopes of the different parties can sometimes build up pressure to achieve the impossible, so keeping a sense of proportion is essential.

(iv) **Organisational Structures**

Finally, it is important to check that all the organisational resources involved are suitable for the tasks outlined for them. For example, in the case of a child who is depressed, possible options might include counselling. It is important to ensure that the relevant persons in school consider such support to be part of their role and are equipped to give it.

This discussion around objectives is often difficult — and often fudged. It is sometimes argued that it is pointless to discuss with parents or pupils options that might not come to pass. But, in working with pupils and parents who are already hostile to the services provided, by presenting a false picture of the situation to avoid difficulty is not helpful in the long run. Achieving shared concern is worth the effort, even if it is only partial at this stage.

PHASE 1. Step 3. The definition of role.

This issue was mentioned briefly in the original training manuals but deserves more attention. It is apparent from increasing research into patterns of service delivery, that individuals do have certain expectations about the role that they believe others will play. Is the parent looking to the teacher as an 'Expert', who can offer clear advice, or is a partnership in joint problem-solving preferred. Does an external advisor, teacher, social worker, or psychologist prefer a shared approach to the issue, when the teacher just wants to be told what to do. Does the child think a psychologist is a psychiatrist whose role is to lock them up, or is the child a highly sophisticated user of support services, who can tell the professionals the limits of their powers?

It is not for the professional to state what role the parent or child might play, but to find out what role they prefer and negotiate a mutually acceptable method of working. We were certainly aware of this problem (Lane, 1972, 1973), particularly so as we used an open file system at the Islington Centre from its inception, but the complexity of this issue was glossed over in the early work.

A discussion around each party's expectation about the role they are going to play in the analysis of the problem is, therefore, essential. This will include: who provides/collects what information and the ownership of any data: who decides what will be done and, if statutory issues apply, how they will operate.

If we return to the problem presented by Jack, we can explore this initial phase of the process.

Jack is a mean vicious boy and somebody ought to do something about him.

The strength of feeling of the teacher may well be expressed in this statement but it does not define the problem. It was originally redefined by asking the teacher to provide examples of what she meant by the phrase 'mean and vicious'.

The example given was: punching and kicking Mary.

Discussions with the Head Teacher, Jack and his parents led to a partial shared concern but also disagreement. Jack and his parents agreed the behaviour should stop but disagreed about why he was doing it. The teacher's insistence that it was his problem was met by their insistence that it was not

Jack took the view that Mary deserved to be hit because she insulted him.

It was possible to negotiate a limited shared concern, namely that the difficulty seemed to need more understanding, and it was agreed that observations in class would be useful to clarify: what Jack actually did; when he did it; how often; Mary's role.

The teacher was asked to make specific notes on any incident and this yielded additional information. The incidents recorded were detailed and did in fact clarify 'what, when, and how often'. Mary was seen in the role of purely an innocent victim. Two additional behavioural problems were raised: 'dancing on the tables', and 'impulsiveness'. Dancing on the tables was defined adequately, but impulsiveness was not. However, discussion with those involved led to an agreement to explore the behaviour in more detail.

The teacher's role was defined at this stage as primary data collector, but Jack was to be involved in providing commentary on any data from his perspective. His parents preferred not to be involved but wanted to be consulted about any decisions. The Headteacher would facilitate discussion on decisions. The Advisor

---

(Islington Centre in this case but it could have been another member of staff, psychologist, special needs teacher, etc.,) would assist the teacher to devise observation methods or assist with them.

Discussion of possible outcomes was difficult since the teacher felt that an external placement was the answer. The parents were opposed to this and wanted a school-based solution to be found. They also felt that too much blame was attributed to Jack .

The shared concern at this stage was defined as:

The problems

... Jack was seen punching and kicking Mary on at least one occasion per day. He danced on the tables when told not to do so. He was generally impulsive (a description too ill-defined to be useful, but a compromise on this was reached).

The objectives were identified as ... To explore the factors which caused Jack to punch and kick Mary; for Jack to stop dancing on the tables — parents and teachers agreed that this was unacceptable and Jack was simply told to stop it, and to reach an agreement about the definition of impulsive behaviour so that the alternative to it could be defined.

The roles were also decided... the teacher was to collect data on incidents; Jack was to comment on the data; the advisor was to suggest methods for data collection; the parents and Headteacher to take part in a meeting to discuss the results and agree the next stage.

All this preparatory work had laid the ground for analysing the problem. Before moving on to Phase Two and an analysis of the problem it is wise to recapitulate the process.

1. Someone has identified a problem.

2. A statement of the problem and the objective has been obtained and clarified.

3. The expectations of the participants have been considered.

4. The possible range of interventions has, in general, been discussed and acceptable ones identified.

5. The feasibility of the proposal has been assessed, taking into account available resources.

6. The situation/organisation in which change is proposed is one which is amenable to that change.

7. The roles have been defined.

8. A shared concern has been established, even if it is only partial.

This process is primarily about each party becoming aware of the issues of concern and agreeing to explore them in the next phase.

CHAPTER FOURTEEN

Exploring the problem

PHASE TWO: EXPLORATION

The task now is to observe the problem in context and its surrounding circumstances in sufficient detail to gather data that will allow us to explain it. We are moving from a statement of the problem itself towards consideration of why the problem occurs.

The potential number of explanations is very large and to make the exploration viable, some hypothesis of cause is necessary. Hypotheses of cause emerge from a number of sources but they must be specified in some way which will allow information to be gathered on their validity.

In part this process is an exploration of the possible, of unknown parameters. If the situation was understood it would be possible to move through a restricted framework. (Lane, 1990) For example:

1. Definition of the problem
2. Establishment of the shared concern
3. Generation of options
4. Commitment to a chosen option
5. Evaluation of outcome

The process could proceed in a circular fashion until an adequate solution was implemented. In many cases this is exactly the process that is used in work with children in school situations. I used it myself, frequently, as a Departmental Head. However, in the case of more complex problems and certainly in respect of the Impossible Child, immediate or crises solutions have been found wanting. An exploration of possibilities is necessary. It is important to the success of the exploration to suspend judgement on solutions and the 'realism' of the data obtained. Too often, colleagues prevented themselves from finding workable ideas because they quickly dismissed ideas as unrealistic. At this stage forget about realism, explore possibilities. Later in the process, a comparison is made against real world constraints and realistic, practical decisions are made.

During the exploration phase you are dealing with possibilities and moving towards the creation of a model of the real world. In phase three 'Formulation', you build that model and test it. The extent to which it provides a viable explanation determines the success of any intervention plan constructed upon it. It is more time-consuming to explore rather than prescribe, but our experience has demonstrated that in the case of children presenting long term problems, it is worth while. In fact data we collected on the process indicated that the resources consumed were fewer than those used in abortive attempts at crisis management.

PHASE 2. Step 4. Generating hypotheses.

We are concerned at this stage with determining the areas in which we are going to look for explanations of cause; we are not determining cause.

Two key questions provide the starting point.

1.   Is the problem specific to a given situation or does it occur more generally?

If the problem is specific, then it is factors in that situation which concern us. If the problem is more general, then a broader range of situations may have to be explored which may include organisational or individual explanations.

2.   When did the problem first occur? Is it something new or have similar/identical problems happened in the past?

If the problem is specific to the here and now, exploration will focus on current events. However, if it represents part of an ongoing or repeating pattern, an exploration of the history may be required.

At this stage we are, in effect, creating hypotheses to be tested. We might be saying that the problem is of recent origin and occurs only in a specific situation and in the presence of certain people.

The distinction between 'past and general' and 'present and specific' helps to choose methods based on Trait or State approaches respectively.

Beyond these two areas, the specific attributions of cause that the participants hold provide the starting point for formally defining hypotheses. What is it that Jack, his teacher, his parents, the advisor, think is the likely cause of the problem? These are personal hypotheses and will be expressed in different forms, but they do need to be recognised. Some will be based on a theory of behaviour, some on experience in the situation, but all are valid as hypotheses.

Once we have identified the existing hypotheses, alternative possible explanations of cause relevant to context can be discussed. The aim is not to reach agreement on the hypotheses, only to agree that they will be explored.

Once the hypotheses to be explored can be agreed, the issue of proof and disproof can be considered.

The aim is to specify the type of information which would support any hypothesis, and that which would throw doubt upon it.

For Jack we have two hypotheses:

---

1. In respect of Mary:

We are saying that there is a specific problem and that it may relate to a set of circumstances in a specific classroom or in respect of something between Jack and Mary. We are looking for an exploration of those circumstances. However, the problem seems to have a history. Concern has been evident for some time so a limited history of this may be necessary.

2. In respect of Jack's impulsiveness:

This is still not defined but the impression given by the teacher is that it is a general problem. An analysis of Jack's behaviour in a variety of settings may be required but since it is still ill-defined we need to define rather than explore it. So we must choose a method to define the problem. (This is still a Phase One issue, but the reality of classroom life necessitates taking the issues forward together, but keeping hold of the fact that this issue is still being defined.)

The source of the hypotheses are Jack, his teacher and parents. They can probably be specified more precisely than this and will need to be, before any data is collected, but for the purpose of choosing methods to collect the observations this will do.

PHASE 2. Step 5. Selection of the Observation Technologies

How are we to undertake our observations? We have to keep several principles in mind to make sure that the data we collect is useful to our final analysis.

The prerequisite concerns:

(a) Reliability

Observations must be reliable — that is to say, they should not vary noticeably if collected by different observers. This is relatively easy to achieve if standardised tests are used. It is more difficult in more unstructured areas, such as classroom observation or interviews. Structured forms of observation can help, such as ticking off every five minutes whether a student is on-off task, and so on. The important thing is to avoid biased observations for data purposes.

(b) **Validity**

Observations can be considered valid if they measure what they purport to measure. Take for example a situation where we have been asked to see if a student is unusually impulsive in certain situations. If we were undertaking standard five minute observations we would want to ensure that we had (a) observed for long enough, (b) observed in all the relevant situations, (c) compared these observations with those of another randomly chosen student and (d) compared with other observations, such as BSAG. To put it another way, a one-off observation of a student being easily distracted would not constitute a valid measure of impulsiveness.

(c) **Economy**

Schools are not laboratories where detailed and prolonged observations can be unhurriedly carried out. Teachers and other professionals have great demands on their time and energy. If they are constantly being asked to fill in detailed forms and write long reports, the results will soon be not worth having or will not appear at all. So thinking of easy and economic ways of eliciting information is part of the selection process. The example of providing teachers with tick-off charts for assessing situations may be a practical way into this. In a large and busy school it might be asking too much of a group of teachers to assemble together for a long case conference on a child. On the other hand, if a brief checklist were provided in advance a twenty minute meeting of all the concerned teachers might prove a quick and economical way of getting answers based on a series of well thought out questions, made possible by the checklist.

(d) **Ease**

Similarly, data should be sought which is easy rather than difficult to obtain. The more complex the procedure needed, the greater the potential for error. If you find yourself involved in collecting data which requires observations five times a day in different settings over a period of three weeks, you are probably on the wrong track!

(e) **Accessibility**

Elaborate techniques of observation and intervention may be effective but if they require a degree of expertise or resources not generally available, little is gained. For example, calling in an outside expert to administer an elaborate test, the results of which would be obscure to most of the parties involved, is unlikely to be really useful. The principle: 'least intervention to achieve significant gain', should always be applied.

(f) Ethics

The question of ethics will always arise when someone with greater power is investigating someone with less. Where a shared concern has been established, the issue of consent is partly tackled although the power differential remains.

Take for example the question of observation. Is it right to observe students in the classroom without their prior knowledge? A simple first test to apply is to ask whether, if the position were reversed and you the subject of investigation, you would be happy with the approach adopted. The best position to start from is that of assuming that the students we work with have the right to informed consent or rejection of the work we do. Then, if we wish to depart from the general principle, we have to offer clear justification.

There may be circumstances in which a teacher may wish to undertake detailed observations of certain children without their knowledge. If it can be clearly justified, okay, but can it? To illustrate:

In my work I frequently observed a child as a comparison with the child who was the centre of the analysis. That comparison child was never consulted. The justification was that the data on that child was never used or recorded in the name of the child. Is that just?

On many occasions, teachers asked me to look at a child in class and discuss my observations with them. The teacher was thinking about a referral but did not want to make one at that point. The justification was that it would prevent unnecessary referrals, and no data was recorded which could subsequently be used. Is that just?

Frequently, teachers would ask for observations and advice on the management of a problem. No data was recorded and classroom management is a legitimate concern of the teacher. So advice on management was given. Is that just?

In circumstances where a child was formally referred, parental permission was always obtained and the child involved. But if the advice needed by the teacher was relatively simple, a parent's anxieties were raised — perhaps unnecessarily. Is that just?

The Choice of an Analytic Technology

We have defined the problem and objectives and given some consideration to the observation methods we might use. Now we come to collect those observations that we hope will provide us with an idea of cause and effect - that is, we are collecting material to help us answer the question,

What factors influence the occurrence of the problem?

There is a whole universe of approaches that may be adopted. Some may focus primarily on the individual (Eg psychoanalytic or developmental approaches), others on the individual and significant persons, (interaction analysis, transactional analysis), and others on more general aspects (e.g. organisation and systems theory). When choosing an approach, we will be influenced by the nature of the problem we are analysing, by our own general theoretical approach, and by our own competence in different areas.

In analysing and assisting with human problems, there is no one 'right' way to analyse or work with a problem. Working with a troubled child, a psychoanalyst might obtain a personal history and use psychoanalysis; a behaviourist might analyse the precipitating and contingent aspects of the problem behaviours and work with a programme of behaviour modification; a teacher might analyse the strengths and weaknesses of the curricula offer and design new teaching materials to engage the interest of the child; and so on. Each of these methods might be equally effective. All that we can ask is that a method of analysis and a method of intervention are made quite clear and specific; that the choice of analytic method is justified; that the method of analysis is appropriate to the intervention carried out; and that a method of assessing the effectiveness of the work is built into the programme. Beyond this there is always the question of justifying the work ethically, in terms of available research, and to those involved.

We summarise some available methods, relating to the hypotheses issue of the 'specific and present' and the 'general and past'.

In choosing a technique for analysis, it is important to remember that the choice is not an arbitrary one. Practitioners do not in effect choose an historical analysis (discussed below) because they happened to fancy doing an historical analysis. Their choice is determined by the problem, objectives and hypotheses previously listed.

The techniques (devices for determining problem and factors of influence) are based on a technology (body of knowledge about problems, and factors of influence).

For example, test data approaches may include the technique of administering a personality or I.Q. test, but that technique carries with it certain assumptions about individuals. That is, that they can be usefully defined by virtue of their position, compared with others, against a given criterion or 'norm'. On the other hand, functional analysis (also discussed below) contains the assumption that each individual behaviour must be treated as a unique environmental event, so reference to norms (the rated scores of others by test) is irrelevant. The choice of analytic technology must reflect the nature of the problem and the objective to be met.

Thus: processes which see the individual's behaviour as:

(A) **Unique:** historical analysis — functional analysis — experimentation

(B) **Comparative**: test data — developmental analysis

The choice of approach is made according to its appropriateness to determining relevant factors in the particular case and not at random or by predetermination (attaching a 'problem' label). The approach adopted here assumes the unique nature of the individual and his situation but assumes also that it may be useful to compare one child with another. We can sum up what may need to be determined in a given case as follows:

(A) **General and past features (potential traits)** These are factors of influence in the individual's situation or life experience. They include constitutional factors such as specific impairments, developmental status and temperament, and experiential factors such as the significant models to whom the individual has been exposed. The entire history, physiology etc. of the child is not investigated, only aspects which could be considered relevant. For example, if a child were referred for aggressive behaviour, his temperament (personality data) would be a constitutional feature of interest. Likewise, the existence of an aggressive father as a model would be an experiential factor worth considering. Trait is defined in more detail later but, basically, any event which may predispose towards the likelihood of the difficulty occurring is investigated.

(B) **Specific and present features (state)** These are factors of influence in the current situation. They include:

General setting factors — such as a generally unruly classroom in which aggressive behaviour is more likely to occur. Precipitating factors — such as the child being told off 'unfairly' by the teacher.

Maintaining factors — such as peer status for being aggressive towards an unfair teacher.

In undertaking an analysis, therefore, the problem behaviour(s) as previously defined is analysed by two components:

The general factors likely to act as predispositions (traits) and the specific factors likely to precipitate and maintain the behaviour(s).

Remember that the choice is determined by the hypotheses. You may not explore trait factors in certain cases, but you will always need to understand the current (state) situation.

The trait and state division is offered as a useful way of managing the task of data collection. It is not necessary to buy into the concept, in order to make use of the step-by-step process, since it is the hypotheses of cause by the participants which are the subject of investigation.

It is not claimed that this is the only valid form of analysis. The process of working through the given steps, from definition (Step 1) to re-evaluation (Step 15) is, however, appropriate to most objective, analytic systems.

The technologies relevant to the understanding of trait and state components are now considered.

Formulation of technologies to analyse the problem

There are a range of available methods, a few of which are covered here. The organisation of the techniques is in terms of those useful in understanding trait and state elements. Technologies for understanding trait elements

In analysing trait elements, the concern is with factors that predispose the likelihood of one response rather than another to a given situation. Thus the interest is not in every aspect of the individual's existence but only in factors which could result in consistent, enduring potential for a given pattern of response.

The technologies discussed below are used to gain information about enduring predispositions, whether constitutionally or experientially acquired.

Developmental assessment — This is based on comparative conceptions, that is, a child is considered in relation to experimental or clinical norms. But, in working with children, it must never be forgotten that they vary in their rate of development and differ over time. The child's position on an overall developmental framework must be taken into account, not simply his position on one aspect at one moment. Many children suffer temporary problems. Awareness of these has to guide the individual so that inappropriate and premature interventions do not take place. Of interest is the overall pattern of development of the child in relation to peers. One asks whether there are any areas in which they seem to be 'out of step'. The medical history of the children and families should be checked for any evidence of disorders. The general health of the child should be considered. Do they frequently suffer from a particular illness, or several minor illnesses? Any evidence of speech, language, sensory or motor problems would require suitable investigation.

Professional clinical assessment must be sought if there are any indications that the general health or developmental status of the child is in question.

Of particular interest in relation to constitutional aspects are any signs of problem behaviour which appear to be unmotivated — the child doing things without reason. If it really does appear that there is no reasonable basis, in terms of the 'state' factors discussed later, for an explanation of the child's behaviour, the possibility of a constitutional impairment must be explored. For example, in three recent cases of children referred for sporadic aggression or impulsivity, it proved impossible to find 'state' explanations and, on further investigation (by medical practitioners), evidence of epilepsy was revealed. The concern is with patterns of change in the pupil's behaviour over time and situation, in relation to peers.

Further discussions of this complex area are available in Illingworth (1975). The value of a development perspective is emphasised by Christie (et.al., 1990).

Historical analysis — This acknowledges importance of the uniqueness of each individual. No individual will have had the identical experiences of another. The importance of the history of the problem should never be forgotten. The history provides clues to predisposing factors (in the acquisition of patterns of response) but does not explain its present status. Only currently operating factors ('state') can do that. Obtaining a history helps unravel the development of the problem (its acquisition), the general influence to which the child has been exposed (general background factors) and the child's experience of different models of behaviour (imitation learning).

Acquisition — The value of understanding the way in which a problem evolved varies from situation to situation. Any suddenly occurring behaviour problem (a crisis) should be considered in terms of acquisition. Additionally, fear reactions are often better understood in the light of an acquisition history. However, histories of anti-social behaviours of long standing are usually difficult to obtain and consequently of less value.

One asks when the problem first appeared (onset), the circumstances under which it appeared, what happened prior to and following it, any changes since onset, and the consequences for the individual and others of the behaviour.

General background — The general situation of the school child, family and circumstances and biographic information not supplied on the initial referral, is obtained. This is of interest in providing an orientation, more rarely of value in determining controlling factors. Data should be treated with caution, therefore, and only included if they can be realistically related to the explanation of the problem.

Model exposure — Across the whole range of problem areas, details of significant others who provide models of behaviour to the child should be elicited. Again, it should be stressed that the existence of an aggressive father as a model for an aggressive pupil does not explain current behaviour. It provides a clue to experiential factors which may have led to the learning of particular patterns of response. These patterns provide a predisposing influence. The existence of significant models from whom the child may imitate behaviour and who may encourage the child's inappropriate behaviour, must be noted.

Their presence may indicate the need for training the child in alternative behaviours and for the provision of alternative encouragement, to counter the effect of the model.

Wolpe (1973) provides examples of the way the history of the problem is related to current events and further examples or discussions are available in Lane and Green (1978) and Meyer and Chesser (1970). Unfortunately, in work with children, a clear history is not often available. In such situations other indications of predisposing traits in behaviour must be used such as test data or observations of general behaviour patterns in different situations.

Organisational analysis — Since problems for the individual may occur in several settings including institutions, the analysis of those settings is necessary. It is useful to consider organisations in the same way as individuals, that is, as being governed by trait and state elements. (This is not meant in a literal sense, of course, but it does help to clarify analysis.)

1. **Traits** — Organisational traits, that is, predispositions to respond in a definite way arise from two basic sources:

    (a) **Constitutional factors** — The formal role definition and structures of an organisation act both to limit the potential and to provide the basic building blocks for its achievements.

    (b) **Experiential factors** — The informal roles and modifications to formal constitutional structures which arise from experience in operation shape the constitutional potential of the organisation.

2. **States** — Although the above provide the potential for action, it is the current events (states or situation) which determine actual achievement. Although techniques for unravelling trait and state elements overlap, the distinction can usually be kept in mind. Some of the relevant, essentially trait issues are discussed below. The consideration of the other areas, i.e., states, can be tackled in terms of sociological models of functional analysis, discussed later. The aim is to try to create an organisational structure in which both the individual and the organisation can achieve the optimal satisfaction of goals.

This is a complex area and the reader might care to refer to studies such as Argyis (1957) and Buckley (1967) for a more detailed theoretical basis. The 'Soft Systems Methodology' of Checkland (1989) is also worth exploration. Certain aspects in relation to schools are covered in Lane (1973, 1978). The use of systems or ecological analysis provides a number of ways to look at organisational aspects (Gillham, 1978, Apter, 1982). A broader perspective on ecological factors is provided by Eggleston (1977). The idea of negotiated realities is also important, and in particular achieving an understanding how rules of conduct emerge. (Hammersley and Woods, 1984)

Factors which might need to be considered include the following areas:

1. **Organisational goal and structure**

    (a) Organisations are constructed to achieve specific goals: what are they and is there any conflict between the goals of the organisation and those of the pupil, other members, or the external environment?

    (b) Organisational goals do change over time: what changes might be taking place which may create difficulties for the pupil or help to resolve present difficulties?

    (c) Organisational goals will have a priority structure: what is it and what implications might it have for the pupil?

    (d) What degree of specialisation of role for the achievement of goals exists in the organisation? Who (in relation to the child) fulfils which role and what position (status) does the role take in the formal organisational hierarchy?

    (e) What communications networks exist for the administration of power, execution of action or transmission of information? How might these relate to the child or how might they be used to initiate change?

    (f) Informal goals, as well as formal, tend to emerge in organisations. Is any information available and what are the implications for the pupil?

2. **Role, rules and expectations**

    (a) What expectations do the various parties have about the roles occupied? That is, what do teachers think it is that pupils should or should not do, and what are the pupils' expectations about teachers?

    (b) What rights and obligations are stated or assumed in respect of the various roles? Are these accepted and acted upon by the relevant parties?

    (c) What degree of clarity of expectation is there and with what degree of concensus are the expectations held? Lack of clarity or consensus usually creates difficulties.

    (d) Are the expected behaviours clear, not simply in terms of the defined action required, but also in terms of situation and outcome. For example, does the pupil know:

- the situation in which a given behaviour should occur;
- the details of the expected behaviour (the range of behaviours which count as adequate performance);
- the outcome (pay-off) for behaving in the expected way?

(e) What process of initiation into the expected roles exist, to enable participants to learn appropriate behaviour? It cannot be assumed that pupils/teachers know what is expected of them.

(f) Are any of the expectations of the individual or organisation incompatible? Given incompatibility, what is the pay-off in respect of performing each of the incompatible roles?

(g) Are the processes discernable by which individuals come to be identified (labelled) as in need of change? What implications arise?

(h) How are pupils and teachers negotiating the rules governing their interactions in the classroom?

3. **Resolution of conflict**

(a) Organisations rarely optimally achieve their stated goals. What is considered, in reality, an acceptable level of achievement/behaviour in the organisation? Given achievement at that level, would the organisation/pupil be reasonably satisfied?

(b) Development of and progression for both the individual the organisation requires periods of passivity/activity, dependence/independence, limitation of range/expansion of range, short term interest/long term interest (and time perspective), subordination/superordination, external control/internal control, crisis/stability, etc. Given the need for opportunities to develop, what provision for temporary adjustments and resolution of conflict exist in the organisation?

(c) To what extent are the rules of permitted tolerance clear? Can these be usefully further clarified? To what extent does flexibility exist in the implementation of sanctions (rewards and punishments) to allow for individual need?

(d) Does any conflict of role occur through the use of multiple role occupation? For example, does the House tutor hold counselling role and disciplinary roles which may conflict? How is this resolved in the organisation?

(e) What is the respective power of the holders of different roles? What permitted procedures for the exercise of that power, or challenge to it, exist?

(f) Does the pupil (other members, and the organisation) consider that other parties have the 'right' to a given position or behaviour, in terms of:

   (i) **Legitimacy** — where individuals see the role or behaviour as a legitimate one, they are likely to accept it.

   (ii) **Priority** — where individuals have a hierarchy of values, they may give up a lower one to achieve a higher one.

   (iii)**Sanctions** — what is the relative strength of the system of sanctions in respect of (i) and (ii)?

   (iv)**What is the basis of compliance** — self interest, similar internalised values?

(g) What rights of exchange (bargaining) exist for parties to trade off one behaviour for another?

Test data approaches — The use of test data encompasses a very wide range of procedures. Usually 'tests' are thought to cover such items as intelligence and personality assessment using standard instruments, but any systematic, numerical system of behaviour observation or description can form part of a test procedure. However, while accepting the broader definition of test data for the purpose of this section and the consideration of trait elements, the narrower conception is used. Test data approaches include any standardised procedure for the categorisation of behaviour based on norms or measured criteria.

A large number of standard tests are available to most practitioners. Yet with the exception of psychologists, most are unaware of their availability to non-psychologists. Of course, readers unfamiliar with tests should not rush into using them or attempt to use restricted tests, but a wider use of standard procedures could be beneficial. Teachers should seek the advice of their Educational Psychologist on the matter of tests. An important distinction exists between norm and criterion referenced tests. In norm referenced tests, an individual's score is compared with those of others; an obvious example is I.Q., tests. In criterion referenced tests, the extent to which an individual meets a given standard is assessed. (The National Foundation for Educational Research in Slough publish test catalogues and will send details on request.

As an example of test data approaches, two tests are considered here, which proved useful in the research. (The first must be used under psychological supervision, the second is available to teachers.) The Eysenck Personality Questionnaire (EPQ) measures three personality dimensions - toughmindedness/tendermindedness, extraversion/introversion and emotional stability/instability. Since this measure proved so predictive in the experimental work, it is useful in assessing pupils. For example, tenderminded, emotional introverts respond better to supportive counselling than do toughminded stable extraverts, the later doing better under token economies. This finding may help in the choice of approach.

It must be said that over the years there was on the part of many colleagues an increasing resistance to using tests of this type. Clients generally felt happy with the way they were used, and pupils found them interesting, but it is important that the context for the work is such that the procedure can be used. It is not helpful to use test material if there is a reluctance, or hostility to its use. The appropriateness of any test to the context must be seriously considered. Advice should be sought on this.

Similarly, the Bristol Social adjustment Guide (BSAG) provides indications of hostility to adults and impulsive behaviours. The existence of varied reports by teachers on the BSAG provided a very useful starting point for exploration with teachers and pupils. The knowledge that the child is seen as particularly hostile may be important in determining the choice of techniques (such as contracts) to overcome hostility, and similarly the impulsive child may need impulse control techniques. The combination of data from the two tests above is also useful. For example, toughminded individuals tend to meet hostility. Where hostility exists on a BSAG in a tenderminded individual (EPQ) one needs to look for situational factors as hypotheses of cause, whereas if the individual were toughminded, that basic trait might have to be tackled directly.

The existence of predisposing (potential) trait elements can be uncovered by the use of such measures.

The concept of preferred action style, tended to replace the idea of traits in later work. We spoke of a child's/teacher's preferred style of response. The concept has certain advantages.

Tests relating to language difficulties and occasionally neurological signs were also found to be helpful. A neurological screening test provided clues for helping a number of pupils. The decision to use a test must be carefully taken. To deny the child access to the potential clues it offers is also problematic.

STATE ELEMENTS

People and institutions bring personality and organisational traits to a situation. However, it is only through an analysis of a particular situation that one can discover the reason why a specific set of behaviours occur. This is the job of state analysis. In looking at state elements one is concerned with:

1. The general setting in which the behaviour occurs.
2. The factors precipitating and maintaining that behaviour.

These are the two most important starting points for consideration. In addition it is necessary to determine:

3. Alternatives possible in the situation.
4. The participant's view of the situation.
5. The level and intensity of the problem in different settings.
6. The individual's potential performance, given changed circumstances.

Understanding the current situation is the most vital part of any analysis. Unfortunately, in the early days at the Islington Centre we had little available to us as a technology other than behavioural analysis. This was a powerful technique; but our case studies frequently raised issues beyond that as a tool. Cognitive and social skills emerged as important, so we had to develop techniques to examine them (Lane, 1975). Learning problems featured and we had to have techniques available to examine them (Lane, 1976). The layout of classrooms, use of space, materials, etc., all featured as individual problems, were analysed. We were making up techniques as we went along, but no theoretical framework was available to encompass it.

Fortunately, a literature began to emerge which encompassed at least part of the problem we faced. We were grateful for help from a variety of sources. Sarason (1975) provided us with unpublished materials on social skills to add to the material we were developing. Meichenbaum (1975) similarly sent us sets of unpublished research. Stott (1976) corresponded with us on our unusual use of the BSAG, and greatly encouraged us. De Bono's Cognitive Research Trust became involved in our attempts to teach thinking skills as a method to work with behaviour problems. Of particular value was involvement with Krasner's (1980) Environmental Design Team. They were taking environmental analysis seriously. Our hesitant attempts to include spacial analysis of the classroom were revitalised.

It became possible to think in terms of analysing the setting for the problem in broad detail and give the findings adequate weight, rather than relying on just a behavioural ABC.

The idea of general setting observation became a powerful tool which had the additional advantage of a high level of face validity with teachers.

General Setting Observation

It is always necessary to obtain information on the general setting in which the problem occurs. For example, in considering a child's disruptive behaviour in a classroom, one must take into account the general behaviour of other children, the interest level of the lesson, teaching style, ventilation and so on. It sounds so obvious now but it has taken many behaviourists a long time to recognise the power of such factors as antecedents to behaviour and a number still fail to do so.

While observation of a general setting starts with a broad orientation, it usually provides a rich field for identifying specific triggers. Taking one

147

referral, a primary school student, as an example it was particularly noticeable that fights with other children occurred in the playground, often near the end of play. This suggested the need to look more closely at peer relations, the structuring of the football game played at school breaks, different methods of control and support between teaching and auxiliary staff and the specific nature of the routines adopted at the end of break.

In considering the general setting, it is often useful to take a leaf out of the functional sociologist's book and look at the differences between the meanings that different individuals attach to situations and the actual outcomes, and then in turn to attempt to uncover the meanings in those outcomes. For example, breaktime is an important time of day in most schools. As teachers, we often say that time in a playground is important for children to 'let off steam'. However, it is noticeable that at breaktime, children often build up steam. Furthermore, schools that encourage a cooperative and nurturing ethos sometimes have unstructured games at breaktimes that actively encourage children to act out and which are particularly stressful for withdrawn or timid children. The result of all this can be overexcited and distressed children pouring back into classrooms in turn increasing the burden on teachers.

One must guard against being too precious with this type of analysis - schools are hard pressed institutions and cannot be perfect. However, it can be fruitful to analyse particular settings in this way.

Five questions (following Merton, 1949) are worth considering:

1. Which participants in any given situation influence the outcome of action taken?

2. Which patterns of response to a situation occur and which are excluded by virtue of that response?

3. What aspects of the situation appear to go unrecognised by the participants?

4. To what extent does the existence of the observed patterns of behaviour and the situation within which they occur help or hinder intentions of the participants?

5. What meaning do the participants attach to the pattern of behaviour?

Thus we might use a sociological analysis (Lane, 1978), and we might undertake a detailed study of the playground, the use of space, games and myths. (Garlovsky, 1984) Three questions can provide the starting point for a General Setting Analysis:

1. In which settings do the problems occur?

2. Are there any settings in which the problems do not occur?

3.   What differentiates the settings?

The initial set of differences might be varied but they could gradually be narrowed down to the factors consistently present in problematic situations. Having narrowed it down, a finer-grained analysis becomes possible.

Factors Precipitating and Maintaining Behaviour (Functional Analysis)

Functional analysis, as defined by learning theorists, is a rigorous approach based on the idea of behaviour as a set of responses to specific stimuli. Once a setting analysis was complete it often provided a mechanism for detailed exploration.

The aim is to discover the chain of events which control a given behaviour. Specifically, we are interested in establishing:

A.   The trigger to the behaviour, what precedes it (an antecedent).

B.   The reaction or response (behaviour).

C.   The events subsequent to the behaviour (consequence).

This is sometimes called the ABC sequence: Antecedent-Behaviour- Consequence. In practice this can operate as a complete loop, with the final consequence providing the stimulus for the next response. For example, a child might be teased (antecedent) and develop a tantrum (behaviour) that has the immediate consequence of stopping the teasing and the longer-term consequence of rewarding it with the tantrum display and thereby increasing the probability of it re-occuring.

This form of analysis can be useful, particularly if the behaviour to be analysed is well defined and episodic in character. It does require very careful observation and this can also prove a hindrance. More than 10,000 individual ABC sequences were traced in the case studies. Sometimes the effort involved was not repaid and unravelling the sequence proved unsatisfactory. Other devices were used, such as the construction of a critical path sequence for the behaviour. Perhaps the most useful alternative was to look at the behaviour and setting as a process. It would then be seen as a whole rather than as specific events. In particular, each pattern could be seen in the light of the alternative responses that could have been made and have been made on other occasions. The idea of alternative responses, and meaning component from sociology can then be incorporated and behaviour is seen as a chosen (or set of alternative) option(s). (Lane, 1972, 1973, 1989)

In this approach no special status is accorded to the ABCs — each is simply a part of a single meaningful behavioural act.

The analysis process therefore centres on the whole rather than the parts. A model using some of these ideas has recently appeared under the title of the Response Process Model (O'Connor, 1987).

A process approach also leads naturally to the use of ecological or environmental design principles (Krasner, 1980, Apter, 1982). The origin of this work owes much to the open classroom of the British Primary School, as US commentators such as Krasner acknowledge. The real origin lay with those many teachers such as Ella Flagg Young who struggled to open horizons for children against all the odds: the source of many of Dewey's ideas on education according to Herrick (Herrick, 1971). The essence of the environmental/ecological approach is to look at all the factors in the current situation which impact on the behaviour and then to tackle those that are amenable to change. It represents a belief in the power to change, by changing environments.

A detailed account of these techniques and others are found in the references quoted and in Lane (1978). The key starting point is the General Setting Analysis — from that, the rest of the techniques fan out.

Alternatives possible in the situation
The whole basis of the idea of performance discrepancy is that of alternatives. In the data collection this can be focused through consideration of the paths through which behaviours pass.

For each behavioural act, the situation is examined and the question asked: What factors need to be present for that act to be chosen or take place?

The alternative to that act is then discussed. The factors required to enhance the possibility of the alternative being chosen are then outlined.

The next behaviour in the sequence is then considered and the question repeated. In this way, a path of acts, (choices) and the factors which led to them is established. The pattern necessary to the acts and the pattern necessary to the alternatives are clarified.

This simple analysis of the alternative paths often produces valuable information.

Participants' view of the situation
There are four ideas which are particularly useful in considering the participants' view of the situation.

a) Attribution theory
Attribution theory provides a particular method for classifying the explanations individuals use. If the attributes are coded according to the system it helps to explain some of the difficulties encountered in changing beliefs. The idea is to understand the causes individuals attribute to behaviours.

The key classifications according to Brewin (1989) are:

Internal — causes that arise from within a person such as effort or character, or

External — causes such as luck or the actions of others.

Personal — causes that imply something unique about the person, or

Universal — causes that are likely to affect many people in the same way.

Unstable — temporary causes, or

Stable — permanent ones.

Global — causes that effect many events in a person's life, or

Specific — causes that effect only a particular event.

Controllable — causes over which the individual has power, or

Uncontrollable — causes outside the individual's influence.

If a teacher attributes the cause of the child's behaviour to internal, controllable factors, it can be seen that the child is more likely to be blamed for his behaviour than if it were seen as external and uncontrollable.

b) **Theory of Planned Action**

In the data on effective Heads of Year it was indicated that a pattern of examination of the relationship between intention and behaviour was often used. Ajzen (1988) has presented a theory of 'Planned Behaviour' which incorporates such an approach. Two key factors are seen as important determinants of behaviour.

1. The theory assumes that perceived behavioural control has motivational implications for intentions. People who believe that they have neither the resources nor the opportunities to perform a certain behaviour are unlikely to form strong behavioural intentions to engage in it even if they hold favourable attitudes toward the behaviour and believe that important others would approve of their performing the behaviour.

2. A direct link may exist between perceived behavioural control and behaviour. Thus if individuals perceive that they have control over the situation, that increases the prediction that they will engage in the behaviour as a partial substitute for a measure of actual control.

Careful questioning can elicit salient beliefs about factors which might help or hinder the performance of the behaviour in question.

c) Sussing out

It is apparent from a number of studies that pupils use a process of experimentation with behaviour in the classroom to test out and create 'rules of exchange'. This 'sussing out' (Beynon, 1984) is an important process. Specific discussion of the rules of exchange which pupils believe are in operation and comparison with those which the teacher believes exist can be highly informative and may pinpoint conflict issues.

The ideas continued in Personal Construct Psychology are useful, theoretically, to explore the sussing out process. PCP is based on the idea that behaviour is an experiment designed to test ways of construing the world (Fransella, 1989). The use of a 'grid' to explore the way the child saw the classroom, compared teachers, constructed rules, etc., proved very valuable in many specific case studies at the Islington Centre. (An approach to grids is provided by Thomas and Harri Augstein, 1985.)

Consistency Management (Tattum, 1986) is particularly important in the areas of rules. Tattum points to the stages of rule creation, surveillance, adjudication and sanction as of importance for both inconsistency and discrimination.

d) Totally unreasonable or irrational?

There are times when the beliefs expressed are over-demanding to the point of irrationality. Examining demands that individuals must/should behave in a given way can be usefully explored within the framework of Rational Emotive Therapy (Ellis, 1989). Ellis makes the point that it is not events which disturb us but rather the view we take of them. He provides an alternative 'ABC' to the behavioural perspective.

A = Antecedent events B = Belief about the antecedent event C = Consequence (feelings/behaviour) of belief about the events.

This type of ABC analysis provides a way to examine the seemingly irrational aspects of behaviour, and a further series of 'letters' (D, E,) in the model provide a mechanism for changing them. (Dryden, 1987, and Ellis and Grieger, 1977, provide examples of the approach.)

The level and intensity of the problem in different settings

Behavioural targeting has been extensively used in behavioural work. Baselines for the occurrence of specific behaviours are established. Particular attention is paid to the duration, intensity and frequency of behaviours. Comparison of the settings in which the same behaviour occurs but less frequently, intensely, or for a shorter duration, provides clues to the key differences which control the behaviour.

152

The individual's potential given changed circumstances

Experimentation — simple experiments with behaviour settings can be highly informative. The aim is to change systematically features of the setting, while keeping other aspects unaltered to observe any improvement in performance. These changes are introduced on a temporary basis to provide observations to test hypotheses. They are not interventions and, even if successful, should not be retained at this stage. They are introduced, reversed and the effects monitored. (a reversal design)

Two aspects of the experimentation process are particularly valuable, the examination of learning and of environmental design.

A learning analysis — Given the evidence that learning problems are a part of the difficulties likely to be experienced by the child, specific analysis of the child's learning patterns is necessary. A detailed approach to this task has previously been provided (Lane, 1976). Ainscow and Tweedle (1988) have developed a concise and powerful plan of value in this context. They analyse in particular:

- How we determine appropriate objectives for all our pupils.

- How we help pupils to be actively engaged in the tasks and activities that are set.

- How we make effective use of the resources available to facilitate learning.

Environmental Design — The design of environments within which behaviours are enacted can be powerful determinants of behaviours. An ethnographic analysis (Pollard, 1986) highlights the patterns of classroom life. He points to the 'interests at hand' which pupils and teachers are engaged upon in a primary concern with the maintenance of their 'self'.

Krasner (1980) and Eggleston (1977), from a psychological and sociological perspective respectively, discuss an ecological framework.

These techniques can be used to test hypotheses concerning the current factors (states) which influence the occurrence of the behaviour and the non-occurrence of the alternative.

Points to consider before proceeding:

1. Will the observations which it is intended to obtain make it possible to unravel predisposing factors of personality, history, general influence and so forth - Trait Factors?

2. Do the observations which it is intended to obtain make it possible to indicate the general setting in which problems occur and factors which precipitate and maintain the behaviour -State Factors?

3. Have relevant alternative perspectives been considered?

Jack — In considering Jack, techniques are necessary to determine state and trait influences on the three behaviours listed, but also to obtain some measure of their occurrence. The following techniques might be used:

General (potential trait) elements

Historical Analysis: A history of the development of problems between Jack and Mary is obviously required, together with some idea of the onset of the general impulsivity. The parents' attitudes may provide some encouragement to him, but a more specific check on possible models for this type of behaviour is necessary. Interview parents and teachers, also check school records.

Test data: A check is needed on his pattern of impulsiveness compared with the 'norm' so a test, the BSAG, is administered. If he turns out to be severely impulsive that might require further investigation, e.g., is he clinically hyperactive? Give the BSAG to two teachers, in case the problems occur only with the referring teacher.

Specific (potential state) elements

General setting observation: General observation is required in the classroom of the behaviour of other children and the pattern of teacher behaviour in response to Jack.

Base line measures: The level (number and severity) of the specific problems listed has to be established. Further observations in class can be made and charted.

Functional analysis: From the observations, 'trigger' and 'consequence' factors can be elicited.

Techniques not initially used.

Developmental assessment — since there is no suggestion that Jack is 'childish for his age' or has specific impairments, a developmental assessment is not sought initially. However, if the level of impulsivity is extreme, a developmental 'history/ assessment' might have to be requested from the School Health Service.

Organisational analysis: Since, initially at least, the problem appears to be specific to Jack and his relationships with two others (Mary and the teacher), analysis of organisation is unnecessary. However it may become so if the general observations in class reveal more broadly based problems.

Experimentation: If the observations reveal considerable levels of impulsive type behaviours, it might prove necessary to test out Jack's ability to control himself given adequate guidance.

PHASE TWO. Step 6: Obtain observation base data to check hypotheses.

The data is obtained as suggested. A check is made to see that all required data has been collected. It is helpful to organise it provisionally under trait and state headings. If the data cannot be ascribed as a trait or state factor, it is listed 'to be clarified'. It is not analysed at this stage.

State factors are specific factors operating in a current situation, that is, precipitating and maintaining elements and alternatives. For example, if Jack hit Mary when she called him a Sambo, that might be a precipitating factor, as would Jack's mood at the time if he was angry about something else. If Mary stopped calling Jack a Sambo when he hit her, the cessation of the name-calling might be the maintaining factor. Alternatively, if one of Jack's friends said, 'Good old Jack, Mary deserved that', the praise from his friend might be the maintaining factor. Trait factors are those general factors from the individual's (organisational) experience or constitutional aspects which make a behaviour more likely. This would include evidence of a particular impairment, or personality features such as high levels of toughmindness or emotional instability, evidence of consistency of behaviour across situations, general attitudes, positive and negative, of the people involved, a family history of violence towards the children. Or it might entail a detailed history of the problem behaviour itself, showing how it arose and factors influential in its development which may be continuing to exert an influence, such as being unable to trust adults because of a previous history of punishments from adults or more appropriately, this teacher. These elements may indicate predisposition to respond to current events in one way rather than another.

Points to consider before proceeding:
1. Has all the data listed been obtained?
2. Has the data been organised under trait and state headings where possible?
3. Has data not ascribed as a trait or state factor been listed to be clarified?
4. When 1, 2 and 3 are complete, the adequacy of the data as a hypothesis test can be considered.

The purpose of initial analysis is to consider the adequacy of the data obtained for the purpose proposed.

Phase Two Overview
Points to consider before proceeding:
1. Does the data obtained meet the objectives defined? If not and it appears that the problem was not properly defined, return to definition stage. If not and it appears that the analysis was inadequate, return to hypothesis selection. They may need to be more tightly specified.
2. Have any new areas arisen which require definition? If so, return to definition phase. If new areas can be defined but require analysis, return to hypothesis selection.
3. Can relevant trait and state factors be listed? If so, proceed to phase three.
4. If the data is adequate to proceed but areas remain to be clarified, can the problem be partially analysed while continuing to explore the other areas?

If so, proceed with analysis but return to definition to clarify unresolved questions. Keep in mind that the continuing analysis will be provisional and may need to be adapted

Jack — All the data required was obtained except for a failure to observe any examples of 'dancing on tables'. The data could provisionally be listed under trait and state headings, but the role of dancing remained to be clarified.

Trait data:
From the history impulsiveness appears always to have been a problem (not taking time to think out actions, not sitting still at the desk etc). It also appeared that Jack did get into fights but this had not appeared as a particular problem until recently and then only in relation to Mary. No specific models for aggressive, impulsive behaviour appear.

From the test data, Jack showed highish levels of general impulsiveness (inconsequence), including desire for adult attention, but not extremely so. That is, it represented the top end of the 'normal' range. The scores were similar on both BSAGs obtained.

State data:

From the general observations the classroom appeared relatively well organised, although there were difficulties over management of the use of artwork materials, at which times more problems occurred.

From the base line measures: Two fights with Mary were observed but no dancing.

From the functional analysis, it appeared that during times when the class was more than usually disorganised (art work), Jack found it impossible to get help from the teacher. In such a situation, if Mary insulted him (her role, it appeared, was not wholly innocent) he punched her. Whereas if he was busy and the class not disorganised, he ignored her. Any such incident of punching was immediately followed by teacher attention. He was the centre of her attention for several minutes following such an incident.

Data to be clarified

From the observations — since no dancing was observed, further discussion of it it necessary. The issue was confused since it had originally been seen as separate but was mentioned again. Was it still happening or not?

Initial analysis of the data indicated that it was adequate, that is, some understanding of the situation was possible. Clarification was sought on the 'dancing' and it appeared to represent little more than a silly prank. Jack was caught dancing on the tables, cheered on by peers, on two occasions when the teacher arrived late in class. In discussion with the teacher, it was decided to ignore this problem. So analysis could proceed given the data obtained.

CHAPTER FIFTEEN

Phase three: formulating explanations

Introduction

The collection of information to explore the problem provides the data for the formulation phase. A series of hypotheses have been tested. Some have been found wanting and others have proved useful.

A statement of the problem has been obtained, objectives provisionally agreed and data collected on predisposing, precipitating and maintaining factors. A great deal is already known about the problem. That information must now be integrated into an explanation of why the problem behaviour occurs — the formulation. The formulation is a model of the problem in context. It represents the participants agreed and tested view of the world. It has to be stated in a way that the various parties can agree:

'Yes, that's it ... we do understand what is causing this and we can see a way forward.' It cannot be stressed too strongly that until a formulation has been worked out, an intervention cannot be designed. The techniques used for change will depend on the formulation obtained.

The distinction must be quite clear between:

1. A statement of the problem — (free of interpretation)

2. A statement of objectives

3. The data collected

4. The explanation (formulation) of why the problem occurs.

Those undertaking an analysis must be clear about the distinction between these components. If it is not clear, do not go on. Go back, revisit. When you are ready, go on.

PHASE 3. Step 7: Checking the hypotheses.

Factors of past and general influence: Analysis by trait.

Analysis is here concerned with factors of enduring influence, 'past and general'. It is primarily about historical, developmental, organisational and individual differences. They are defined as trait items to emphasise that only elements of enduring interest, rather than any historical factor, should be taken into account.

The aim in looking for trait factors is to obtain some understanding of elements which lead to the development of the problem of continuing influence. Trait factors do not explain the current problem, they help to explain why a particular situation is influential for one person rather than another. It is unfortunate that some teachers think of behaviour which is simply a response to a given situation in terms of traits not states. That is, a child who is behaving badly in response to a particularly difficult situation in school is always regarded as someone who behaves badly irrespective of the actual situation. The research revealed this to be a frequent problem.

A child who had worked very hard at change, receiving daily reports of 'good' rather than 'bad' behaviour, would still receive an end of term report listing bad behaviour because the teacher claimed that, 'that is what he is really like', quite irrespective of the child's actual behaviour. This naturally generated considerable hostility among children who had made genuine efforts at change and were beginning to trust adults again. It is vital that traits of behaviour are not seen as negative labels for use against the child.

Traits, as used here, are relatively consistent responses to a given situation or across situations which arise from factors in the individual's constitutional endowment or his experience, which increase the likelihood of a given behavioural response occurring. It excludes patterns which vary considerably across situations. At the level of personality they represent a 'preferred response style', not an immutable characteristic.

The term is also applied to organisational factors of an enduring nature such as policy or curricula aspects of the school.

Constitutional factors — These include among other things personality dimensions, behavioural deficits arising from specific impairments, and the influence of enduring organic/physiological factors — and of enduring features of school organisation.

Experiential components — These include, among other things, the impact of a particular conditioning experience resulting in, for example, the individual being unable to trust adults, the model the individual has been exposed to and learnt from, and the impact of background, educational, familial and societal factors.

These elements are only considered in the analysis if they relate directly to the understanding of the present problem. The accumulation of vast quantities of historical information about the individual's breast feeding experience, what happened to Uncle Fred on holiday, and the comments of all and sundry should not be collected unless the observer can seriously argue that they have a direct bearing on the current problem. The effect of the successive accumulation of quantities of such information is to make files unreadable, and the isolation of significant elements a lifetime's work. Data not directly related must be ruthlessly discarded otherwise any attempt to develop realistic intervention strategies will be doomed to fail.

You cannot change the past, only its current effects, but where predisposing effects operate, they have to be taken into account. For example, a child might be currently operating in a manipulative, aggressive way because that is what he has been taught to do by his father. He might be highly extravert and emotionally stable, and therefore poorly responsive to conditioning. These are trait elements because the style of response that the child brings to the situation increases the likelihood of a poor response to sympathetic counselling. The child might respond to a token economy in which he can see a direct benefit, immediately available. Knowledge of that fact can help to design appropriate intervention.

Points to consider before proceeding:
Trait factors predispose the likelihood of one response to a situation rather than another. The question is asked: Does the data obtained really help to explain the response(s) seen in the current situation?

Jack — Analysis by trait:
Jack appears to be a generally impulsive child demanding high levels of adult attention, who would consequently tend to get into trouble because he did not think before acting. There was no evidence, however, of a history of extreme violence towards others. Given his general impulsivity in any situation which lacked clear guidance, more problems were likely but, since the level of difficulty was within the normal range, direct action to help Jack to modify his response was not necessary.

Factors of specific and present influence: Analysis by state:
State analysis explains why a behaviour pattern currently occurs. It clarifies the precipitating and maintaining factors by identifying the actual sequence of

161

events in a problem behaviour. In undertaking a state analysis, one is concerned with all the factors currently operating, in particular details of:

1. **General setting factors** — These factors indicate the setting in which the difficulties currently occur. Setting factors include classroom layout, teaching materials, teaching style, subject matter, people, etc. They may be open to change (or not) by a variety of methods.

2. **Precipitating factors** — Those elements which precede the behaviour in question and appear to act as a trigger to it. These factors are open to change by techniques such as stimulus control.

3. **Reaction** — This is the problem behaviour itself, that is, what happens when the individual is triggered (responds). The behaviour may be changed directly through such techniques as the pairing of incompatible responses.

4. **Maintaining factors** — These are the events which follow the reaction and potentially maintain it (consequences) and also act as a further trigger to action in the feedback chain. These factors are open to change via techniques such as reinforcement .

5. Beliefs of those involved about the behaviours in question (meaning).

6. Other factors relevant to the current situation which arose in Phase 2, hypothesis testing.

Points to consider before proceeding:
1. What general features of the current situation are of potential influence? This excludes features (traits) which hold true across situations.

2. Can you identify the factors which precipitate the behaviour in question? Triggers.

3. Can you define the reaction carefully? Response.

4. Can you identify maintaining factors in the behaviour which increase the likelihood of its recurrence? Consequence.

5. What do those involved believe about the situation?

Jack — Analysis by state
General setting — Problems were more likely to occur in situations in which clear rules and procedures were not available and in which Jack could not receive the teacher's help when requested.

Precipitating factors — The combination of the setting factors, together with a specific insult from Mary, tended to trigger a reaction.

Reaction — The motor behaviour of punching Mary was the obvious reaction but other components, given the situation in which the problem occurred, might include: the autonomic one (his general anxiety at not getting teacher attention) and a cognitive one (his belief that Mary deserved to be hit). Since only the motor behaviour was observed at this stage, that had to represent the defined reaction. (Clarification of the other components would however be possible.)

Maintaining factors — Two possibilities exist, that of teacher attention, and/or the cessation of the insult from Mary. However, the latter is less likely, since he ignored insults at other times but appeared to seek teacher attention.

PHASE 3. Step 8: Formulation of the problem and intervention hypotheses

The trait and state factors are drawn together to provide a formulation of the problem, why it occurs, and, out of this formulation, intervention hypotheses arise.

If the general behaviour pattern (trait) and not simply the response to the situation (state) needs to be changed, it requires a direct programme. Where such trait factors are important, they may need to be dealt with. For example, a generally impulsive child may need to learn impulse control and a hostile child to develop contractual relationships (Lane 1978). This can be undertaken quite separately from attempts to change the specific factors in the presenting situation. The state factors normally represent the main focus of attention and may represent the only focus of attention. Either the elements which precipitate the reaction itself or those which maintain the behaviour will need to be changed.

The formulation of the problem, that is, the explanation of why the problem occurs, is stated. For example, if specifically (state) a pupil danced on tables in school and received a great deal of teacher attention for this but not at other times, it might be recorded that inappropriate dancing on the table behaviour occurred because of the attention it earned and the absence of attention for other, more appropriate, behaviours. If the pupil was also a generally (trait) impulsive individual, inclined to do unusual things, this would add to the formulation. The

163

intervention hypotheses are stated. In this example, it might be argued specifically (state) that teacher attention be focused on behaviour other than dancing on the tables and generally (trait) that the pupil be taught to control his impulsiveness.

The aim is to state clearly the formulation: *why* the problem occurs, and the general intervention options which arise. The point by point specification of techniques of change to be used does not take place until the intervention phase. There is little to be gained by doing that until basic agreement has been reached with the participants on the stated formulation.

The formulation is the agreed model of the world which explains why this set of behaviours occur in this context. As such it is open to further test. It can itself be tested. The intervention which follows is in fact a test of the validity of the formulation. If the formulation makes sense, the intervention should work.

Points to consider before proceeding:
1. Can you explain why the behaviour occurs, in a way which takes account of trait and state factors where relevant and leads on to direct intervention possibilities?

2. Can general approaches to intervention be suggested, which take account of the formulation but which could be discussed with the participants?

3. If a satisfactory formulation cannot be found, five options are open:

    (a) If key data appears to be missing, and a hypothesis can be made as to what that data might be return to phase 2.

    (b) If the explanation does not really meet the original statement of the problem, return to phase 1.

    (c) If an explanation is not possible and the practitioner has no clue as to the missing factors, then the case must be discussed with other professional colleagues including relevant external agencies. A referral for specialist investigation may then follow.

    (d) If a relatively satisfactory explanation is available, the practitioner, may recognise shortcomings but, nevertheless, feel able to proceed with a partial, albeit cautious, explanation.

    (e) If an explanation and general intervention is possible but intervention techniques cannot be found later, even following a review of case studies, the literature and discussion with colleagues (or contact with the appropriate professional agencies or bodies) then it is time to invent a technique. Look carefully at the formulation, the data and the implications, and consider possibilities. Discuss them carefully with all concerned and introduce them with caution and very careful evaluation of outcome.

4. If the formulation is satisfactory and intervention hypotheses are possible but beyond the resources of the practitioner, the matter must be referred 'up the line'. Resources may be available elsewhere, or if not, a clear presentation of the need may help generate an interest in providing a new resource.

5. Note well: The intervention hypotheses are statements of 'What needs to be done' arising out of the formulation: they are not lists of techniques. Thus, one might state that the child needs attention from the teacher for appropriate behaviour; one does not state at this stage that, for example, the technique of token economy should be used to increase appropriate behaviour. They are called hypotheses because they remain exactly that — ideas to be tested in step 9 and in the intervention phase.

Jack — Formulation:

Jack is a generally impulsive, attention-seeking individual inclined to get into trouble but not at levels beyond the normal range. Problems occur in relation to specific events. He punched Mary apparently in response to her insults, at times when the class was more than usually disorganised and help from the teacher difficult to obtain. The behaviour appears to be maintained by teacher attention consequent to the problem occurring.

Intervention hypotheses: Four possibilities exist:

1. To help Jack to be less impulsive (act directly on the trait component).

2. To deal with Mary's insulting behaviour.

3. To help the teacher to organise the art work lessons better so that rules and procedures are clear.

4. To provide Jack with a way of obtaining help from the teacher without resort to violence.

PHASE 3. Step 9: Discussion with the participants and redefinition of objectives

It is vital that discussion should take place with all the participants and include not only the formulation and general treatment hypotheses but also the consequence of the programme and alternatives to it.

The objectives of all participating agents are restated with each participant's role and objectives defined.

It is at that point that the suspension of reality, sought in the early phases, must give way to hard thinking. It is the opportunity to test the formulation against real world issues.

At this point the actual objectives to be met, which may for reasons of practicality, ethics or choice, form only a part of the overall explanatory outline, must be clarified. If this step is omitted considerable dispute may later arise over who was supposed to do what. Given the likelihood of mutual hostility, that possibility must be reduced to a minimum.

This discussion serves several purposes:

S *Strengths:* The particular strengths of the formulation as a model can be explored.

T *Threats:* The likely benefits can be compared with the likely costs, to whom might it be a threat (victim) and who might benefit.

O *Opportunities:* The opportunities created by the formulation can be outlined, the possibilities it opens up can be discussed.

P *Practicalities:* The practicalities of any ideas can be explored and likely problems of implementation considered.

T *Test:* What is an appropriate validity test? Are we happy with the formulation and intervention hypotheses?

H *Harness:* The discussion provides a means to harness the energy of those involved in the programme, to provide motivation and gain commitment.

E *Evaluate:* The initial issues of feasibility, choice of objectives, ethics, etc., can be revisited. Provisional thinking about the evaluation of the programme can begin, in the sense of asking questions about the performance criteria, which are sought.

N *Negotiate:* Alternatives can be discussed and the rights of each party to be active participants can be ensured.

G *Generate:* Generation of new ideas, and the brainstorming of possible interventions can take place.

O *Options:* Options can be agreed and commitment can be confirmed.

STOP, THEN GO — provides a device to think through the implications before the intervention is designed. In practice it turns out to be a very important step. Early programmes failed to take adequate account of this step to their peril.

Points to consider before proceeding:

1. Has agreement been reached with the participants on the formulation and intervention hypotheses?

2. Do all parties fully understand the implications of any formulation and intervention proposed?

3. Are all parties willing to proceed to a commitment to an intervention contract?

4. If the parties do not agree and further discussion does not resolve the issue, return to phase 3 and reformulate to meet the objections. If this fails, return to phase 1. If even that fails, send back to referring agent with a statement of the position and offering future help. 5. Are all the participants clear as to the end product and what each party is expected to be responsible for to reach the objectives?

Jack

Initially the formulation was discussed with the teacher, who agreed with it. In relation to the intervention hypotheses she felt, however, that action on points 3 and 4 were the most practical, in the light of the difficulty in art periods. The formulation and hypotheses, particularly in relation to point 4 (getting attention), was discussed with Jack. (Point 3 is the teacher's concern and points 1 and 2 were not to be included initially.) He agreed with them.

The objectives were restated as:

1. To introduce a new procedure for the organisation of art lessons: the teacher was responsible for this, the end-product being a generally less disruptive class.

2. To provide Jack with an appropriate means for getting the teacher's help: He was responsible for following whatever procedure was eventually agreed and the end-product would lie in not having to wait for help when needed.

CHAPTER SIXTEEN

Intervention plans

PHASE FOUR: INTERVENTION

An understanding of the problems has now been achieved and the general format and objectives of an intervention agreed. The validity of the formulation has been considered and a commitment established. The fourth stage of the analysis consists of the technical design of the intervention and its implementation.

Many practitioners worry that they will not be able to design appropriate interventions. The concern is usually misplaced. The process of working towards a shared concern and through hypothesis-testing on to a formulation generates many ideas for intervention. The experience practitioners bring to the situation and ideas that other colleagues, pupils and parents contribute, will provide the basis for intervention design. If stuck, a full discussion with the appropriate psychologist will provide further ideas. Two basic approaches to the design of any change process are always available:

1. The targets are defined and agreed.

2. Steps (or option paths) to reach those targets are established.

3. Each step (or option) is practised, assessed, retaught, until achieved. This approach applies as much to social as academic behaviours. Those involved in the programme are simply asking each other what it is they want to achieve and are defining the paths to reach it. An alternative approach lies in experiential learning in which an individual's preferred style of learning is examined. This approach is discussed in Thomas and Harri-Augstein (1985). In an experiential approach one is concerned as much with how people learn as with what they learn. The approach is highly consistent with the results of the research in this study and more particularly, earlier studies on learning problems. These studies (Lane, 1976) clearly indicated that style of learning/teaching was a feature of the disabling of pupils' learning.

A useful distinction in the field of learning exists when the objective in the situation is to increase, decrease or instil new behaviours. This distinction is not absolute but it does help to focus attention on the direction of change needed and potential techniques. It is important, however, for practitioners not to allow themselves to get caught up in concerns about specific techniques. It is more useful to focus on the issue, 'what has been learned' in the process of developing the formulation and then to generate options based on that. Eight times out of ten (we counted) the ideas will come to you. The procedure adopted here works from the assumption that the practitioner needs to assist with a change in behaviour in one or more of the following ways:

1. **Increase** — appropriate behaviour — that is behaviour which, while occurring, does so too infrequently, with too little intensity or on the wrong occasion.

2. **Decrease** — inappropriate behaviour — that is behaviour which occurs on the wrong occasions, or on appropriate occasions but either too intensely or too infrequently.

3. **Instil** — new behaviour — that is, a desired behaviour which does not occur in any form and must be taught from scratch.

The number of techniques for behaviour change or evaluation are many and varied, and a few are discussed in Appendix One. These represent potential ideas when you are stuck (the two out of ten occasions), or starting points for thinking, or discussion with professional colleagues. The issues raised below simply outline the steps the practitioner must take to convert the options agreed in the previous phase into a clear, achievable programme of intervention.

PHASE FOUR. Step 10: Specification of behaviours to be changed and procedures to be used

There are three key aspects involved in the attempt to change behaviour: it can be increased, decreased or instilled. The basic procedures are discussed later. The critical point, however, is to ensure that the approaches adopted meet the formulation of the problem. For example, if an individual's generally impulsive traits were important, a direct technique to teach impulsive control would be needed. Where the response of the teacher in a given situation (state) was the important factor, that response would have to be changed to achieve gain. Some of the techniques available under increase, decrease and instil sections are discussed in Appendix One.

Specification is a technical function. Once objectives, etc., have been agreed, the actual details of the intervention are worked out and explained. The example of Jack, below, illustrates the point that the techniques needed are usually available to the practitioner.

Points to consider before proceeding:
1. Is it clear which (and how) behaviours are to be increased, decreased or instilled?
2. Have the techniques to be used been clearly explained to the participants? (Who, What, Where, When, How)
3. Does the approach to be adopted arise directly out of the formulation and discussion of it and does it meet these objectives?

Jack — The specification of the programme was as follows:

1. To increase level of organisation in art lessons:

It was agreed to list all the tasks involved in setting up, carrying out and clearing away art lessons. They were listed and displayed on the wall of the classroom. The pupils were split into five groups and each group made responsible for specific tasks from the list. A rota was established so that groups did different tasks each week. Each group 'elected' a group leader whose job was to organise the pupils in the group. The time taken to complete each task properly was measured by the teacher and the groups 'earned' extra free time in proportion to task completion for activities of their own choice.

2. To increase use of appropriate attention-seeking behaviour by Jack.

To achieve this Jack was given two paper triangles (one orange and one red) which could be stood up on his desk. Whenever he wanted the teacher's help, he was to stand a triangle up and wait quietly. The choice of colour was determined by the urgency of his request. The teacher then attended to him as soon as practically possible, and also encouraged an appropriate use of colour, i.e. not using red if it wasn't urgent.

No decrease and instill elements were used.

PHASE FOUR. Step 11: Intervention contracts

The theoretical basis for such contracts has been discussed elsewhere (Lane 1972, 1978). The contract system provides an agreed basis for the mutual exchange of benefits between participants. It is the essence of an approach which is based on exchange between participants. The performance discrepancy has been agreed, each party knows what to do and so a contract between them is possible.

These are not contracts which 'children are put on', to control them. They are not the contingency contracts many behavioural programmes employ.

Since the appearance of the original materials and volumes (Lane, 1974, 1978) the use of contracts has become widespread. Unfortunately, they are as often misused as well used. The essential feature of a contract, that it is a mutual exchange of benefits, is simply ignored. A contract works when both parties enter into it freely, and believe that the benefit to them is worth the cost. The contract has to be reasonable. Excessive benefits to either side encourage manipulation not cooperation. Of course, there is no necessity to have a formal intervention contract. An agreement with each party knowing exactly what is expected can work. A issue which does arise is the legal status of such contracts. Most are not intended to be legally binding they are simply an agreement to act in a given way. However, since many are formally drawn, are called contracts, and are signed and dated, the issue of legal status does arise. Some practitioners do add clauses to contracts to make the point that neither party considers them legally binding. Some call them 'agreements' not contracts. The contracts need to be carefully drawn so that the obligation and rights of the parties are clearly established and the details of who does what, where and when, clarified, leaving no room for doubt.

Each party benefits from these contracts, so have an interest in their satisfactory completion. It is that commitment which enhances success.

Once objectives and methods have been decided, a contract between the parties is agreed.

PHASE FOUR. Step 12: The programme is enacted:

The programme agreed in the contract is now operated and monitored on a continuing basis.

The enactment step is itself a part of the continuing process of hypothesis testing. Each component of the plan has been included because it was predicted by the formulation. The intervention as a whole should work and each part should make a contribution.

If the programme does not proceed satisfactorily, that is, in accordance with the predictions inherent in the formulation, then a revsion is necessary. You do not wait months or weeks, or even days or hours (in some cases) for an effect. Your agreement states that this or that will happen. It should happen. If it does not, find out why.

Continual monitoring is necessary and each party is responsible for doing so. The intervention is planned so that it works, not suggested in the hope that it will work. This concept is very different from common practice in programmes with difficult or challenging behaviours in school. It is not the same as sending the child to a clinic, or unit, in the hope that whatever it is they do at such places will solve the problem. You have not put all the work into designing the intervention for a vague hope. Make it happen.

Points to consider before proceeding:
1. Does each party to the contract consider that sacrifices made are worth the gains to be achieved?

2. Are all the participants clear about what they have contracted to do, when and where they will be doing it, how they will complete it, and what they can expect in return for sticking to the contract?

3. (if the participants are distrustful of each other) Are the implications of breach of contract clear?

Jack — Jack and his teacher have a written agreement covering the use of the triangles (see below). The organisation of art lessons was undertaken by the teacher herself, although a verbal contract between her and the class was operated.

A contract for three weeks between Jack and Ms ....

It is agreed that:

Teacher — *Ms ... is to provide Jack with a red and an orange paper triangle to be used to attract attention from her. Ms... will watch for the triangles on Jack's desk and if she sees one raised, she will indicate by raising her hand that she has seen it, and will attend to him as soon as she can. She will attend to Jack within five minutes if he puts up an orange triangle and within one minute in the case of the red triangle.*

Jack: — *will not attract his teacher's attention in any way other than by using the triangles. He will wait quietly by his desk until Ms... arrives. The orange triangle is to be used if he wants help but not urgently. The red triangle is to be used if help is needed straight away. Both Jack and Ms... agree to try this system for three weeks. If either of them is unhappy with it, they will talk to the other during break, lunch or after school about their complaints. They will not complain during lessons.*

Signed...............................Date........................Signed........................__.

CHAPTER SEVENTEEN

Phase five: evaluating change

PHASE FIVE. Step 13: Evaluation

Evaluation is a continuous process. In the same way that the design of the programme was the result of experimental testing of hypotheses, the intervention is itself a test of the validity of the formulation, intervention hypotheses and objectives. Failure of the child to respond is evidence of a failure in the formulation, hypotheses or objectives and is not regarded as bloodymindedness, laziness or lack of motivation on the part of the participants.

Evaluation also serves to provide feedback on the procedures adopted so that any adaptions may be made. Where success has been achieved through the completion of contract terms, the analysis proceeds to an optimisation of gains.

Where the programme is partly successful, a return to formulation is made to identify reasons for the failure, by reconsidering the formulation in the light of subsequent events.

Where the intervention proves a total failure, a return to PHASE ONE (definition) is made, to try to find out if the problem or objectives are in fact different from those originally assumed.

Points to consider before proceeding:

- If the programme has worked well, decide why and proceed.

- If success is only partial, review the formulation for possible errors in the light of the failure.

- If the programme proves a complete failure, the initial definition and objective should be looked at

---

Jack — After three weeks the teacher and Jack reported satisfaction with the system. Further observation in class confirmed the success.

PHASE FIVE. Step 14: Optimisation and Maintenance.

There is a critical stage in the analysis beyond the successful change of behaviour. It is important not only to change behaviour, but also to do so in the most efficient manner possible, and then to enable the individual (or group) to meet the present environment from the position reached, rather than from where s/he previously stood. Additionally, not simply for the pupil but for the benefit of the practitioner and future participants, a period of follow-up and reflection is essential, so that ideas can be rethought in the light of experience.

The reader should avoid the temptation to bypass this stage. One's skills as a practitioner cannot improve without periods of reflection: avoiding it can only be to the detriment of those one is seeking to help.

Running a successful programme is not all there is to it. In order to achieve maximum gain, the level of intervention must be reduced to the absolute minimum. It sounds paradoxical but it is usually the case that you try to use the mimimum intervention possible. The contribution of each factor in a programme needs to be assessed for each case and from time to time across cases. This process in the present study had led to the down-grading of tokens (although they retain importance) and to an upgrading of teaching generalisable skills (thinking processes, scripts, etc.) and to the ability of the pupil to control his/her own situation.

The establishment of new behaviour patterns opens up new situations and relationships. The implications of the likely impact of these for all the participants, active and passive, need to be considered.

This is particularly true when generalised survival skills such as impulse control, interpersonal or work skills are taught. Following such training, the individual is more competent in dealing with the situations encountered, so new objectives not previously available are likely to arise.

An issue which arose in a number of cases concerned the difficulty pupils often faced in the new situation of being successful. They faced a new sense of their 'being in the world'. A process to help pupils across the abyss they felt existed was needed. They moved between the world they knew, its consequences and friendships and their sense of self (being) within it, and the new world with its uncertainties and often sense of loss, and actual loss of supports and contacts. They often felt as if they did so without replacement by new contacts and support. As the research data indicated practitioners who maintained support for pupils through this period were more successful at assisting them than those who ignored this phase in the process. There is little point in introducing change (except under rare circumstances) if it cannot be maintained once the intervention is complete. In many respects the problem of maintaining and generalising gain to other situations is tackled long before this step. If valid, not assumed, survival skills are taught, they are likely to be maintained since they bring their own reward. For example, being able to read is more likely to be reinforcing than being unable to read, since the skill itself is valuable. Selecting behaviours which are likely to be reinforced in the natural environment, such as responding to an individual in a way which facilitates a positive response — a polite answer rather than a punch on the nose — is also preferable to teaching behaviours relevant only to a limited area.

There are additional actions that can be taken post-intervention to ensure the continuance of the gains of the programme, particularly since new objectives often need to be met. These might include the use of a post-intervention contract, with each party agreeing to take necessary action. The introduction of new patterns of reinforcement for continuance of change rather than its establishment, and the transfer of parts of the programme to other workers in daily contact, or to the client himself, can also be helpful.

The critical point is not to assume that gains will be maintained but actively to plan for it.

Points to consider before proceeding:
1. Can the level of intervention be optimised?
2. Have new objectives arisen which require clarification and action?
3. Have the implications of the new behaviour for all involved been considered?
4. Has a programme to maintain gains and/or meet the new objectives been introduced?
5. Has a post-intervention contract been established so that each participant is aware of his/her role in maintaining gains and in taking necessary action in the event of difficulties or further new objectives arising?

Jack — The programme seemed to be optimally successful: a small amount of effort brought considerable payoff. New objectives arose. The success of the triangles strategy with Jack encouraged the teacher to use the same idea with the rest of the class. A programme for this was agreed with the pupils (and Jack).

To maintain gains, it was decided to send letters of praise about Jack to his parents. Jack liked this idea.

PHASE FIVE. Step 15: Re-evaluation

It is important to follow up cases, for several reasons:

- To check the current situation.
- To obtain necessary statistical data and feed it back to participants. To advise as necessary.
- To update records and rethink ideas.

Without this process, the validity of the work being carried out cannot be established. Only by continuous re-evaluation can adjustments be made, invalid or uneconomic techniques be rejected and accurate data be collected, to provide a basis for planning and advisory services. Interventions must not only work at the time they take place but the effects must be of lasting value. More than this, the intervention must take place with maximum economy.

Experimental and economic principles are demanding when applied to educational and clinical work. Yet if the practitioner is really concerned about the client, evaluation must take place in the long run, for it is only approaches that stand up to scrutiny which offer any real hope for the child's progress. Some events may be so rare and some human concerns so metaphysical that they cannot be usefully measured, but these are not the concern of education. Nothing that cannot be defined has any place in education for it is too open to abuse and manipulation. Without definition, neither the child nor anyone else has a means of discovering whether or not any programmes with pupils really are in their own interest.

If something can be defined, it can be measured in some form. Measurements need not rely on a computer. Indeed, in most of the studies in this research, relatively simple procedures have been used, to make them accessible to the widest possible audience. In the same way, evaluation data might include a simple rating scale (has improved/not improved, etc.), or observations or a simple test such as the BSAG which is available to most practitioners. Many who do excellent work tend to reject measurement, but if they continue to fail to evaluate they will find themselves isolated sooner or later. Measurement is not a complex process and can form part of any intervention programme of whatever orientation. It can involve no more than stating one's initial objectives in observable terms and then taking the trouble at a future date to find out if the objectives have been met. Such a procedure can form a fundamental part of the work of any competent professional.

Points to consider before proceeding:
1. Have the gains been maintained?
2. What changes have taken place?

3. What can be learnt from the follow-up data relevant to future programmes?

4. Which areas need to be rethought and which can be consolidated?

5. What information can be usefully fed back to participants?

Jack — Revaluation indicated that gains were being maintained. Additionally, the class teacher was now taking a different attitude to problems. She now saw them as not 'in the child' but tried instead to analyse why they occurred and then adapt her teaching to the situation.

Conclusions

A detailed step by step procedure has been provided. Short cuts should not be attempted until considerable experience with the full procedure gives some justification for doing so. The reader should not make use of techniques of change until the principles outlined here of definition and observation have been thoroughly understood and the idea grasped that the intervention used depends upon the formulation which arises out of the data obtained.

There is no cookbook of techniques that lets one categorise a pupil and pick a technique accordingly, along the lines: disruption of lessons equals time out from reinforcement. Unfortunately a number of such cookbooks have appeared.

The methods discussed here seem complex but we are dealing with children who are not responding to traditional interventions. They have now been used with several thousand children, in various parts of the UK and abroad. They work.

CONTEXT-FOCUSED ANALYSIS: Summary of steps:
PHASE ONE: Definition.
1. Obtain statement of the problem from those involved.
2. Clarify initial objectives of those involved.
3. On the basis of initial information received consider roles.

Theme: A process of awareness aimed at achieving a shared concern.

PHASE TWO: Exploration.
4. Hypotheses of cause are generated.
5. Observation technologies are chosen.
6. Data is collected to test the hypotheses.

Theme: The process is one of increasingly refined observations.

PHASE THREE: Formulation.
7. The adequacy of the hypotheses are checked.
8. A formulation and intervention hypotheses are established.
9. Discussion with participants and redefinition of objectives takes place.

Theme: The process is one of testing the hypotheses until an adequate explanation is available.

PHASE FOUR: Intervention.
10. The procedures to be used are specified.
11. An intervention contract is established.
12. The agreed programme is enacted and monitored.

Theme: The process is one of structured practice.

PHASE FIVE: Evaluation.
13. Outcomes achieved are evaluated.
14. Any gains made are maintained, the programme optimised and new objectives which arise are tackled.
15. Re-evaluate, re-think and review outcome and ideas.

Theme: The process is one of monitored achievement...

WITHIN A SUPPORTIVE ENVIRONMENT.

CHAPTER EIGHTEEN

Three case studies

Introduction

This chapter describes three examples of our approach. (Further case studies are in, Lane, 1978, Lane and Tattum, 1990)

The first case provides a commentary on one of the early studies. Information not previously included is added and areas of negotiation highlighted. It typifies the range of interventions which may be required. The second case is particularly concerned with the way hypotheses can be tested and with the interrelation of school and individual components. The third case concerns an initial referral of five pupils and the emergence of some changes in the school system to deal with the situation (Corlett, 1986, based on a previous case report).

CASE STUDY ONE

Phase One:

Winston was referred by his school for behaviour problems consisting of impulsive and violent outbursts towards teachers and peers. He was said to have come from a difficult family and a social work report was available, containing very detailed information. He was also reported to have communication problems in reading and speech.

His school was not sure whether to remove him or to attempt to change his behaviour so that he can be contained. He is regarded by staff as a boy who has no ambition other than to be a menace. A few members of staff like him, but admit to being unable to do anything with him. Separate objectives appear from teachers: some want him removed and a few are prepared to work with him. From comments supplied by his social worker it appears that he is very much rejected by mother, and father is absent. A fair bit of hostility at home and in school is reported and mother's objectives seem to be to get him removed.

From this information, the advisor to whom the case was referred formed the belief (provisional hypotheses) that Winston is possibly facing rejection all round, including by his peers, if his violent behaviour towards them is accurately reported.

Hostility from mother and evidence from the social work report indicate little chance of improvement in the home situation at present, so effort will need to be concentrated on his school problems. His reported communication problems may relate to his general interpersonal difficulties. If hostility is severe in school, an attempt to modify teachers' attitudes may be necessary, but if their expectation and objective is to remove him this might be difficult, as it would require a commitment to change by teachers. Winston's possible expectation of removal, which has been threatened several times, may make him resistant to outside placement.

Given the history of difficulties it is highly unlikely that several teachers can be induced to cooperate, and cooperation from home seems less likely still, but the options should be kept open.

His communication difficulties remain ill-defined but the behaviour problems can be fairly clearly defined from the extensive anecdotal material provided:

1. Running around the classroom and dancing on tables when requested not to do so.

2. Fighting with other pupils in class when they tell him to keep quiet.

3. Refusing to carry out teachers' instructions.

4. Not completing set work.

5. Not working for longer than a few (five) minutes at a time before getting up and wandering around the class.

6. Swearing at teachers when corrected and refusing to go to the 'punishment' class when asked and going there when not asked.

7 . Leaving school without permission and truanting.

The discussion of these problems between Head of Year, pupil and advisor raised a number of issues. The pupil was very pessimistic about the situation and believed that the school was determined to throw him out. The Head of Year agreed that the most likely outcome was a suspension followed by removal 'to a special school'. Most teachers were not prepared to work with Winston any longer. The problems could be defined and Winston and the Year Head seemed agreed on the behaviours of concern. Winston's position was that he was not being given a real chance to improve. This was disputed since several interventions had been tried. He felt that the past was always dragged up.

Winston and the Year Head agreed to the limited objective of exploring the problem areas to see if there was anything that might be tackled, but they were equally clear that if nothing changed very soon, suspension was inevitable. They estimated three weeks as about the limit of tolerance. The priority identified was to determine the factors which caused certain behaviours to occur, discover who was prepared to work with the pupil and begin to explore his learning difficulties. Roles as data gatherers were allocated among the three: pupil, Year Head, and advisor.

Phase Two:

It was decided to observe or test the following general and specific problems:

General factors (potential traits)

1. Determine the level of hostility towards adults and peers.
2. Ask the senior teacher which teachers were still prepared to work with him.
3. Obtain from teachers a list of his communication and work difficulties, what it that he is supposed to do that he cannot do.
4. Test the length of his attention span on work set in class.
5. List the influence of personality factors on the behaviour.
6. Review social work, educational welfare, educational and psychological reports available for evidence of historical/experiential factors potentially influential in predisposing the behaviours.

Specific factors (potential state)

7. Based on the list of behaviours considered inappropriate, discover what triggers and maintains the behaviour.

Observation techniques:

To meet the seven observations listed for Winston, the following procedure was adopted, in order of the objectives as previously listed.

General factors (potential traits)

1. Two teachers who saw him in different lessons were requested to complete a BSAG form independently.
2. The senior teacher responsible for the pupil was asked to list the names of teachers or, if that was not acceptable, the number who were prepared to cooperate in a programme and those who were not.
3. Teachers complaining of Winston's communication/work difficulty were asked to list the things he could not do in class that they felt he should be able to do.
4. On the basis of the data raised in point three, two lessons were chosen in which to monitor him, one in which he had difficulty and one in which he

183

had less. His attention spans were recorded, from the time of starting a piece of work to finally stopping it. Another randomly chosen pupil in class was recorded for comparison. It was not possible to find a lesson in which he had no difficulty, for comparison purposes.

5.   An EPQ was administered to check personality influence, together with a BSAG filled out by the pupil himself to gauge his own view of his behaviour.

6.   All reports on the pupil were reviewed to look for factors which might explain hostility to adults, the availability of aggressive/non-aggressive models and inconsistency in relationships with parents.

Specific factors (potential states)

7.   A check list was constructed, based on a list of the behaviours previously obtained, so that each occurrence during two thirty minute observation periods could be marked and factors preceding and   following the occurrence noted.

Observation data

The general (trait) data obtained was as follows:

BSAG — This indicated severe inconsequence (impulsiveness, distractibility), severe hostility (loss of faith in adults) and peer maladaptiveness. No significant difference was found between the ratings of the two teachers.

Teacher cooperation — Only the senior teacher was prepared to work with Winston. He felt he could persuade a few teachers to 'be nice' to him to aid the experiment, provided that his behaviour changed quickly.

History — The family is known to the police and social services as delinquent. The father is a very violent man who beats the children and mother is seldom in work. Three of the seven children are under supervision orders and one is in gaol. School reports consistently refer to problems of fighting, which becomes more frequent with age and impulsiveness. Winston had been referred for child guidance but this failed to bring any change, likewise attempts at family therapy. Social work support was having limited but positive influence in establishing some stability. The teacher's action towards Winston appears as inconsistent as the family's, varying between sympathetic concern because of his deprived background and harsh control. Neither has resulted in change, although increasing comments in his reports on his sullenness and provocative behaviour possibly indicate increasing hostility to adults. This ties in with the BSAG result.

View of self — The self-administered BSAG form shows considerable agreement with the teacher-administered profile. Winston sees himself as very impulsive and hostile to adults. He commented, while filling in the form, that his impulsiveness was getting him into more and more trouble and he would like help to change it. He felt that teachers disliked him and did not help him with work. He said he would like help and would like to change the behaviour of teachers towards him. He added that he would change if they did.

Personality — High levels of P, E and N were obtained.

The specific (state) data obtained were as follows:

Observation in class — Winston showed no interest in both lessons observed, which was hardly surprising. He did not understand the work set. He asked one teacher for help four times, was ignored once, told to wait once but did not receive help, told to keep quiet once when he said 'I can't do this bloody work', and told finally that if he shouted out any more he would be sent to the punishment class. Other pupils dealt with the boredom of the lesson by getting on quietly with some other work and, when the teacher was not distracted, asked him for help with requests like, 'Please Sir, can you help me with this work now?' The teacher was very inconsistent in reward/punishment, ignoring Winston when he was quiet and tried to tackle the work, ignoring him when he became fed up and wandered about the room despite the teacher's requests to work, and attending to him only when he hit another pupil or danced on the tables.

His peers attended to his dancing and shouting but eventually lost interest and moved to another part of the room. They then started telling him to keep quiet and let them get some work done for a test coming up next week. This test seems to have been a spur of the moment suggestion by the teacher, to try to obtain some order; the pupils complained that they didn't know about it. Winston did not stop in response to his peers but, upon the sudden arrival in the class of an even noisier and louder pupil, he stopped messing about to watch.

Data to be clarified were as follows:

Work and attention — Winston's attention span was limited, in both lessons, from a minimum of under one minute to a maximum of ten. But the randomly chosen pupil showed a similar pattern. The teachers had made no suggestion that Winston had any specific disability in work or communication skills. It appeared from their reports that he communicated and worked effectively when he chose. The main problem seemed to be communicating with those in authority who confronted him. But it remains to be clarified whether his attention span is generally limited (trait) or is simply a reflection of the situation (state).

Initial Analysis

The data appeared adequate for a provisional formulation, therefore it was decided to proceed but to return to definition to look at attention variables.

Following further observations and discussions with teachers, it was decided to list his generally poor attention span as a state factor, since it did vary greatly according to the situation in class. It was then possible to proceed with the analysis of all the behaviours.

Phase Three
Analysis by trait:
The pattern shows considerable consistency. Winston shows high levels of toughmindedness (P), extraversion (E) and emotional instability (N), so an excitable, demanding, impulsive, aggressive reaction would be expected. His high level of emotionality (N) also shows itself in his concern about his behaviour.

The personality profile also shows its impact in the high levels of inconsequence and hostility on BSAG across situations.

The adult models available to him are aggressive, delinquent or inconsistent. He has no reason to trust adults since they have proved unreliable in the past. He feels, and is, rejected.

The evidence of his work/communication difficulties suggests a state rather than a trait influence, although general impulsivity would make learning difficult, particularly when he is provided with inconsistent learning experiences or lack of positive experience.

Analysis by state:
General aspects — Highly inconsistent response from adults, resulting in little opportunity to learn, was also reflected in inconsistent peer behaviour being reinforcing then rejecting, all within a few minutes.

Precipitating factors — Boredom or failure in lessons and inability to get a helpful response from the teacher.

Reaction — He would start making a noise, banging desks and dancing on them.

Maintaining factors — Initially peer attention for the behaviour plus possibly enjoyment at the teacher's inability to stop him. (A sequence of disputes with the teacher often lead to his being sent to the punishment class, which apparently he quite liked, where he received considerable controlled teacher attention and later peer status for his punishment.)

Formulation and intervention hypotheses:
Formulation — The formulation initially concentrates on limited areas, since there is an urgent need to address concerns and an immediate threat of suspension.

Winston's behaviour is being maintained by intermittent peer attention. He received no attention from the teacher for brief appropriate behaviour and very little for inappropriate behaviour except when it was highly disturbing to the teacher. Where he has work difficulties he is not receiving help.

Winston is reacting to the all-round rejection he receives but this is partly due to his very impulsive, distractible and toughminded temperament.

He recognises this as a problem and wants to change it and the hostility he faces. When he encounters antagonism towards him from staff he finds generating the motivation for such change difficult and expresses anxiety about his position. Some possibility of intervention cooperation from staff exists and he says that he is prepared to change provided that others also change, so a programme may be feasible.

Intervention hypotheses
1. Get cooperation from the teachers prepared to do so try to bypass others initially.
2. Ask teachers to provide Winston with help for specific work difficulties in a consistent fashion.
3. Provide Winston with a means to control his impulsiveness.
4. Teach him techniques for communicating with authority and handling peer reactions.
5. Provide a basis for a contractual rather than a confrontational relationship with teachers.
6. Teach him to control anxiety/instability reaction.

Discussion
In discussion, Winston said that he would welcome the chance to avoid certain lessons and teachers. He felt that teachers disliked him but he would like to help to change their behaviour toward him and his work. He gave clear evidence of awareness of his own impulsive behaviour and particularly that it caused a problem which he would like to change. His senior teacher was prepared to cooperate and believed he could persuade a few teachers to be nice to Winston experimentally provided that his behaviour quickly changed.

Given the range of issues and level of teacher hostility, it was thought that he might have to work part-time out of the school.

Full agreement was obtained (in discussion with the social worker, who spoke to Winston's mother) although it was apparent that part of the work, for example, initial impulse and anxiety control training, would have to take place outside the school setting as no one at the school had time to learn the procedures. It was agreed that Winston should visit a Guidance Centre to see if he would be willing to attend on one day a week for such training. After his visit the programme was agreed.

Restated objectives

The intervention programme was to be based partly in school and partly in the Guidance Centre. The Guidance Centre's role was to teach impulse and anxiety control techniques and to arrange follow-up practice in school. Winston was to be considered responsible for the success of his end of the programme by attending the special lessons and practising what he learnt there. He was also to agree to sacrifice certain gains if he did not complete his side of the programme. The end product for Winston was the control of impulsiveness/anxiety, easier communication with teachers, less rejection from peers and less hostility from the teachers.

The teachers' role was to undertake a fixed response to him — a be-nice-to-Winston attempt — and filling in a report book on his appropriate behaviour. They were to note examples of change by Winston, to assume his good faith and intention to change, and to encourage him to do so. The end-product for the teachers was an easier life through the reduction of impulsive behaviours.

PHASE FOUR:

The details of the programme were grouped into increase, decrease and instil elements.

Increase — Reflective behaviour and verbal control of thinking. Impulsiveness consists of a failure to reflect upon alternatives before acting. Therefore the intention was to increase reflective behaviour and verbal control of thinking to overcome Winston's impulsiveness. Since this appeared to be in part a trait (preferred style), it could be dealt with directly as follows:

(a) Thinking lessons

In order to intervene in the sequence of events that lead to his usual impulsive rejection of learning that involved problem solving, a stimulus control sequence was taught (Lane, 1975). In a carefully graded set of maths puzzles, Winston was instructed to solve the puzzle and, at the point at which he felt that he could not do it, to say out loud, 'Now, how can I go about solving this?' in replacement of his usual response of throwing the work away or walking away. Thus a verbal facilitative response replaced an active retarding one. He was instructed to talk out loud to himself, following a model provided by the teacher. For example, in reconstructing a square from its divided pieces, he was given the following model. 'Now, how can I go about solving this? Well it's a square, perhaps if I find the corners first that will help. Good, well done ...'

In solving other problems such as the reasons for having 'all standing room only buses', the model given was that of looking for good and bad points, as follows.

'Now how can I go about solving this? Perhaps if I got the good points about the idea first then the bad points ...'

Once this verbal control of thinking was established, the talking was gradually faded in volume until it was silent (internalised). This approach provided a method to learn an alternative general (trait) response pattern.

(b) Contingency management of appropriate behaviour.

Since, as well as being a trait, his impulsiveness was also a reflection of state events such as inconsistency in the teachers, state factors also had to be dealt with. When Winston behaved in a learning or relationship facilitating way, he was rewarded at the Guidance Centre with a token exchangeable for goods. In this way, appropriate behaviour was gradually shaped and increased. In order to ensure its continuation back in school, a good-report book was introduced. His teachers were required to write in it positive and true statements about improved work, attitude and behaviour. This introduced consistency into the teachers' relationship with him. All these comments earned tokens back in the Centre. In order to increase deferred rather than immediate gratification (a feature of impulsiveness), tokens became more valuable when saved — 200 was worth four times as much as 100.

Decrease — Impulsiveness and inappropriate response to frustrations.

As he had apparently been receiving reinforcement for impulsiveness and inappropriate response to frustration, it was also deemed necessary to act directly to reduce the reinforcement from this and provide an alternative method of handling frustration, as follows:

(a) Time out

Whenever inappropriate behaviour occurred (not doing work and so forth), Winston was denied access to token-earning activities, and could only earn them again when he started behaving appropriately.

(b) Relaxation

He was taught to control rate of breathing to help him relax in the face of frustration. Now, when a frustrating situation occurred, he was to use this breathing routine.

Instil — An attitude that relationships can be pleasant and not manipulative and provide an alternative way of handling authority. In addition to the increase and decrease elements, there existed his general hostility to authority/adults and a possible lack of skill in relating to them. So it was necessary to instil a new skill in handling authority and establish a contractual basis to relationships as follows:

(a) **Reinforced role play and modelling.**

Winston took part in story and script sessions in which problem situations, such as confrontations with authority figures, were enacted and alternative behaviours were taught and practised.

(b) **Written contract**

Winston's evident hostility made it crucial that a guarantee that he could not be manipulated by centre staff or those in school came before trying to build a trusting relationship. He was told by the staff of the centre, 'Right, you don't know me from Adam. I might be a right pig for all you know. So, we will have this written contract stating what we have agreed to do. I can't make you do anything that's not in the contract. If you think I am trying to, you can tell me to clear off'.

The signed contract bound the Centre to reward effort and provide the programmes, Winston to carry out agreed tasks and the school to keep their end of the bargain, to try and be nice to Winston and to provide help with work. The report book specifically cued teachers to look for appropriate behaviour and comment on it.

The programme elements of increase, decrease and instil were very detailed, but the techniques themselves were simple and readily usable in teaching situations.

PHASE FIVE: Evaluation

Evaluation of the programme at six weeks with a BSAG form and statements from the teachers and Winston indicated that all was proceeding satisfactorily.

The main contributory factors to success were felt to be the impulse control training, scripts and the positive consistency of the teachers. The tokens were rated as less important by the pupil and relaxation was rarely used, as the need had not arisen. Time out was only used once and was not therefore a critical element.

Optimisation

The programme was optimised. It was decided and agreed to start introducing other teachers, one lesson at a time, into the programme. Winston retained a right of veto until the end of the three month contract. It was believed likely that the new objective of introducing further teachers could be met, since he had achieved good impulse control. Since time out had contributed little, it was abolished and relaxation training was suspended, at least temporarily.

At the three month evaluation progress was still being maintained.

New objectives were formulated. It was decided that, on completion of the remedial work which was to continue past three months, Winston should be allowed to join an examination group for certain lessons in which he was

CONTRACT

A contract for three months between Winston, the Centre and his school

It is agreed that:

Winston: *will attend special sessions at the Centre on Monday and Thursday mornings starting promptly at 9.30am and finishing at 12.30pm. He will take part in training sessions as follows:*

9.30-10.00	*Learning to think less impulsively.*
10.00-10.30	*He will choose a lesson from a list covering work difficulties at school supplied by himself and agreed with the school.*
10.30-11.00	*Coffee Break*
11.00-11.30	*Story and script sessions on alternative ways to handle problems.*
11.30-12.00	*Relaxation sessions.*
12.00-12.30	*Free time for activities, coffee or to talk to staff.*

All work completed and behaviour carried out in accordance with the rules set (on the separate sheet of rules), will earn tokens which can be exchanged for items from the menu provided. (Menu items include biscuits, extra activities, coffee, coke or other items by agreement). Any non-completion of work or breach of rules will result in the loss of opportunity to earn tokens for a period to be decided at the discretion of the Centre staff. Winston may recover token-earning time by behaving appropriately or completing the work.

In school, Winston will attend lessons with agreed teachers and behave in accordance with the same rules as are in operation at the Centre. He will carry the report book at all times and ask teachers to complete it at the end of lessons. These comments will earn tokens back in the Centre.

Head of House *will ensure that Winston is placed in classes appropriate to his need for extra help with his work; will arrange for him to attend the lessons only of teachers who have agreed to act in a positive manner and complete the report book; will take responsibility for ensuring that teachers complete their part of this contract.*

Centre staff *will provide lessons and tokens as agreed but will not make additional demands without the agreement of all parties. They will also provide a report book and list in it the behaviour expected so that teachers in school can make a note of its occurrence. Any comments received in the book will earn tokens back in the Centre.*

General agreement *This contract is to run for three months. It will be reviewed in six weeks, or earlier if one party feels aggrieved. All agree to do their best to meet the terms of the contract and state their belief that each party will act in good faith and try their best to carry out their part.*

Signed.......................... Signed.......................... Signed.........................

showing some ability. Contact with the social worker was to be maintained in case family intervention became possible. The sessions at the Centre were ended.

Maintenance

A post-intervention contract between Winston and his senior teacher was written, to include rights to negotiate new teaching arrangements so that Winston's reintegration into classes could proceed smoothly. It was also apparent that Winston was actively working to improve the family situation. Support was promised to him in this area, should he ask for it in future. He was also given the right to contact the Centre to keep them in touch with his progress or difficulties. An additional right, in conjunction with his school, was offered, namely, extra tuition should his examination studies raise difficulties because he had missed so much work in the past. In return, he had to agree to take up any disputes with the senior teacher rather than in confrontation with other staff, and he agreed to try his best to keep school rules and accept the disciplinary authority of the teachers.

Re-evaluation

Winston was followed up at six, twelve and twenty four months after the intervention using an improvement rating, the BSAG and discussion. At six months, things were still going well. At twelve months, they started going wrong. Winston made use of his right to contact the Centre and it quickly transpired that the teacher with whom he had his contract had left. The new senior teacher knew nothing of the contract so did not act in accordance with it. Discussion with this teacher was held and he agreed to talk to Winston about a new contract. The matter was therefore left between them. A modification in procedure was introduced to ensure that prior notice was given of such fundamental changes. At twenty four months Winston had left school and was attending college. His change from delinquency to college entrant was having a positive effect on the rest of his family.

Comment

This is not an entirely satisfactory study since far too much was attempted too quickly. The pressure of the situation ensured that a comprehensive programme was enacted when a more controlled, step by step approach might have been preferable. With a slower pacing, it might have been possible to carry the whole programme within the school setting.

(Subsequent programmes in the school used such an approach, with teachers being taught the programme management skills.)

Much of the data collected which could have been incorporated in the formulation was left out because of pressure to act quickly, but intervention techniques were applied without reference to the data and the construction of an appropriate formulation. No serious attempt to check the validity of the formulation was made and it was good fortune that it held up. Nevertheless, a child who was clearly on his way out and who had failed to respond to previous interventions, did change his patterns, and the teachers greatly modified their approach to him.

A number of his teachers used this experience to re-think some of their work with other pupils, and a programme of school-focused training for teachers was established to spread the skills.

The hypotheses used were too vague in some areas and consequently a broad spread of data was collected when more focused hypotheses could have reduced the requirements. Given the time and effort involved in data collection, this would have been preferable. More focused hypotheses would also have revealed the requirement for higher levels of skills training and consistency instead of tokens as key intervention points. Certain teachers had resisted the use of tokens but were persuaded to use them. Yet tokens contributed little to the programme and the benefits did not warrant the costs. The case demonstrates the effectiveness of the approach, but also underlines the need for tightly developed hypotheses where possible. If the hypotheses had been more clearly defined and tested, a less elaborate programme would probably have been enacted.

This case certainly demonstrates just how much work teachers are prepared to undertake if they see some benefit.

CASE STUDY TWO (described in Tattum and Lane, 1988)

John is the youngest of five children. His father was in regular work but had always been aggressive towards the children, according to the mother's and child's accounts. She used to intervene to prevent the children being hit, but gave up after receiving beatings herself. She reported that the father had a poor relationship with all the children. Attempts over the years to involve the family in Family Therapy failed. The older brother had been suspended from school for bullying and was increasingly involved with the police. John spent several months in hospital in his early years for a series of operations to correct birth defects. He remembered that period clearly and his feelings of fear. Difficulties with language development added to his problems. Speech therapy over several years, two years in a specialist unit for language difficulties and, later, a period in a unit for the 'emotionally disturbed', preceded his transfer to mainstream secondary education. At this time, he was still a non-reader and had poorly developed social skills, although his speech had improved. He developed a severe stutter at the age of twelve when he was becoming increasingly involved in violence and vandalism and, subsequently, football hooliganism.

The school he attended made extensive use of the cane as a punishment, in spite of the fact that, as the Deputy Head said, 'You might as well cane the wall as some of these children for all the good it does'. (Such non-response to discipline and therapy was a feature of many of the toughminded, stable extravert children in the study).

In terms of the research findings reported previously, John is an example of a child with multiple problems. However, there were also several positive compensatory features. John had established a very good relationship with the special needs teacher in the school, who made a determined and successful attempt to teach him to read. A number of other teachers felt there were positive aspects in his behaviour, although they neither accepted nor tolerated his bullying. Several teachers wanted him further beaten, suspended, prosecuted or 'xxxxed'. His mother, although powerless against the father, did provide a compassionate model and he felt loved by her.

The school decided to make a referral for Child Guidance but that broke down. (Psychotherapy is often sought - 'perhaps he needs individual help' — but is rarely useful for a toughminded, extravert pupil, who has learned a pattern of violent response and has been consistently reinforced for using it.) They then made a referral to the Islington Centre. A complex analysis and intervention followed. In brief, it identified certain key elements:

a) Both his father and some male teachers provided models of aggressive behaviour. John disliked them but saw them as powerful models.

b) He valued the compassion he was shown but saw it as weakness.

c) He greatly valued being in school, at least that part of it which gave him some sense of success. He feared the prospect of further suspension.

d) His speech difficulty and lack of social skills prevented his expressing/asserting himself effectively. When confronted, he found that hitting out worked: children did not tease you if you terrorised them, and being unpredictable made teachers uncertain about confronting you. Violence worked; reason did not.

e) The school did not have a consistent policy, and conflicts were apparent between staff over dealing with these issues and this pupil.

A programme was introduced to teach John mechanisms to deal with stress situations and to develop his social skills. A review of the models in his environment took place, to help him to identify power as legitimate assertion rather than aggression. A contracted set of relationships was established with teachers so that events were rendered predictable, with defined consequences. It was made clear that any incident of bullying would be followed by a suspension, but that the issue of provocation by others would also be tackled, that is, he would feel that he was treated fairly. Over a nine month period, the programme took effect with only two incidents being reported. No violence was reported in his final year at school. He left without qualifications but did eventually obtain work. Two years later, he was involved in an incident with others (his old football gang) but, following a period of probation and good social work support, stayed out of further trouble. Five years on he was working, developing an ongoing relationship and feeling positive about himself.

Hypotheses testing
One particular aspect of the case will be considered. Point (d) above looked at the problem of hitting out as a result of stress. The way the hypotheses were tested in this area provides an example of the process.

Three situations of violence were identified for consideration;
1. Bullying other children.
2. Attacks on certain teachers.
3. Fights in other contexts.

The initial hypotheses linked the idea of stress to violence as follows:-

When faced with a confrontation situation, John's level of stress is increased. As a result, his speech difficulty becomes worse, he has difficulty expressing himself and he hits out, which reduces his anxiety.

The various components in this sequence can be tested. The situations in which confrontations occur can be listed, the levels of stress he feels can be established on a scale on which he rates the level (say 1-10). Speech fluency could be checked, and the occasions on which he hits out could be recorded. Specific 'Attribution' or 'ABC' techniques could be used to provide a fine-grain analysis of the contexts in which violent or non-violent outcomes were observed.

This process of observation led to the realisation that there were in fact at least four different patterns.

1. **Cognitive justification**

   In some settings when faced with stress, John became angry, told himself that it was wrong that he was treated that way and chose to hit out.

2. **Stress Management/Skills deficit**

   In some settings he would become anxious, be unable to talk his way out because of his stutter, and hit others in frustration.

3. **Just World**

   In some settings where he saw someone acting unjustly, he would 'punish' the offender by hitting him. This was cold, calculated violence.

4. **Sheer pleasure**

   Certain settings, mostly involving football, were ones in which he sought out fights for the pleasure involved. This was entertainment, not stress.

Given these very different patterns, the hypothesis that stress leads to violence cannot be sustained. It might do, but the circumstances in which it did were very specific.

Alternative hypotheses were needed to cover the varied situations. The case-study describes one of these patterns to devise a formulation and intervention, but it would not cover other settings which give rise to the violence. Hence the intervention had to include issues to do with the 'just world' and direct control was needed in other contexts.

The one area not covered in the original programme was 'sheer pleasure', and it is not surprising, therefore, that no change occurred in that area.

Comment

Testing out the hypotheses in a systematic way reveals the key elements which must be included in the formulation and enables disproof of hypotheses to take place.

Unlike the first case, of Winston, more careful hypothesis testing did take place here. This allowed for very tight control on the situation.

CASE STUDY THREE

The Headteacher of a Primary School referred five boys from one class, who had been the centre of considerable disturbance for two years. They were said, to be impulsive and easily distracted, to interfere with the work of other children and to fail to respond to correction. All had been seen for additional (although varied) professional help, including child guidance, social/family work, and individual remedial tuition. No progress having been made, the Headteacher now felt that 'reducing the damage to the rest of the class' should be the major priority.

So, initially, the definition of the problem related to certain 'difficult' children. However, discussion with the class teacher and preliminary observation in class revealed a number of problems of organisation. The 'problem five' represented a focal point, but the issues raised were applicable to several other members of the class. The way their individual difficulties were expressed reflected these broader organisational issues.

The school staff felt strongly that they had done their best to meet the children's 'needs' in offering additional professional help, both outside the school and through extra help in special groups in school.

Certain features were apparent:

(1) They had received considerable individual and family intervention for their 'maladaptive' behaviour, but the contribution of classroom and school organization had been neglected, and so had the interactive effect of individual differences and classroom organisation.

(2) An observer placed in the class could not distinguish between the 'problem five' and certain other pupils in terms of the behaviour in question, but could do so in terms of the level of negative response from the teacher.

(3) Certain children (the five) were more likely to receive an order to carry out a task when the other pupils received a request. They were more likely to be warned of the consequences of non-compliance in advance of completing a task.

(4) The level of praise available to pupils generally in the class was low, but when a task was completed, praise was more often directed to 'better behaved' children than to the 'five'.

(5) The level of attention from the teacher gained by pupils generally for non-compliance with a request/order was low, but was more often directed to the 'worse behaved'.

(6) The class was divided into groups by ability and a wide and imaginative range of resources was available. However, budgetary considerations meant that there had to be a high degree of sharing, sometimes necessitating

197

a frustrating wait. The materials were not well located and certain traffic lanes existed for pupils to fetch the materials they needed. The pupils who were said to be the most easily distracted were positioned at the junctions of these lanes, so suffered the most distractions. The rationale offered for this was that they were close to the teacher's desk/assistance.

(7) Several support groups for language and remedial work existed and some of the pupils (three of the five, plus a few other pupils) spent part of the time in them. Instead of all going out together, they went at various times, further disrupting classroom routine and requiring the pupils at times to pick up the threads of a lesson in the middle. Little effective communication existed between the support groups and the classroom teacher. Discussion about the pupils took place, but there was no joint teaching or preparation of materials to ensure that the learning in one setting reinforced or extended that in the other.

(8) Much support was available to the classroom teacher, on paper. Advice — psychological, remedial, psychiatric, social, etc. — was abundant. In reality, this advice was unhelpful and unstructured; it offered much theoretical explanation but no realistic way to translate theory into classroom practice. Although interesting, it was not useful for a teacher to hear about problems of sibling rivalry as a possible explanation for difficulties with peers, if no practical intervention was designed to help the teacher to deal with its impact on the classroom.

Following an analysis (primarily based on the state elements) which determined the relative importance of the issues, various suggestions were developed to meet these difficulties, which were then initiated by the school. When followed up, it was found that the head and staff were beginning to resolve issues of organisation and to define problems in more objective terms. Significantly, they had begun to look at resources available within the school to meet the problems. This contrasted with the previous pattern of assuming that children who were difficult had 'special needs requiring special help'.

In the classroom originally observed, desks and materials had been repositioned, quiet areas set aside, and the timetables of the different staff more satisfactorily blended. More effective support between remedial and classroom situations had also developed. As a result of this action by the school there were considerable improvements in the behaviour of all the children, not simply the 'five'.

CONCLUSIONS

Difficulties in schools are not a product of specific deficits in the child or the school; the process is interactive and dynamic. You do not explore this process in order to blame the teacher, the child, the family, or the curriculum. Schools which look at themselves and this process are often surprised at what they find and the strengths that are revealed. This case-study highlights the positive way a school can use the analysis of a difficult group of children to look at itself. Certain principles need to be applied, however, if the process by which an individual school achieves or fails to achieve perceived objectives is to be made explicit. It is argued that:

(1) Problems may be multifaceted, they exist in a context and they are amenable to understanding only in so far as that context is understood.

(2) A framework of formal analysis is necessary for understanding without preconceptions or 'explanatory fictions' in order that the unstated may be revealed and unused skills recognized.

(3) Understanding is not enough: it needs to be followed by agreement on objectives and intervention.

(4) Planned action must follow understanding, for without action there is no significant learning.

(5) Schools are dynamic, needs and resources change, consequently programmes must be evaluated and objectives periodically challenged and, if necessary, altered.

The 'impossible child', or the difficult class, provides a challenge to the school. If the school can respond to that challenge and recognize it as part of its own construction and reconstruction, then more positive classroom behaviour can be promoted.

CHAPTER NINETEEN

Some Outcome Studies

Introduction

This chapter discusses the nature of outcome data. Some of that data has been reported previously and some will form part of a forthcoming detailed outcome study.

The discussion has been forced upon me through the gradual realisation that several competing tasks were required, each valid in its own way but contradictory in origin. What is the purpose of a chapter on outcome data in a short book like this? To demonstrate that the techniques work, perhaps? That seems like a fair assumption, but how do you actually decide if they work? Whose criteria do you use? Those of objective external data maybe — but what are we then measuring? We could take the child's score on a test (the BSAG) then measure on a re-test. That would surely be an objective measure. (Findings for our pupils on BSAG were reported by Topping 1983.) But what if we find that a child can show substantial statistical improvement in such a measure but still be suspended from school? Is the child still to be judged a success (this is not hypothetical — it happened)?

The problem is complicated by the fact that several different tasks were attempted. The work with the individual pupils is primarily about performance. The appraisal of performance based on agreed outcomes is what the case study material is all about. Because the Islington Centre operated an open file system, these outcome measures had to be shared. In sharing them, two concerns were raised. Firstly, the child's performance on agreed outcomes had to be measured, not the child as a person. The child's competence might also be assessed, but this raised the second concern. You cannot effectively measure performance or competence except within the context of the performance. The demand characteristics of the situation featured strongly. Thus the child in possession of the file will argue that a particular measure of success makes no sense in the case of reports received from Mr X — because that teacher marks far more severely than anyone else. Or the child might argue that expecting consistent performance (or marking) when the class has had three changes of teacher in a year, is unrealistic.

There has been much talk in education (and industry) in recent years about performance indicators and competencies. It is a new language to be learned and yet I am not sure that a grammar to support the words really exists. When Gene Stone and a group of educators from Harvard founded Clayton University, based on the idea of competence-led education, they were criticised or ignored by traditional educators. Their system has more recently been widely copied (although never attributed to the source). But they did not just use a set of words but linked it all to a philosophy of life-long education (much influenced by Carl Rogers, one of their advisors) and provided a grammatical structure against which to assess learning. Essentially, they did not separate learning from the context in which performance occurred. They looked at the process by which knowledge and skills were acquired, in order to achieve competence in a defined area and they demonstrated that competence in the relevant context. The process was encompassed within an agreed learning plan (contract), which included a negotiated method to measure competence. A learning dialogue was involved. Outside of that learning dialogue, the concept does not make as much sense. Yet it is a 'context free' set of assumptions about what constitutes adequate performance/competence which is currently sweeping education. Even if the role of context is acknowledged, no systematic way of assessing it is provided.

The approach to appraisal adopted here was influenced by this work, but also by the idea of a social exchange process. It was given substantial shape by complementary work in industry and the need to design 'Personal Development Plans' which delivered performance output and long term development for the individual concerned (Lane, 1980, Lane, 1988, Grieve and Lane, 1989, and Lane and Van Oudtshoorn, 1990). Since I was arguing that for teachers, managers etc., individual targets could not be assessed outside of organisational constraints, I could hardly deny children the same principle. At the Islington Centre (from 1975), each child started with an open file which became the working document for his progress reflecting the organisational and individual constraints. It was a profile, in the current sense of the term, in name only. It was concerned with context, not with the measurement of the whole child. We argued that we could not or would not measure the whole person (Lane, 1974, 1978). Any such claim we saw as arrogant and also coercive. If the whole person is seen as 'I', then it becomes easy to slip into blaming the child. We preferred to measure performances rather than persons. The actor may give a bad performance without being a bad person, so why not the child.

We could give meaning to contextual issues through correlations of factors with different outcomes. We could indicate the elements which influenced outcome and we could identify the child's role. We can take a sample from the three thousand or so pupils who went through the process (300 was the sample) and we can demonstrate that they achieve certain performance targets but not others. So what?

Does that tell us that the 'programmes' were responsible for the successes and teachers for the failures? In the earlier data, change points were identified and correlates established: they tell us something. But for the individual, it is the change in his life space that matters, not the correlates. Discussion of the way it feels now and agreement on outcomes with key power brokers, is more important than any statistics produced.

There are therefore at least three types of outcome data:

1. Data agreed on the basis of the dialogue between child and referring agent; the noteworthy difficulty that comes to be seen as no longer noteworthy.

2. The experimental data of interest to a world outside of the child's immediate concern.

3. A public agenda based on reports which have real consequences for the child's life but over which there is no direct control. We can look at all three types.

The noteworthy difficulty

Some three thousand case studies were reduced to a sample of 300. For each of these a shared agreement is reached. A programme is agreed. An evaluation is undertaken for each objective.

We can thereby explore the variations in patterns of improvement. If we take various samples from within the group, we find very high levels of improvement. That is the objectives are reached. But is that good, bad or only to be expected? For the child and teacher concerned, this is the key data. The noteworthy difficulties are no longer a concern. Two aspects of this will be considered here, prior to a more detailed forthcoming study. How many objectives might be tackled?

The programmes for 100 pupils were examined and a mean number of objectives established. A figure of 7.8 was obtained. There were, therefore, approximately eight objectives in each programme and a range of techniques was used. The top ten programme components for this sample group were:

Contract: 98%, report system/tokens: 90%, parental involvement: 85%, specific targeting of school reports: 75%, specific targeting of behaviours: 75%, help with work difficulties: 70%, social/cognitive skills training: 60%, specific time limit 'what by when': 35%, additional monitoring systems (additional to contract/report system): 25%, counselling/psychotherapy: 10%

How much did they improve?

In the original data one of the criteria for success was judged to be the attitude of the school to the need for continuing involvement. It was found that the decision by the school that they no longer needed support for the child was a crucial one.

Based on this criterion over 95% were judged sufficiently improved by their school for programme termination. For a specific group who had additional intervention programmes based on a partial withdrawal to the Islington Centre, the rate drops to 90%.

Is that good or bad? It is certainly above the rate of spontaneous remission established in the earlier data but how does it compare? It is only by asking the question 'How does it compare?', that the figures become meaningful, yet that question is meaningless to the individual at the centre of the programme. Thus we have to obtain some experimental comparisons to satisfy an agenda different from that of the child involved.

But for the teachers and pupils involved it is this judgement, the end of noteworthy difficulties, that matters.

Experimental data

Establishing a direct comparison group is difficult and does present some political difficulties. However, the ILEA did monitor outcome data for different types of support service over the years. We have some difficulty with the data for they only included in the figures for Islington those pupils whom we took off-site, when the whole thrust of our work was to keep pupils on site. They include for us, therefore, only the most difficult of our pupils. They also include pupils with long-term truancy problems, although they formed part of a separate component of our work.

Nevertheless it does provide some level of comparison.

The Inner London Education Authority, in its monitoring of the school support programme, produced figures on rates of return to school.

The rates of return to school reported by ILEA for On and Off Site Units (RS744/80) ranged from 25% for Off-site Units, 54 % for Guidance Centres (such as Islington) to 75% for On-site Units.

The figure for Islington using the artificial restriction referred to above produces a finding of 79% for our sample. This includes pupils involved in long-term truancy. Excluding that group, and only counting the standard population of the units, that is those referred for behaviour problems, produces a figure of 87% in one test period. This, as we point out, is at the bottom end of our calculation.

The figures sound good and are higher than those reported above. Of course, all the units were admitting different children and attempting different things, so is a comparison realistic?

A more effective comparison can be made between pupils who received an intervention in one of the various facilities and those who received no specific additional programmes. Any statistical difference between the groups can provide a base line for judging the relevance of any of the improvement rates.

For our research we followed a sample of 114 pupils involved in programmes (but not at the Islington Centre) compared with untreated controls based on a three year follow up. No statistically significant difference was found between them. That is, treated groups showed no significant improvement over the untreated groups. Splitting the groups into children primarily referred for anxiety or for conduct disorders did produce some positive trends for both treatment groups. The improvement rates for the anxiety group were 63% untreated, and 80% treated. For the conduct group, the figures were 35% untreated and 52% treated. (The figures failed to reach significance.)

This provides a possible base line to consider the figures above.

The problem is that the groups who formed the database for the ILEA study were varied. They certainly found that those most likely to improve were, girls, younger pupils, and those with anxiety problems of recent duration. They clearly do not fit our criteria for the Impossible Child. We are therefore comparing our pupils against a less difficult group.

An alternative comparison is to take two groups of pupils matched prior to admission and then involved in different intervention programmes. This was attempted for our follow-up study. Two groups of fifty pupils attending other provision or the Islington Centre were matched by BSAG patterns, age, sex and school. Two years after completion of programmes provided at Islington or other provision, a comparison was made of those who were re-referred for further intervention or suspension from school. The alternative programme pupils were re-referred in 66% of cases and the Islington pupils in 25% of cases, a significant difference.

It appeared that the rates of return and long-term outcome were significantly better than a base-line based on spontaneous remission or other comparison groups/interventions. But does that really answer the question?

The public agenda

The issue of statistics is of more than ideal concern since, as the data in the first part of this study indicated, a measure of behaviour change did not correlate with a rating of change: the label involved something more.

The label is the part that has consequences for the child's life. The issue of shared concern is critical here, for if we can come to share the concern we can also come to share a view about what constitutes evidence of change. The consequences for some children of a failure to achieve a shared view are substantial i.e., suspension, negative court reports, possible imprisonment.

The issue of the public agenda is a very real one. In an earlier paper I had referred to the problem facing pupils in relation to reports made by teachers to courts and the very damning effect such reports could have on outcome. (Lane, 1985) A recent major study of decision-making in the courts has pointed to this problem. The authors argue that reports from teachers have a major influence on the decisions reached. Yet these reports are often inaccurate, contain unsubstantiated allegations, and as we have shown may not reflect the child's attempts at change. (Parker, et.al., 1989)

The research data previously reported provided evidence of the important link between behaviour difficulties and later criminality. A specific study of the impact of programmes on patterns of offending would be a of interest as a public agenda issue. Such a study was undertaken.

The patterns of offending for the pupils were studied over a ten year period. Control groups of pupils involved with various other programmes and no programmes at all were included. Offending during different age periods was also traced. One study traced the cumulative patterns on convictions from ten to twenty years of age. Effective intervention had a significant impact and reduced patterns of offending. (Full details will appear in a subsequent report.) A chart is included here.

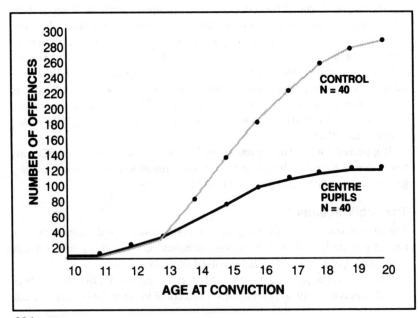

The findings above are promising but such comparisons are difficult to make and the subject therefore requires a detailed report of its own. A further report is planned. However, the findings above remain: programmes for change are viable even with groups of pupils written off as impossible.

Conclusion

This chapter introduced some of the outcome data for the Impossible Child, although of course the main results are contained in the first half of the study. It also raised questions about the purpose of outcome data. For the child, the main concern is the change they make which is recognised by those who have the power to influence them. For those trying to decide if the programmes are worth trying, a comparison with other outcome data is reported.

But the key measure is contained in the changes that individuals make. The Impossible Child, as the earlier data indicated, was at loggerheads with the world over extended periods. A myth can be created around the child, a myth that nothing changes. Yet it can be changed. The child can break the label, the teacher can see through the immediate concern to a new pattern and a new life-chance can be opened up. The Impossible Child, it seems, need not be impossible. I leave the last word to one of the pupils:

"I'll give you a ******* break when you give me a ******* chance."

APPENDIX

Sources for techniques of intervention

INTRODUCTION

The following details provide some sources for instituting an intervention programme. Case-studies in the previous edition (Lane, 1978) provide something of the flavour of various techniques. (Case-numbers quoted refer to the 1978 volume.) There is no substitute for referring to the original sources quoted and the reader should not attempt to institute programmes without reference to the original works.

Techniques are chosen because they fit the analysis of the individual case, thus, full analysis always precedes selection of technique. Very often, a technique suggests itself once the formulation of the case is complete. The arrangement of techniques follows the pattern established previously. The techniques discussed vary in difficulty but should be used in a professional way, not as 'ad hoc' flirtations. The techniques to increase behaviour could, for the most part, be used by any competent professional. The techniques to decrease behaviours should normally be used only under specialist psychological/psychiatric guidance. Instil techniques fall into both categories.

The practitioner contemplating trying any of the techniques should discuss them with professional colleagues and gain support for their use. Given that support, and a professional approach, there is no reason why the practitioner should not be able to design effective interventions.

Techniques to increase behaviour

Techniques to increase behaviour are used when the desired behaviour, or something similar to it, exists in the individual's repertoire of skills but is under-utilised, or not performed in appropriate circumstances.

Behavioural counselling: When counselling is seen as an action-oriented process, behavioural approaches offer a contribution through:

(a) getting the client to define problems objectively;

(b) deciding upon a course of action with the client and

(c) instituting a programme to change behaviour based on scientific principles.

A review of techniques and principles in behavioural counselling can be found in Thoresen and Hosford (1973) and Krumboltz and Thoresen (1976). The supportive approaches developed in client-centred and eclectic schools provide an alternative format. A review of their strengths and weaknesses is provided in Carkhuff and Berenson (1967). (Case Number 4 provides an example of it).

Biofeedback: Biofeedback training provides a means to enable individuals to obtain direct information about the reaction of their nervous system, in a form which makes it possible for them to control those reactions. Its application to stress situations has been widespread but it also has an application in, for example, the rehabilitation of the disabled (Lane and Sturgess 1978) and preventive programmes (Lane 1978). The case of Enrico (No. 5) provides an example of its use. It can be used as an increase or decrease technique. See also Meichenbaum (1976), and Birbaumer (1977).

Cognitive behaviour modification: The integration of interest in the functioning of the autonomic system, with concern for cognitive processes, has opened up a whole new range of applications for behavioural techniques. Examples of its use for stress, anger and pain are found in Meichenbaum and Turk (1975) and simplified step by step procedures are described in Lane (1978). Its application to work with impulsive children has been demonstrated by Meichenbaum and Goodman (1973). Many examples of current thinking are found in Meichenbaum (1976), Dryden and Golden (1986) and Karoly and Kanfer (1982).

Increasing cognitive skills: The key element involved in attempts to increase cognitive skills is the analysis of them. It is important to determine not simply what the child can or cannot do, but also what conditions cause variations in performance, and to analyse sequentially the skill itself so that adequate training can be designed. Patterns of remediation in psycholinguistic skills are described in some detail in Kirk and Kirk (1972). The use of academic skills to reduce behaviour problems is discussed in Ayllon and Roberts (1974). The cases of John (No. 2), Charles (No. 19) and Benny (No. 6) are other relevant examples. Examples are also found in Lane (1975), Ashman and Conway (1989).

Reinforcement: When the consequence of a behaviour serves to increase that behaviour (in frequency or intensity) it can be said to reinforce it. Behaviour can be reinforced positively or negatively. Detailed introductions to these behavioural techniques can be found in Wedell and Merritt (1988) and Gelfand and Hartman (1984). There are various ways of using reinforcement principles, as follows:

Positive reinforcement strengthens the behaviour on which it is focused. For example, if a teacher attends to a pupil when he asks politely for help, that teacher's attention can reinforce the child's behaviour. Similarly, if the child only receives attention when he shouts out inappropriately, that behaviour is increased. Becker et.al. (1967) reports on the use of teacher attention and praise in reducing classroom behaviour problems. Madsen et.al. (1968) have looked at the use of rules, praise and ignoring behaviour as control techniques. The principles have been applied in delinquency and community settings by Fo and O'Donnoll (1974).

Negative reinforcement occurs when behaviour is strengthened or increased by escape or avoidance of a particular consequence. Phobias, because the individual avoids the feared object by his phobic behaviour, provide an example of negative reinforcement.

Contingency management is simply an effective means of organising reinforcements, and involves ensuring that rewards follow desired behaviour in appropriate situations. The teacher needs to recognise the behaviour that is to be rewarded and ensure that rewards follow it. For example, the impulsive child who only occasionally sits still should be rewarded when so doing. Numerous opportunities for good contingency management exist in schools and it provides the single most effective, yet simple, technique available. Case No. 3 provides an example. (Tattum, 1986 has provided an alternative discussion.)

According to the Premack Principle (1959), any behaviour which is preferred or frequently engaged in, 'a high probability response' when it is made to follow a behaviour which is not frequently engaged in, 'a low probability response' increases the likelihood of the low probability response occurring. Thus, if a child would prefer to run about (high probability response) rather than sit still (low probability response) allowing the child to run about after a period of sitting still increases the chance of sitting still. A list can be made of activities the child would normally choose to engage in if given the chance, and each of them could be used as reinforcers for other behaviours less likely to occur. Danaher (1974) provides a review (See case No. 13).

Token Economy is based on contingency management theory. Token economies work on the assumption that certain tasks or behaviours are worth more than others. These valuable tasks are heavily reinforced with tokens which can be redeemed for actual rewards. In establishing an economy, the basic concepts must be discussed with the participants. They must understand why they are getting tokens and there must be time set aside to cash them in. Participants must also understand that tokens will vary from child to child depending on behaviour. For example, John gets several tokens for not kicking chairs; Mary for not kicking John. A list of rewards (menu) should be compiled. This menu should have a variety of rewards costing only a few tokens and some larger bonuses which the children can work towards. Rewards might include time with the teacher, free time, time to read, or more tangible goods. This menu can often be established from suggestions by the pupils themselves. Various case studies using reinforcement techniques with children are available in Galloway (1976). See also paper in Eisler and Miller, (1975) and the Association for Behavioural Approaches with Children Journal (edited by Frank Merritt of Birmingham University) for examples of advantages and problems faced by British practitioners in various settings in using the technology. Also see study No. 15.

Report Book: The report book system mentioned in the case of Winston (No.3), provides a means to extend token economy or contingency management systems into various classrooms without having to establish full blown economies in each setting. It also provides a means of cueing teachers to behaviour that they should observe or to which they should attend. The report book also offers a non-threatening way to express positive regard for adults who find it difficult to give praise in a face-to-face situation. The case (No.7) of Michael provides an example of its value. Essentially, a report book system consists of providing the child with a book into which only positive comments are written by each teacher working with the child. Each comment counts as a token. At the end of the day, or week, the book can be taken to someone nominated in the school or some outside agency who then counts up the tokens and grants the child the reward earned. This can be made more precise by listing the behaviours in the book on which teachers are required to comment. Taking a book with positive comments home to show to parents may create a possibility of changing the often negative attitude of parents to school. It can also establish a positive mental set, for the teacher, who has to look for positive behaviours to comment on, rather than negative ones which occur when letters or reports on misdemeanours are used. It stimulates the potential for positive reinforcement.

Shaping: The process of reinforcing desired behaviour to increase it, is only applicable if the behaviour required does actually, albeit infrequently occur. If not, there is nothing to reinforce. If there is no behaviour even remotely resembling that desired, an instill programme will be needed. If a behaviour similar to the required one occurs, then that behaviour can be shaped into the desired one through the process of reinforcing successive approximations of the desired behaviour. It should not be attempted without experience of reinforcement procedures or reading examples and discussions of shaping, such as in Liberman (1972). An interesting comparison of shaping (an increase procedure) and modelling (an instil procedure) is provided by O'Connors (1972) — see case No.11.

Stimulus control: In the analysis of State factors outlined previously, the sequence: trigger-reaction-maintenance was discussed. Behaviour can be changed by influencing the maintaining (reinforcing) factors, using the principles of reinforcement, or by changing the trigger (stimulus) factors which set the response in the first place. The principles of stimulus control, or rather its lack of application, is a major source of faulty learning. The stimulus that is to control behaviour must actually do so, e.g., when a child enters the room and leaves a coat on the floor instead of on the coat hook, do not ask him or her to put it on the coat hook, but rather get them to go outside with the coat on, come in again, take the coat off and hang it up. Thus, the stimulus of opening the door is linked with taking off the coat, is linked with hanging it up, and not with the inappropriate stimulus of telling the child to hang it up. Remember always that the stimulus is the event immediately preceding the response. The principle of stimulus control, then, is to link an appropriate, naturally occurring event immediately prior to the behaviour with that behaviour, not telling the child 'a thousand and one times' after the event. (An alternative stimulus control was used in Case 3).

Stimulus control procedures have a variety of applications. They require identification by asking or observation of:

1. the stimulus currently controlling the behaviour - the 'wrong' one.
2. a definition of the appropriate stimulus - the one you want to control the behaviour.
3. a procedure to bring the behaviour under appropriate stimulus control.

The possibilities include:

1. instructions to the individual on appropriate response, prompts, etc.
2. manual guidance of the individual's response.
3. starting off with guidance, then fading it out.
4. modelling of the appropriate behaviour (an instill technique) can also be used, although this involves more than stimulus control. The application of stimulus control is particularly useful in dealing with learning disabilities in, for example, teaching:

   a. discrimination between words in reading.
   b. generalisation of response for teaching similarities, e.g. two
       equals 2.
   c. concept formulation: when the individual has to learn both what
       is and what is not an example of a class of behaviour e.g. what
       is a letter and what is a number.

Sixty second therapy: Sixty second therapy was developed in the research to
meet the demands of teachers who had no extra time but were generally positive
and is based on four principles. (I had thought of calling it 'one minute
management' when I first described it in Lane, 1973)

1. For some children who crave, but are deprived of positive teacher-attention,
    even small amounts of such attention are reinforcing.

2. If the mental set (expectancy) of the teacher and pupil at the beginning of
    the day is positive, the chances are increased of further positive reinforce-
    ments occurring.

3. If the mental set of the teacher and pupil at the very end of the day is
    positive, the good feeling is likely to be remembered.

4. The initial and finally occurring events in a sequence are more readily
    remembered than the intervening ones, particularly if some way is found
    to cue the individual specifically to attend those events.

Good results were achieved with sixty second therapy although no fundamental
long-term change is expected and the technique loses power if over-used. The
case of Jerry (No.1) provides an example. The procedure is to devote ten seconds
at the beginning of the day to welcoming this particular child into class by name
and telling him briefly that there is some interesting work, or inviting him to sit
down, as the lesson is about to begin and it is pleasant to see him. At the end of
the day, fifty seconds is devoted to discussing anything positive that the child
did during the day but no mention is made of negative aspects.

Techniques to decrease behaviour

Techniques to decrease a behaviour are used when an existing behaviour in the
child's repertoire occurs more frequently or intensely than is appropriate to the
situation, or when the right behaviour occurs but in the wrong situation.

Anxiety relief conditioning: This consists of directly conditioning an anxiety
inhibiting response to a neutral word (calm). The word 'calm', uttered sub-vo-
cally in distressing situations, can greatly reduce anxiety after this conditioning.
It is discussed in Wolpe (1973).

Assertive training: Assertive training can be used to teach social skills, in which case it forms part of the 'instill' element, as it is based on the learning of a new response. An alternative is to use assertive training to decondition anxiety, in which case it belongs in the 'decrease' category. One cannot be anxious and assertive at the same time in a relationship with another person. If the individual is taught assertion in an anxiety provoking situation, the anxiety is diminished. It is discussed in Wolpe (1973). Case No.10 provides an example. A detailed discussion occurs in Charlesworth and Nathan (1987).

Behavioural rehearsal: This approach is based on the same principles as applied to assertive training in anxiety deconditioning. The aim is to practise situations which evoke anxiety so that anxiety in relation to those situations is reduced. An interview between an employee and employer, teacher and pupil or child and parent might be practised with the intention of helping the individual to feel less anxious when confronting the real situation. Wolpe (1973) provides detailed examples and, more briefly, Case No.10 provides an example.

Covert sensitisation: see Cantela 1976. Essentially the technique consists of pairing a verbally suggested aversive response with an imagined stimulus. For example, an obese individual who wishes to prevent himself eating an extra helping of a favourite food, might imagine himself eating the food and then vomiting all over himself, the table, other people, then seeing the terrible looks from others, the putrid smell rising up, etc., but when he turns away from the food, he imagines feeling better and clean.

Extinction: If behaviour is reinforced, it is likely to be repeated or strengthened. Conversely, if a behaviour is no longer reinforced, it is less likely to be repeated. When a behaviour decreases as a result of non-reinforcement, it is said to have been extinguished. This is not the same as directly punishing the response but is a useful device for reducing the occurrence of a behaviour. Since attention from an adult is often reinforcing, ignoring a maladaptive behaviour can extinguish it. This process is effective by itself, provided that the individual has an alternative response available to him which can be reinforced. Normally extinction is used in association with reinforcement. The undesired behaviour is ignored and the desired behaviour reinforced. The technique is particularly useful in eliminating tantrum behaviour, as most parents will realise: the more attention a child receives for his tantrums the longer they persist. There are of course some behaviours which are so damaging that they cannot be ignored. An alternative is to make use of the principles of marginal utility (Lane 1972, 1978) or satiation (Ayllon 1963). These principles rely on the old adage that you can have too much of a good thing. While one cigarette might be pleasant a smoker forced to smoke huge quantities one after another will eventually find smoking unpleasant. Too much reinforcement becomes unpleasant.

Punishment: Punishment is defined behaviourally as, 'Any consequence of behaviour that reduces the future probability of that behaviour' (Azrin and Holz 1966). Hitting a child or using any similar physical procedure which does not reduce the probability is not, by this definition, punishment, nor is it the concern of this present discussion. (Since the publication of the first volume it is good to note that it is now it is considered that no physical punishment has any place in education.) There is considerable controversy among researchers, even on non-physical punishment techniques. While their careful use had been demonstrated to be effective in the classroom (Hall et.al.,1971, O'Leary and O'Leary 1972), some workers feel that it has no place. (Azrin and Holz 1966). I have argued (Lane 1973) in keeping with the principle of consent in this present study that where punishment procedures are agreed with all parties, they have a limited use since agreement enables the nature of the power structure and psychological compliance variables to be taken into account. In contingency management, more effective alternatives to punishment are normally available, but two may be useful:

(i) Response cost consists of requiring a payment or fine for inappropriate behaviour. This might entail losing an extra privilege or having to give up one's own time and so forth. It is a technique which should be used sparingly. See Kazin (1972).

(ii) Time out consists of withdrawing from the offender the opportunity to earn reinforcement for a defined but limited period. Critical to its success is the right to return to reinforcement by behaving appropriately. See Burchard and Bareara (1972) and Hobbs and Forehand (1975). A useful discussion of the technique is found in Topping (1983). There are twelve rules for making punishment effective, but many are seldom applied in teaching situations.

1. The punishing consequence (or a symbolic representation of it) to a behaviour must be applied immediately after the behaviour. If time is allowed to elapse, the immediate consequence of the behaviour might be reinforcing and act to maintain it, irrespective of later consequences.

2. The consequence must be applied consistently and systematically and not according to the mood or need of the punisher.

3. The recipient of punishment must consider (on reflection) that it was fairly administered.

4. The recipient must be unable to escape the punishment by avoiding the punisher.

5. The punisher must be a regular source of alternative reinforcement to the recipient, ensuring that the recipient needs to retain contact.

6. Punishment is more effective if preceded by a warning signal. This signal can then serve, by stimulating anticipatory anxiety, to make the immediate consequence of the act aversive.

7. Punishment is more effective if used in conjunction with reinforcement of a response which is incompatible to the one being punished.

8. Punishment will be undermined if the behaviour is simultaneously being reinforced in some other way such as through peer status.

9. Punishment by taking away reinforcement and providing a means to earn it back is more effective than direct aversive consequence alone.

10. The design of a punishment system is more effective as part of an overall system of control and reward agreed with those likely to be punished, so that their form of compliance (identification, internalisation or self-interest) is incorporated.

11. The limits of behaviour must be rigidly defined so that the range of permitted tolerance is clear and understood.

12. The system of control must be flexibly applied once notification of offence and immediate consequence (warning or symbolic punishment, e.g. a note that the pupil has to report for detention) has taken place, so that appropriateness to the situation and the possibility of error in notification can be taken into account.

There are potentially undesirable side effects to the use of punishment procedures. In the absence of the punisher, the behaviour may reappear and the punisher may serve as a model of aggressive behaviour, teaching the pupil that 'might is right' (see Gardner 1969 for a review). An interesting alternative to direct punishment is the use of self punishment. Case No.4 Richard provides an example of self punishment.

Systematic desensitisation: The major technique available for overcoming anxiety-based problems is that of systematic desensitisation. It is based on the principle of reciprocal inhibition, the pairing of responses incompatible with anxiety to overcome anxiety. The client is taught how to relax and maintain that relaxation in the face of the anxiety-provoking stimulus. The major source is Wolpe (1973): examples of its use with children can be found in Graziano and Kean (1967), Tasto (1969), Lane (1978) and Lane and Green (1978).

Stress Management/ Control: Stress control provides an extension of the use of relaxation training in combination with positive self talk. In many emotion-evoking situations, it is the combination of physical arousal and negative cognitive thoughts which act in a feedback system to cause the individual to lose effective control over the situation. The individual tells him/herself that he/she cannot cope, becomes more anxious, is thereby less able to cope, confirm that inability, becomes more anxious and so on. Teaching the individual both to control the arousal and to self instruct positively in coping techniques, can overcome the negative feedback cycle. A detailed but simplified account of such a procedure (anxiety management) is available in Lane (1975) and Charlesworth and Nathan (1987) offers a comprehensive source. A problem arises in this area when sources of organisational stress are seen as an individual problem. In early work at the Islington Centre, stress management training included work on analysis of organisational factors (Lane, 1976). Recently Cooper, Sloan and Williams (1988) have provided a study of organisational and individual sources of stress.

Tension relief through imaginal release: The use of imaginal release in connection with controlled breathing can be very effective when individuals can identify or locate a point of tension. Some individuals feel their tension in particular parts of their body. The procedures and an alternative is available (Case No.11)

Thought stopping: Thought stopping is used to control unwanted thoughts. Examples of its varied use have been reported by Wolpe (1958), Yamagami (1971) and Campbell (1974). When an unwanted thought comes to mind the client might shout the word 'stop' or count backwards or name days of the week, that is, to use a device to interrupt the thought. The thought ceases temporarily. The repetition of the technique gradually diminishes the reccurrence of the unwanted thought, particularly if the individual deliberately concentrates on positive or pleasant thoughts after interrupting the unwanted one (Case No.4).

Techniques to instil behaviour

Techniques to instil behaviour are used if a completely new response needs to be taught.

Assertive training: The ability to assert one's rights appropriately is a valuable skill, which many people, and particularly the impossible child, have never learnt. Essentially it consists of teaching the individual the negative consequences of failing to assert oneself. The client is then taught, through practice in real or imaginal situations, relevant assertive behaviour, with the practitioner providing a model. When used simply to teach a desired response assertive training can be considered as part of social skills training. Wolpe (1973) and Alberti and Emmons (1974) provide a discussion of it and the case of Peter (No.10) a brief example, together with case 8 on alternative approach.

218

Contract therapy: The use of a contract is based on the assumption that an individual's exchange with his environment is based on the action that will bring greatest relative advantage or least relative disadvantage in the fulfilment of needs. A contract, even a simple one like 'If you do this I'll do that', whether verbally or in writing, provides a statement of the rights and obligations of both parties to it. The value of a piece of behaviour (its price) is measured in terms of what the individual has to give up for it; if you ask a child to give up behaving in a certain way, there must be something gained by that sacrifice. We all exchange behaviours in this way. This is discussed in more detail in Lane (1972, 1978) together with several case examples. The case of Mrs Selby (No.12) provides a primary school level example, and case 14 an example in a secondary school.

Imitative learning (modelling): Imitating others is a major source of learning. This normally-occurring learning process can be utilised as an educational tool. Instead of relying on the tedious process of reinforcing small steps in a behavioural repertoire, one can greatly speed up the learning process by providing a model. If a pupil can observe another person behaving in a desirable fashion and be motivated to do likewise, long sequences of behaviour can be easily learnt. In 1924, Jones demonstrated that children could overcome phobias of animals if they could observe other children handling them fearlessly. Bandura (1969) has successfully repeated and extended such experiments. Liberman (1972) summarised the factors influencing imitation learning. Imitation proceeds best when:

(a) The model has status, (i.e. has access to rewards).

(b) The model has power, (i.e. can give rewards).

(c) The model is reinforced for the exemplified behaviour.

(d) The model is similar to the observer.

(e) The observer has components of the modelled behaviour already in the repertoire.

(f) The observer has a chance to practice the behaviour soon after watching the model.

(g) The observer is reinforced for performing the model's behaviour. Kazdin (1974) is a useful source.

Social skills training: Any social skill can be taught if it is broken down into its component parts and a systematic training programme for teaching those parts and practising them in appropriate situations is introduced. A particularly useful approach is through scripts or stories of situations which provide an outline of the required behaviour (see Lane 1975) for full details). The case of

Winston (No.3) was one which used social skills training. Sarason and Sarason (1974) is an excellent source for teachers, and Jelfs (1982) provides an extensive range of group work techniques valuable in this area. Orlick (1982) provides games useful for work with younger children. Group tutoring manuals, now widely available in schools, are an important source and Button, (1982), an important original source.

Self-management: Teaching the individual to monitor and control own behaviour is a technique receiving increasing attention. In an earlier study (1972), this author designed an entire remedial programme around the principles of self-management of work and behaviour, which resulted in a considerable improvement in learning skills in secondary remedial pupils. The programme included self-monitoring of progress by the pupils, design of their own work contracts, marking their own work and rewarding themselves for doing so. The case of John (No.2) provides a simplified example. O'Leary and O'Leary (1972) and Thoreson and Mahoney (1974) provide some examples of its use. Worth reading is work in peer-tutoring (Topping, 1988), in self-organised learning (Thomas and Harri-Augstein, 1985), and in self-instruction learning (Goldstein, 1981). It became clear in the study of the Impossible Child that the extent to which the pupil was taught self control of the situation significantly enhanced success. So one should always exploit any opportunity to include self-management in each programme.

There are now a wide number of general texts available as well as detailed 'packages'. The list could be endless so we end with a few general recommendations from recent texts: Ainscow and Tweddle (1989), Fontana (1985), Herbert (1988), Tattum (1986), Widlake (1986), Shearar, et.al., (1990) and the Elton Report (1989).

A final reminder:

Please do not use the appendix like a cookbook of ideas. No technique makes sense without a formulation. As my colleague Julius Malkin was fond of saying,
  "We are all accountable to our formulation."

Bibliography

Adams, P.L. (1973) *Obsessive children: a socio-psychiatric study*, Butterworth, London.

Adams, F. (1986) *Special Education*, Longman, Harlow.

Ainscow, M. & Tweddle, D.A. (1979) *Preventing classroom failure: an objectives approach*, David Fulton Publishers: London.

Ainscow, M. & Tweddle, D.A. (1988) *Encouraging classroom success*, David Fulton, London.

Ajzen, I. (1988) *Attitudes, personality and behaviour*. Open University Press. Milton Keynes.

Alberti, R.E. & Emmons, M.L. (1974) *Assertive behaviour*. San Luis Obispo, California.

Allsopp, J.F. & Feldman, M.P. (1974) Extraversion, neuroticism, psychoticism and antisocial behaviour in schoolgirls. *Soc. Beh. Pers.*, 2, pp. 184-190.

Andry, R.G. (1960) *Delinquency and parental pathology*. Methuen, London.

Apter, S.J. (1982) *Troubled children, troubled systems*. Pergamon, New York.

Argyis, C. (1957) *Personality and organisation*, Harper Row, New York.

Argyle, M. (1964) *Psychology and social problems*. Methuen, London.

Ashman, A.F. & Conway, R.N.P, (1989) *Cognitive strategies for special education*. Routledge. London.

Askew, S.(1988) Aggressive behaviour in boys: to what extent is it institutionalised? In Tattum D.P. & Lane D.A., *Bullying in schools*. Trentham Books.Stoke on Trent.

Azrin N.H. & Holz, W. (1966) Punishment. in Honig, W.K. (1966) *Operant behaviour: areas of research and application*. Appleton-Century Craofts, New York.

Azrin, N.H., Hutchinson, R.R., & Hake, D.F. (1966) *Extinction-induced aggression. J. Exp. Anal. Beh.*, 9. p. 191-204.

Ayllon, T. (1963) Intensive treatment of psychotic behaviour. *Beh. Res. & Ther.* 1. pp. 53-81

Bakwin, H. (1973) *The genetics of bedwetting.* in Kolvin, I., MacKeith, R., & Meadow, S.R. *Bladder control and enuresis.* Heinemann, London.

Bandura, A. & Walters, R.H. (1959) *Adolescent aggression.* Ronald, New York.

Bandura, A. (1969) *Principles of behaviour modification.* New York, Holt, Rinehart & Winston.

Batchelor, I.R.C. (1969) *Textbook of psychiatry.* Oxford Univ. Press, London.

Bateson, G., *et. al.* (1956) Towards a theory of schizophrenia. *Beh. Sci.,* 1 pp. 251-264.

Bayley, J. (1990) *Southwark EGS Handbook.* Southwark, LEA.

Beck, A.T. (1976) *Cognitive therapy and the emotional disorders.* International Universities Press, New York.

Becker, H.S. (1963) *Outsiders: studies in the sociology of deviance.* Free Press, Glencoe.

Becker, W.C., *et. al.* (1967) The contingent use of praise in reducing classroom behaviour problems. *J Spec. Educ.* 1.3. pp. 287-307.

Bennett, I. (1960) *Delinquent and neurotic children: A comparative study.* Basic Books. New York.

Berger, M. (1977) Learning Theories. in Rutter & Hersov *op. cit.* (1977)

Beynon, J. (1984) 'Sussing out' teachers: pupils as data gatherers in Hammersley, M. & Woods, P. *Life in schools: the sociology of pupil culture.* Open University Press, Milton Keynes.

Birbaumer, N. (1977) Biofeedback training: a review. *European Journal of Behaviour Analysis and Modification.* 1.4. pp.235-251.

Blau, P.M. (1964) *Exchange and power in social life.* John Wiley, New York.

Bolles, R. (1970) Species-specific defence reactions and avoidance learning. *Psychol. Rev.* 77. pp. 32-48.

Bowlby, J. (1951) *Maternal care and mental health,* World Health Organisation, New York.

Brewin, C.R. (1989) Attribution, emotion and counselling psychology. in Lane, D.A: *Attributions, beliefs and constructs in counselling psychology.* British Psychological Society, Leicester.

Brown, M. & Madge, N. (1982) *Despite the Welfare State.* Heinemann, London.

B.S.C. (1988) Behaviour Support Conference. Inst. of Ed. London.

Buckley, W. (1967) *Sociology and modern systems theory.* Englewood, New Jersey.

Buhler, C. (1951) Maturation and motivation. *Personality.* 1. pp. 184-211.

Burchard, J. & Bareara, F. (1972) An analysis of time out and response cost in a programmed environment. *J. App. Beh. Anal.* 5. pp. 271.282

Burt, C. (1925) *The Sub-normal school-child: 1. the young delinquent.* University of London Press.

Butler, N., Peckham, C. & Sheridan, M. (1975) Speech defects in children aged seven years: a national study. *Brit. Med. J.* 3.2.1975.

Button, L. (1982) *Group tutoring for the form teacher.* Hodder and Stoughton, London.

Callias, M. (1990) Child therapy and outcome. in Lane, D.A. & Dryden, W. (1990) *Child and adolescent therapy in Britain.* Open University Press, Milton Keynes.

Campbell, L.M. (1974) A variation of thought-stopping in a twelve year old boy. *J. Beh. Ther. & Exp. Psych.* 4. pp. 69-70.

Cantela, J.R. (1976) The present status of covert modelling. *J. Beh. Ther. & Exp. Psych.* 6. pp. 323-326.

Cantwell, D. (1977) Hyperkinetic Syndrome. in Rutter & Hersov (1977) *op. cit.*

Caplan, H.L. (1970) Hysterical conversion symptoms in childhood. M. Phil. London. (unpub.)

Carkhuff, R.R. & Berenson, B.G. (1967) *Beyond counselling and therapy.* Holt Reinhart & Winston, New York.

Carroll, H.C.M. (1972) Remedial teaching of reading: an evaluation. *Rem. Educ.* 7.1.

Cattell, R.B. & Cattell, M.D.L. (1969) *Handbook for the high school personality questionnaire.* IPAT, Illinois.

Cattell, R.B., Shrader, R.R. & Barton, K. (1974) The definition and measurement of anxiety as a trait and a state in the 12 to 17 year range. *Brit. Soc. Clin. Psychol.* 13. pp. 173-182.

Chazan, M. (1967) The effects of remedial teaching in reading: a review of research. *Rem. Educ.* 2.1. pp. 4-12.

Checkland, P. (1989) An application of soft systems methodology. in Rosenhead, S. *Rational analysis for a problematic world.* Wiley, Chichester.

Clarizo, H. (1968) Stability of deviant behaviour through time. *Mental Hygiene.* 52. pp. 288-293.

Clarke, R.V.G. & Cornish, D.B. (1978) The effectiveness of residential treatment for delinquents. in Hersov, Berger & Shaffer *op. cit.*

Cloward, R.A. & Ohlin, L.E. (1961) *Delinquency and opportunity.* Routledge and Kegan Paul, London.

Cohen, A.K. (1955) *Delinquent boys: the culture of the Gang.* The Free Press. New York.

Cohen, A.K. (1959) *Sociology Today*, edited by Merton, Bloom & Cottrell. New York, Basic Books. pp.473-483.

Cohen, H.L. (1973) Behaviour modification and socially deviant youth. in Thoreson, C.E. *Behaviour modification in education.* NSSE, Chicago.

Colby, K.M. (1964) Psychotherapeutic processes. in Fransworth, P., McNemar, O., & McNemar, Q. *Annual Review of Psychology* 15 pp. 347-370.

Coulby, D. (1981) *Evaluation of the Tower Hamlets School Support Team.* ILEA, London.

Coulby, D. and Harper, T. (1983) *D.O.5. Schools Support Unit. Evaluation: Phase 2.* Croom Helm, London.

Connors, C.K. (1970) Symptom patterns in hyperkinetic, neurotic and normal children. *Child. Dev.* 41. pp. 667-682.

Corbett, J.A. (1971) The Nature of tics and Gilles de la Tourette's Syndrome. J. *Psycho-som. Res.* 15. pp. 403-409.

Corbett, J.A. (1977) Tics and Tourette's Syndrome. in Rutter & Hersov (1977) *op. cit.*

Corbett, L. (1986) quoted in Tattum. D. (1986) *op.cit.*

Corbett, J.A., Matthews, A.M., Connell, P.H. & Shapiro, D.A. (1969) Tics and Gilles de la Tourette's Syndrome: a follow-up study and critical review. *Brit. J. Psychiat.* 115. pp. 1229-1241.

Coser, L.A. (1956) *The Functions of social conflict.* Free Press, Glencoe.

Crown, S (1953) An experimental enquiry into some aspects of the motor behaviour and personality in Ticquers. *J. Ment. Sci.* 99. pp. 84-91.

Cytryn, L. & McKnew, D. (1972) Proposed classification of childhood depression. *AM. J. Psychiat.* 129. pp. 149-155.

Danaher, B. G. (1974) Theoretical foundations and clinical applications of the Premack principle: review and critique. *Beh. Ther.* 5. pp.307-324.

Davids, A., Ryan, R. & Salvatore, P. (1968) Effectiveness of residential treatment for psychotic and other disturbed children. *Am. J. of Orthopsychiat.* 38. pp. 469-475.

Davis, R., Butler, N. & Goldstein, H. (1972) *From birth to seven.* Longmans, London.

Department of Education and Science (1978) *Primary Education in England; HMI Survey.*

Department of Education and Science (1981) *HMI Report on ILEA.*

Dickerson, A. (1987) Animal conditioning and learning theory. in Eysenck and Martin. (1987) *op.cit.*

Di Guiseppe, R.A. & Millar, N.J. (1977) A review of outcome studies on Rational Emotive Therapy. in Ellis & Grieger *op. cit.*

Di Loreto, A. (1971) *Comparative psychotherapy.* Aldine, Chicago.

Dollard, J., Doob, L.W., Miller, N.E., Mowrer, O.H. & Sears, R.R. (1939) *Frustration and aggression.* Yale University Press, New Haven.

Douglas, J.W.B. (1973) Early disturbing events and later enuresis. in Kolvin, I., MacKeith, R. & Meadow, S.R. *Bladder control and enuresis.* Heinemann, London.

Dowling, J.R. (1978) The prediction of children's adjustment after transfer to secondary school. M.Ed. Thesis. Cardiff. (unpub.)

Dryden, W. (1987) *Counselling individuals: the rational-emotional approach.* Taylor & Francis, London.

Dryden, W. & Golden, W. (1986) Cognitive-behavioural approaches to psychotherapy. Harper & Row, London.

Dunham, H.W. & Weinberg, S.K. (1960) *The culture of the state mental hospital.* Wayne State Univ. Press, Detroit.

Durkheim, E. (1938) *The rules of sociological method.* University of Chicago Press. Illinois.

EGC (1975) *The Educational Guidance Centre: introduction to services.* IEGC. London.

Eisler, R.M. & Miller, P.M. (1975) *Progress in behaviour modification.* Vol. 1, Academic Press.

Eggleston, S.J. (1977) *The Ecology of the school.* Metheun. London.

Eggleston, S.J., Dunn, D.K. & Anjali, M. (1986) *Education for some: the educational and vocational experiences of 15-18 year olds from ethnic minority groups.* Trentham Books, Stoke-on-Trent.

Eisenberg, L. (1958) School Phobia: a study in the communication of anxiety. *Am. J. Psychiat.* 114. pp. 712-718.

Ellis, A (1977) Research data supporting the clinical and personality hypotheses of RET and other cognitive behaviour therapies. in Ellis & Grieger. (1977) *op. cit.*

Ellis, A. (1989) Rational and irrational beliefs in counselling psychology. in D.A. Lane. *Attributions, beliefs and constructs in counselling psychology.* British Psychological Society, London.

Ellis A. & Grieger, R. (1977) *Handbook of rational emotive therapy.* Springer, New York.

Ellis, L. (1987) Evidence of neuroendrogenic etiology of sex roles from a combined analysis of human, nonhuman, primate and nonprimate mammalian studies. (discussed in Eysenck & Gudjonsson, 1989, *op.cit.*)

Ellis, L. (1988) The victimful victimless crime distinction, and seven universal demographic correlates of victimful behaviour. *Personality and individual differences.* 9. pp. 525-548

Elton Report (1989) *Discipline in schools: report of the Committee of Enquiry.* HMSO, London.

Erikson, E.H. (1963) *Childhood and society.* Norton, New York.

Eysenck, H.J. (1952) The effects of psychotherapy: an evaluation. *J. Consult. Psychol.* 16. pp. 319-324.

Eysenck, H.J. (1963) Behaviour therapy, spontaneous remission and transference in neurotics. *Am. J. Psychiat.* 119. pp. 867-871.

Eysenck, H.J. (1970) *The structure of human personality.* Methuen, London.

Eysenck, H.J. (1976) The learning model theory of neurosis: a new approach. *Beh. Res. & Therapy.* 14. pp. 251-267.

Eysenck, H.J. & Eysenck, S.B.G. (1975) *The Eysenck personality questionnaire.* Hodder & Stoughton, London.

Eysenck, H.J. & Eysenck, S.B.G. (1976) *Psychoticism.* Hodder & Stoughton, London.

Eysenck, H.J. & Eysenck, S.B.G. (1978) Psychopathy, personality and genetics. In R.D. Hare & D. Schalling (Eds.) *Psychopathic behaviour*. London: Wiley, pp. 197-223.
Eysenck, H.J. & Martin, I. (1987) *Theoretical foundations of behaviour therapy*. Pergamon. New York.
Eysenck, H.J. & Rachman, S (1968) *Causes and cures of neurosis*. Routledge and Kegan Paul. London.
Eysenck, H.J. (1987) The definition of personality disorders and the criteria appropriate for their description. *Journal of personality disorders*, I, pp. 211-219.
Eysenck, H.J. & Gudjonsson, G.H. (1989) *The causes and cures of criminality*. Plenum Press, New York.

Farrington, D.P. (1978) The family background of aggressive youths. in Hersov. Berger & Shaffer. (1978) *op. cit.*
Field, J.R., Corbin, K.B., Goldstein, N.P. & Klass, D.W. (1966) Gilles de la Tourettes syndrome. *Neurology*. 16. p. 453-462.
Fish, B. (1971) The 'one child, one drug' myth of stimulants in hyperkinesis: importance of diagnostic categories in evaluating treatment. *Arch. Gen. Psychiat*. 25. pp. 193-203.
Fitzherbert, K. (1977) *Child care services and the teacher*. Temple Smith, London.
Flynn, J.R.(1989) Rushton, evolution and race: An essay on intelligence and virtue. in *The Psychologist* Vol. 12 No. 9 pp. 363-366.
Fo, W.S. & O'Donnell, C.R. (1974) The buddy system. *J. Consult. Clin. Psych*. 42. pp. 163-169.
Fontana, D. (1985) *Classroom control*. BPS/Methuen, London.
Ford, J., Mongon, D. & Whelan, M. (1982) *Special education and social control: invisible disasters*. Routledge & Kegan Paul, London.
Fransella, F.(1989) What is a construct? In D.A. Lane, *Attributions, beliefs and constructs in counselling psychology*. British Psychological Society, Leicester.

Galloway, D. (1976) *Case studies in classroom management*. Longmans, London.
Galloway, D. (1982) 'Persistent absence from school', in *Educational Research*, 24, 3, pp. 188-96.
Galloway, D., Ball, T., Bloomfield, D. & Seyd, R. (1982) *Schools and disruptive pupils*. Longman, London.
Gardner, W.I. (1969) Use of punishment with the severely retarded: a review. *Am. J. Med. Def*. 74. pp. 56-103.
Garlovsky, D. (1984) Reflections on the wall: murals as educational stimuli. MA Thesis. Antioch University. (*unpub.*)
Gelfand, D.M. (1984) *Child behaviour analysis and therapy*. Pergamon, New York.

Genlin, E.T. (1978) Experimental psychotherapies. in Corsini, R. *Current psychotherapies*. Peacock, Illinois.

Gessell,A., Ilg, F.L. & Ames, L.B. (1974) *Infant and child in the culture of today*. Harper Row, New York.

Graham, J., (1988) *Schools, disruptive behaviour and delinquency*. HMSO, London.

Gillham, W. (1981) *Problem behaviour in the secondary school*. Croom Helm. London.

Gillham, B. (1978) The failure of psychometrics, in B. Gillham (ed.) *Reconstructing educational psychology*. Croom Helm, London.

Glueck, S. & Glueck, E., (1950) *Unraveling juvenile delinquency*. Commonwealth, New York.

Goldstein, A.P. (1971) *Psychotherapeutic attraction*. Pergamon, New York.

Gossett, J.T., *et. al.* (1973) Follow-up study of adolescents treated in a psychiatric hospital. *Am. J. Orthopsychiat.* 43. pp. 602-610.

Gould, S.J. (1981) The Mismeasure of man. Pelican, London.

Graham, P. (1977) Psychosomatic relationships. in Rutter & Hersov. *op. cit.*

Graziano, A.M. & Kean, J.J. (1967) Programmed relaxation and inhibition with psychotic children. *Beh. Res. & Ther.* 6. p.433-437

Green, F. (1980) Becoming a truant. Master's Thesis. *(unpubl.)* Cranfield.

Green, F. & Bayley, J. (1987) *Research papers*. Southwark EGS. Southwark, LEA.

Greenspoon, J. & Lamal, P.A. (1978) Cognitive behaviour modification — who needs it? *Psychol. Record.* 28. pp. 343-351.

Grieve, D. & Lane, D.A. (1989) *Guide to Development Planning*. Birmingham Midshires Building Society & The Professional Development Foundation, London.

Hall, S. (1979) Token economy strategies in criminal institutions. in Trasler & Farrington et al. (1979) *op. cit.*

Hall, R.U., *et. al.* (1971) The effective use of punishment to modify behaviour in the classroom. in O'Leary K.D. & O'Leary, S.G. (1972) *op. cit.*

Halleck, S.L. (1967) *Psychiatry and the dilemmas of crime*. Harper & Row. New York.

Hallgren, B. (1960) Noctural enuresis in twins, *Acta. Psych. Neuro. Scnad.* 35. pp. 73-90.

Halstead, H. & Neal, C.D. (1968) Intelligence and personality in drug addicts: a pilot study. *Brit. J. Addiction.* 63. pp. 237.

Hammersley, M. & Woods, P. (1984) *Life in schools: the sociology of pupil culture*. Open University Press, Milton Keynes.

Hare, M. (1966) Shortened treatment in a child guidance clinic, the results in 119 cases. *Br. J. Pyschiat.* 117. pp. 613-616.

Hare, R.D. (1971) Psychopathic behaviour: some recent theory and research. in Adams, H.E & Boardman, W.K. (1971) *Advances in experimental clinical psychology*. Pergamon, New York.

Harris, R. (1978) Relationships between EEG abnormality and aggressive and antisocial behaviour - a critical appraisal. in Hersov. Berger & Shaffer. (1978) *op. cit.*

Harris, R. (1977) The EEG. in Rutter & Hersov. (1977) *op. cit.*

Hargreaves, D.H. (1967) *Social relations in a secondary school*. Routledge & Kegan Paul, London.

Hargreaves, D.H., Hester, S.K. & Mellor, F.J. (1975) *Deviance in Classrooms*. London, Routledge & Kegan Paul.

Herbert, M. (1988) *Working with children and their families*. BPS/Routledge, London.

Herrick, M.J. (1971) *The Chicago Schools: A Social and Political History*. Sage, Beverly Hills.

Herskovitz, H.H., Levine, M. & Spivak, G. (1959) Anti-social behaviour of adolescents from higher socioeconomic groups. *J. Nerv. Ment. Dis.* 125. pp. 1-9.

Hersov, L. (1977) School refusal. in Rutter & Hersov. (1977) op. cit.

Hersov, L. (1977) Emotional disorders. in Rutter & Hersov. (1977) op. cit.

Hersov, L., Berger, M. & Schaffer, D. (1978) *Aggression and antisocial behaviour in childhood and adolescence*. Pergamon, New York.

Hewitt, L.E. & Jenkins, R.L. (1964) *Fundamental patterns of maladjustment*. Michigan Child Guidance Institute, Illinois.

Hicks, R.C. (1972) *Drugs*. TACADE, Manchester.

Hobbs, S. & Forhand, R. (1975) Effects of differential release from time out on children's deviant behaviour. *J. Beh. Ther. & Exp. Psych.* 6. pp. 256-257.

Homans, G.C. (1957) Social behaviour as exchange. *Am. J. Soc.* 63. pp. 597-600.

Howitt, D., *et.al.* (1989) *Social psychology*. Open University Press, Milton Keynes.

Hullett, G.E. (1966) A symbolic interactionist model of communication. *A.V. Communication Review*. 14. pp. 5-33.

Hoyle, E. (1986) *The politics of school management*. Hodder and Stoughton, London.

Illingworth, R.S (1975) *The development of the infant and young child*. Churchill Livingstone, Edinburgh.

Ingram, T. (1956) A characteristic form of overactive behaviour in brain damaged children. *J. Ment. Sci.* 102. pp. 550-558.

Inner London Education Authority (1988) *Report of survey on ethnic monitoring*. ILEA, London.

Jelfs, M. (1982) *Manual for action*. Action Resources Group, London.

Johnson, J.H., (1986) *Life events as stressors in childhood and adolescence*. Sage, Newbury Park.

Jowett, S., Hegarty, S. & Moses, D. (1988) *Joining forces: a study of links between special and ordinary schools*. NFER-Nelson, Slough.

Judd, G.L. (1965) Obsessive compulsive neurosis in children. *Arch. Gen. Psychiat*. 12. pp. 136-143.

Karoly, P & Kanfer, F.H. (1982) *Self management and behaviour change*. Pergamon, New York.

Karst, S. & Trexler, L. (1970) An initial study using fixed role and rational emotive therapies in treating public speaking anxiety. *J. Consult. & Clin. Psychol*. 34. pp. 360-366.

Kazdin, A.E. (1974) Covert modelling, model similarity and reduction of avoidance behaviour. *Beh. Ther*. 3. pp. 533-546.

Kazdin, A.E. (1972) Response cost: the removal of conditional reinforcers for therapeutic change. *Beh.Ther*. 5. pp. 533-546.

Kelly, G. (1955) *The psychology of personal constructs*. Norton, New York.

Kennedy, W.A. (1965) School phobia: rapid treatment of fifty cases. *J. Abnorm. Psychol*. 70. pp. 285-389.

Klein, J. (1965) *Samples from English cultures*. Vols. 1 & 2. Routledge and Kegan Paul, London.

Kolvin, I. *et.al*. (1981) *Help starts here*. Tavistock, London.

Krasner, L. & Ullman, L.P. (1973) *Behaviour influence and personality*. Holt, Reinhart & Winston, New York.

Krasner, L. (1980) *Environmental design and human behaviour: a psychology of the individual in society*. Pergamon, New York.

Kreitman, N. (1961) The reliability of psychiatric diagnosis. *J. Ment. Sci*. 107. pp. 876-886.

Krumboltz, & Thoresen, C.E. (1976) *Counselling methods*. Holt, Rinehart and Winston, New York.

Lader, M (1969) Psychophysiological aspects of anxiety. in Lader M. (1969) *Studies of Anxiety*. Brit. J. Psychiat. Special Publications 3. Headly, Ashford.

Lader, M. (1972) The nature of anxiety. *Brit. J. Psychiat*. 121. p. 481-491.

Lancet (1971) quoted in MacKeith, R. (1972) *op.cit*.

Lane, D.A. (1970) Drugs: the role of the teacher and youth worker. *Comm. Hlth*. 1.6. pp. 327-329.

Lane, D.A. (1972) Contract therapy: Conference paper. IEGC. London.

Lane, D.A. (1973) Individuals and systems: aspects of educational issues in drug dependence. *Educ. Res*. 16.1. pp. 52-57.

Lane, D.A. (1973) The problem of order. *Rem. Educ*. 8.3. p. 9-11.

Lane, D.A. (1973) Pathology of communcation: a pitfall in community health. *Comm. Hlth.* 5.3. pp. 157-162.

Lane, D.A. (1974) The behavioural analysis of complex cases: Conference paper. IEGC. Islington.

Lane, D.A. (1975) *The BSAG as a self report device.* IEGC, London.

Lane, D.A. (1976) Limitations on Counselling. *Rem. Educ.* 11.3. pp. 120.

Lane, D.A. (1976) *Persistent failure and potential success.* Research Monograph. IEGC, Islington.

Lane, D.A. (1978) *The Impossible Child.* Vols. 1 & 2. ILEA. London.

Lane, D.A. (1980) *Do schools vary in the referrals they make for behaviour problems?* IEGC, London.

Lane, D.A. (1980) *Personal development planning: the autonomous professional model.* IEGC, London. (Revised, 1989, Professional Development Foundation, London.)

Lane, D.A. (1983) *Whatever happened to the Impossible Child?* ILEA, London.

Lane, D.A. (1984) *Self-report of conduct disorder in children.* IEGC, London.

Lane, D.A. (1987) Psychological evidence in the Juvenile Court. in Gudjonsson, G. & Drinkwater, J. *Psychological evidence in court.* British Psychological Society, Leicester.

Lane, D.A. (1986) Promoting positive behaviour in the classroom. in Tattum, D. (1986) op.cit.

Lane, D.A. (1987) *A history of school-focused analysis and intervention.* IEGC, London.

Lane, D.A. (1988) Managing change in organisations: the role of performance counselling. 2nd. European Conference on Assessment Centre Methodology. Runnymede.

Lane, D.A. (1989) *Attributions, beliefs and constructs in counselling psychology.* British Psychological Society, Leicester.

Lane, D.A. & Dryden, W. (1990) *Child and adolescent therapy in Britain.* Open University Press, Milton Keynes. (forthcoming)

Lane, D.A. & Green, F.(1978) *The school refuser.* IEGC, London.

Lane, D.A. & Green, F. (1990) Partnerships with pupils. in Shearer, M, Gersch, I & Fry, L. Macmillan, London, (forthcoming)

Lane, D.A. & Hymans, M.H. (1982) The prediction of delinquency: a correlation between a measure of personality and classroom behaviour. *Person. Ind. Diff.* 3. p. 87-88.

Lane, D.A. & Tattum, D.P. (1990) *Supporting the child in school.* Professional Development Foundation. London.

Lane, D.A, & Van Oudtshoorn, M. (1990) *Counselling and organisational development.* Professional Development Foundation. London.

Lane, D.A. and Zelman, D. (1978) *The disappearing problem.* IEGC, London.

Lawrence, D. (1971) The effects of counselling on retarded readers. *Educ. Res.* 13.2 pp. 119-124.

Lawrence, J. (1973) Comment - on 'The problem child....', vol. 2 no. 2 In London Educational Review vol. 2 no. 3: Autumn. *Aims of education: an interdisciplinary inquiry.* University of London. Institute of Education.

Lawrence, J. Steed, D. & Young, P. (1986) The management of disruptive behaviour in Western Europe. in Tattum, D. (1986) *op.cit.*

Laycock, G. (1979) Behaviour modification in prisons. in Trasler & Farrington. (1979) *op. cit.*

Leeds, A. (1980) Your energy economy. *Yoga Journal.* 31. p. 16-24.

Levitt, E. (1957) A comparison of remainers and defectors among child clinic patients. *J. Consult. Psychol.* 21. pp. 316.

Levitt, E. (1963) Psychotherapy with children: a further evaluation. *Behav. Res. Ther.* 1. pp. 45-51.

Levinson, D.J. (1969) Role, personality and social structure. in Coser, L.A. & Rosenberg, B.R. *Sociological theory.* Macmillan, London.

Liberman, R.P. (1972) *A guide to behavioural analysis and therapy.* Pergamon, New York.

Lidz, T. (1958) Schizophrenia and the family. *Psychiatry.* 21. pp. 21-27.

Lombroso, C. (1917) *Crime, its causes and remedies.* Little Brown. Boston.

Lovell, K., Byrne, C. & Richardson, B. (1963) A further sample of the educational progress of children who had received remedial education. *Brit. J. Educ. Psychol.* 32. pp. 3-9.

Macfarlane, S.W., Honzik, M.O. & Allen, L (1954) *Behaviour problems in normal children.* Univ. of California Press. Berkeley.

MacKeith, R.C. (1972) The prevention of handicap. *Guy's Hospital Reports.* 121. 4 pp. 237-246.

MacKeith, R. (1973) The causes of nocturnal enuresis. in Kolvin, I., MacKeith, R., & Meadow S.R. *op.cit.*

McGuiness, J.B. & Craggs, D. (1986) Disruption as a school-generated problem. In Tattum, D.P. *Management of disruptive pupil behaviour in schools.* Wiley, New York.

McGuire, R.J. (1972) Classification and the problem of diagnosis. in Eysenck, H.J. (1973) *Handbook of abnormal psychology.* Pitman, London.

McWilliams, W. (1975) Sentencing and recidivism: an analysis by personality types. *Br. J. of Social Work.* 3. pp. 311-324.

Madsen, C.H., Becker, W.C. & Thomas, D.R. (1968) Rules, praise and ignoring elements of elementary classroom control. *App.Beh.Anal.* 5.1. pp.139-150

Mahler, M., Luke, J. & Daltroff, W (1945) Clinical and follow-up study of the tic syndrome in children. *Am. J. Orthopsychiat.* 15. pp. 631-647.

Mahoney, D.T. & Laferte, R.O. (1973) Enuresis: a plea for objectivity and sensitivity. *J. Urol.* 109. pp. 531-532.

Mainard, W.A. (1965) A Therapy. in Glasser, W *Reality therapy.* Harper Row. New York.

Malan, D.H., *et. al.* (1968) A study of psychodynamic changes in untreated neurotic patients. *Br. J. Psychiat.* 114. pp. 525-551.

Malinowski, B. (1926) *Crime and custom on savage society.* Humanities Press, New York.

Marzillier, J.S. (1980) Some myths about cognitive behaviour modification. *Behavioural Psychotherapy.* 8.2. pp. 38-44.

Marks, I.M. (1969) *Fears and phobia.* Heinemann. London.

Martin, I. (1987) Theoretical foundations and requirements in behaviour therapy. in Eysenck, H.J, and Martin, I. (1987) *op.cit.*

Marriage, H (1975) in Eysenck & Eysenck (1975) *op. cit.*

Marriage, H. Personal communication in 1981.

Mead, G.H. (1918) The psychology of punitive justice. *Am. J. Soc.* pp. 585, 592. March.

Mechanic, D (1962) The concept of illness behaviour. *J. Chron. Dis.* 15. pp. 189-194.

Meichenbaum, D. (1975) Theoretical and treatment implications of developmental research on verbal control of behaviour. *Canadian Psychological Review,* 16, pp. 22-27.

Meichenbaum, D. (1976) *Cognitive behaviour modification.* Plennum Press, Canada.

Meichenbaum, D. (1975) *Cognitive factors in biofeedback therapy.* University of Waterloo, Ontario.

Meichenbaum, D, & Turk, D. (1975) *The cognitive behavioural management of anxiety, anger and pain.* University of Waterloo. Ontario.

Mendelson, W., Johnson, N & Steward, M. (1971) Hyperactive children as teenagers, a follow up study. *J. Nerv. Ment. Dis.* 153. pp. 273-279.

Menkes, M., Rowe, J. & Menkes, J. (1967) A twenty five year follow up on the hyperkinetic child with minimal brain dysfunction. *Pediatrics.* 39. pp. 393-399.

Merton, R.K. (1949) *Social theory and social structure.* Free Press, New York.

Meyer, A. (1951) The Life Chart. in Winter, E.E. *The collected papers of Adolf Meyer* Vol 3. John Hopkins Press, Baltimore.

Meyer, V. & Chesser, E.S. (1970) *Behaviour therapy in clinical psychiatry.* Penguin, Harmondsworth.

Meyer, V. & Turkat, I.E. (1980) *Behavioural analysis.* Middlesex Hospital Medical School. London.

Michaels, J.J. (1965) *Disorders of character.* Thomas, Illinois.

Minde, K., Weiss, G. & Mendelson, N. (1972) A five year follow up study of 91 hyperactive schoolchildren. *J. Am. Acad. Child.* Psychiat. 11. pp. 595-610.

Morley, M.E. (1957) *Development and disorders of speech in childhood.* Livingstone, Glasgow.

Morrison, J. & Stewart, M. (1974) Bilateral inheritance as evidence for polygenicity in the hyperactive child syndrome. *J. Nerv. Ment. Dis.* 158. pp. 226-228.

Mortimore, P., *et.al.* (1988) *School matters: the junior years.* Open Books, London.

Mowrer, O.H. (1947) On the dual nature of learning as a reinterpretation of 'conditioning' and 'problem solving'. *Harvard Educ. Rev.* pp. 102-148.

Musgrove, F. (1964) *Youth and the social order.* Routledge & Kegan Paul, London.

Naughton, S. & Peters, G. (1976) *Systems and Failures.* Open University Press. Milton Keynes.

Nie, N.H., *et.al.* (1970) *SPSS manual.* McGraw Hill, New York.

Nye, F.I. (1958) *Family relationships and delinquent behaviour.* Wiley, New York.

O'Conner, R.D. (1972) Relative efficacy of modelling, shaping and the combined procedures for modification of social withdrawal. *Jr.Abnorm Psy.* 79.3. pp.327-334.

O'Connor, K.P. (1987) A response process model of behaviour. in Eysenck, H.J. & Martin, I. *op.cit.*

O'Leary, A.D. & O'Leary, S.G. (1972) *Classroom management: the successful use of behaviour modification.* Pergamon, New York.

Olweus, D. (1979) Stability of aggressive reaction patterns in males: a review. *Psychological Bulletin*, 86, pp. 852-975.

Oppel, W.C., Harper, P.A. & Rider, R.V. (1968) Social, psychological and neurological factors associated with nocturnal enuresis. *Pediatrics* 42. pp. 627-641.

Orlick, T. (1982) *The cooperative sports and games book.* Writers and Readers. London.

Osborn, S.C. & West, D.J. (1978) The effectiveness of various predictors of criminal careers. *J. of Adolescence.* 1. pp. 101-117.

Parker, H.,Summer, M., & Jarvis, G. (1989) *Unmasking the magistrates.* Open University Press, Milton Keynes.

Partridge, J. (1966) *Life in a secondary modern school.* Harmondsworth, Penguin Books.

Pasamanick, B. & Knobloch, H (1960) Brain damage and reproductive casualty. *Am. J. Orthopsychiat.* 30. pp. 298-305.

Patterson, G.R., Littman, R.A. & Bricker, W. (1967) Assertive behaviour in children: a step toward a theory of aggression. *Monogr. Soc. Res. Child Dev.* 32, no. 5 (Serial No. 113)

Pavlov, I.P. (1927) *Conditioned reflexes*. (Reprinted 1960.) Dover, New York.

Pearce, W.H. & Thornton, J. (1980) *The Ilderton motor project*. Community Relations Branch. New Scotland Yard.

Pierson, G.R. (1969) The role of the HSPQ in the Greenhill Programme. in Cattell & Cattell (1969) *op. cit.*

Pollard, A. (1986) An ethnographic analysis of classroom conflict. in D.P. Tattum. *Management of disruptive pupil behaviour in schools*. Wiley, New York.

Power, M.S., *et.al.* (1969) Delinquent schools. in *Crime, deviance and social sickness*. New Society Publications. London.

Prechtl, M. & Stemmer, C. (1962) The Choreiform syndrome in children. *Develop. Med. Child. Neurol.* 4. pp. 119-127.

Quinn, P.O. & Rapaport, J.L. (1974) Minor physical anomalies and neurologic status in hyperactive boys. *Pediatrics*, 53, 742-747.

Rachlin, H. (1976) *Behaviour and learning*. Freeman,.San Francisco.

Rachlin, H (1977) A review of M.J. Mahoney: Cognition and behaviour modification. *J. App. Behav. Anal.* 10. pp. 369-374.

Rachman, S. (1971) *The effects of psychotherapy*. Pergamon, Oxford.

Rachman, S.J. & Wilson G.T. (1980) *The effects of psychological therapy* Pergamon, Oxford.

Rahman, M.A. & Eysenck, S.B.G. (1978) Psychoticism and response to treatment in neurotic patients. *Behaviour, Research and Therapy* 16. pp. 183-189.

Raine, A. & Venables, P. (1981) Classical conditioning and socialization: A biosocial interaction. *Personality and Individual Differences*. 2, pp. 273-283.

Reynolds, D. (1982) 'A state of ignorance', in *Education for Development* 7, 2, pp. 4-35.

Robbins, L.N. (1966) *Deviant children grown up*. Williams & Williams, Baltimore.

Robins, E. & O'Neal, P. (1953) Clinical features of hysteria in children. *The Nervous Child*. 10. pp. 246-271.

Rogers,C.R. (1963) Psychotherapy today — or where do we go from here? *Am. J. of Psychotherapy*. 17. pp. 15-16.

Roland, E. (1988) Bullying: the Scandinavian research tradition. In D.P. Tattum & D.A. Lane (1989) *Bullying in schools*. Trentham, Stoke on Trent.

Roland, E. & Munthe, E. (1989) *Bullying: an international perspective*. David Fulton, London.

Rosenberg, C.M. (1969) Young drug addicts. *J Nerv. Ment. Dis.* 148. p. 65.

Rushton, J.P.(1988a) Race differences in behaviour: A review and evolutionary analysis. *Personality and Individual Differences*. 9, pp. 1009-1024.

Rutter, M. (1965) Classification and categorisation in child psychiatry. *Child Psychol. and Psychiat. 6: pp. 71-83.*

Rutter, M. (1971) Parent-Child separations: psychological effects on the children. *J. Child. Psychol. Psychiat.* 11. pp. 259-283.

Rutter, M. (1976) (ed.) *The child, his family and the community.* Wiley, London.

Rutter, M (1978) Family, area and school influences in the genesis of conduct disorders. in Hersov. Berger & Shaffer. *op. cit.*

Rutter, M (1977) Separation, loss and family relationships. in Rutter & Hersov (1977) *op. cit.*

Rutter, M. & Graham P. (1968) Psychiatric disorder in ten and eleven year old children. Proc. Royal Soc. Med. 59. p. 282-387.

Rutter, M., Maughan, B., Mortimore, P. & Ouston, J. (1979) *Fifteen thousand hours.* Open Books. London.

Rutter, M., Tizard, J. & Whitmore, K. (1970) *Education health and behaviour.* Longman, London.

Rutter, M., Yule, W. & Graham, P. (1973) Enuresis and behavioural deviance: some epidemiological considerations. in Kolvin, I., *et.al.* (1975) A multiple classification of child psychiatric disorders. WHO, Geneva.

Rutter, M. & Yule, W. (1975) The concept of specific reading retardation. *J. Child. Psychol. Psychiat.* 16. pp. 181-197.

Rutter, M. & Madge, N. (1976) *Cycles of disadvantage.* Heinemann, London.

Rutter, M. & Hersov, L. (1977) *Child Psychiatry.* Blackwell, Oxford.

Rutter, M. (1979) 'Protective factors in children's responses to stress and disadvantage' in Kent, M.W. & Rolf, J.E. (eds.) *Primary prevention of psychopathology:* Vol. 3 : Social Competence in Children. University Press of New England. Hanover.

Rutter, M. & Giller, H. (1982) *Juvenile delinquency: trends and perspectives.* Penguin, Harmondsworth.

Ryle, R. (1972) *Drug mythologies.* Reprint 728. Kings Fund Centre, London.

Sarason, I.G. (1958) Interrelationships among individual difference variable behaviour in psychotherapy and verbal conditioning. *J. Abnorm. Soc. Psychol.* 56. pp. 339-344.

Sarason, I.G. (1972) *Test anxiety, attention and the general problem of anxiety.* Reprint. NATO Advanced Science Institute.

Sarason, I.G. (1975) Test anxiety and the self-disclosing coping model. *J. of Consulting and Clinical Psychology*, 443, pp. 148-153.

Sarason, I.G. & Johnson, J.H. (1976) *The Life Experiences Survey.* Office of Naval Research. Arlington.

Savage, D.C.L., *et.al.* (1969) Asymptomatic bacteriuria in girl entrants to Dundee primary schools. *Brit. Med. J.* 3. pp. 75-80

Scheff, T. (1966) *Being mentally Ill: a sociological theory.* Aldine, Chicago.

Scheff, T.J. & Sundstorm, E (1970) The stability of deviant behaviour over time: a reassessment. *J. of Health and Social Behaviour.* 11. pp.37-43.

Scott, R.A. (1969) *The Making of Blind Men.* Russel Sage. New York.

Scriven, M (1973) The philosophy of behaviour modification. in Thoresen, C. (1973) *Behaviour Modification in Education.* NSSE, Chicago.

Sears, R.R., Maccoby, J.E. & Leven, H. (1957) *Patterns of child rearing.* Row Patterson. Illinois.

Shaffer, D. (1974) Suicide in childhood and early adolescence. *J. Child. Psychol. Psychiat.* 15. pp. 275-292.

Shaffer, D. (1977) Enuresis. in Rutter & Hersov. (1977) *op. cit.*

Shapiro, D.A. (1980) Science and psychotherapy : the state of the art. *Br. J. Med. Psychol.* 53. pp. 1-10.

Shaw, C.R. & McKay, H.D. (1942) *Juvenile delinquency and urban areas.* University of Chicago Press, Chicago.

Sheldon, W.H., Hartl, E.M. & McDermott, E. (1949) *Varieties of delinquent youth.* Harper, New York.

Shields, J. (1977) Polygenic influences. in Rutter & Hersov, *op. cit.*

Shields, J. & Slater, E. (1960) Heredity and physical abnormality. in Eysenck, H.J. *op.cit.*

Simon, F.H. (1971) *Prediction methods in criminology.* HMSO, London.

Smith, M.L. & Glass, G.U. (1977) Meta-analysis of psychotherapy outcome studies. *Am. Psychol.* 32. pp. 752-760.

Spencer, M. (1875) *The Study of sociology.* Appleton. New York.

Stadden, J.E.R. & Simmelhag, V.L. (1971) The superstition experiment. *Psychol. Rev.* 78. 1. p. 3-16.

Straatmeyer, A.J. & Watkins, J.T. (1974) Rational Emotive Therapy and the reduction of speech anxiety. *Rational Living.* 9.1. pp. 33-37.

Steinberg, D. (1977) Psychotic disorders in adolescence. in Rutter & Hersov. *op. cit.*

Stott, D.H. (1971) *The social adjustment of children.* University of London Press. London.

Stott, D.H. (1975) *Bristol social adjustment guides: manual,* 5th edn. University of London Press. London.

Stott, D.H. (1976) 'Pseudo-retardation as a form of learning disability: the case of Jean', *J. of Learning Disabilities* 9, pp. 354-64.

Stott, D.H., Marston, M.C. & Neill, S.J. (1975) *Taxonomy of behaviour disturbance.* London Univ. Press. London.

Suhl, A.M. (1961) Gonadal hormones and social behaviour in infrahuman vertebrates, in Young, W.C. *Sex and internal secretions.* Williams & Wilkins. Baltimore.

Sutherland, E.H. & Cressey, D.R. (1955) *Principles of criminology.* J. B. Lippincott. Philadelphia.

Szass, T.S. (1961) *The myth of mental illness.* Hoeber-Harper. New York.

Tannenbaum, F. (1938) *Crime and the community,* Columbia University Press Ohio.

Tattum, D.P. (1982) *Disruptive pupils in schools and units.* Wiley, Chichester.
Tattum, D.P. (1986) *Disruptive pupil behaviour in schools.* Wiley, Chichester. (revised edition, 1989.) Fulton, London.
Tattum, D.P. & Lane, D.A. (1989) Bullying in schools. Trentham, Stoke on Trent.
Tennessee State Department of Mental Health (1975) *A prevention intervention model for students' learning and behaviour problems: final report* 1974-75. TSDMH, Nashville.
Teasdale, J.D., Seagrave, R. & Zacune, J. (1971) Psychoticism in Drug Users. *Br. J. Soc. Clin. Psychol.* 10. 2. p. 160.
Thomas, W.I. (1953) *The unadjusted girl.* Dover. New York.
Thomas, A., Chess, S. & Birch, H.G. (1968) *Temperament and behaviour disorders in children.* Unversities Press, New York.
Thomas, L.F. & Harri-Augstein, E.S. (1985) *Self-organised learning: foundations of a conventional science for psychology.* Routledge & Kegan Paul, London.
Thoreson, C. E. & Mahoney, M.F. (1974) *Behavioural self-control.* Holt, Rinehart and Winston, New York.
Thrasler, F. (1936) *The gang.* Chicago University Press. Illinois. Tomlinson, S. (1982) *A sociology of special education.* Routledge & Kegan Paul, London.
Topping, K.J. & Quelch, T. (1976) *Special units and classes for children with behaviour problems.* Calderdale Education Authority, Calderdale.
Topping, K.J. (1983) *Educational systems for disruptive adolescents.* Croom Helm, London.
Topping, K. (1988) *The peer tutoring handbook.* Croom Helm. London.
Trasler, G.B. (1964) Socialisation, a new approach. *Cambridge Opinion.* 38. pp. 17-22.
Trasler, G.B. & Farrington, D.P. (1979) *Behaviour modification with offenders: a criminological symposium.* Institute of Criminology, Cambridge.
Tregerman, S. (1975) Effects of assertive training. (unpublished doctoral dissertation.) Hofstra University.
Traux, C.B. & Carkhuff, R.R. (1966) *An introduction to Counselling and Psychotherapy: Training and Practice.* Aldine, Chicago.

Ullmann, L.P. (1967) *Institution and outcome: a comparative study of psychiatric hospitals.* Pergamon, New York.
Ullmann, L.P. & Giovanni, J.M. (1964) The development of a self-report measure of the process-reactive continuum. *J. Nerv. Ment. Dis.* 138. pp. 38-42.
Ullmann, L.P. & Krasner, L. (1975) *A psychological approach to abnormal behaviour.* Prentice Hall, New Jersey.

237

Volavka, J. (1987) Electroencephalogram among criminals. In Mednick, S.A., Moffitt, T.E. & Stack, S.A. (eds.), *The causes of crime*. pp. 137-145 Cambridge University Press. Cambridge.

Wall, W.D. (1979) *Constructive education for special groups*. Harrap, London.
Walters, R.H. & Brown, M. (1964) A test of the high magnitude theory of aggression. J. *Exp. Child. Psychol*. 1. pp.376-387.
Wardle, C.J. (1961) Two generations of broken homes in the genesis of conduct and behaviour disorders in childhood. *Br. Med. J*. 2. pp.349-354.
Warnock Report (1978) *Special educational needs: report of the Committee of Enquiry into the educational needs of children and young people*. London, HMSO.
Warnock, M. (1983) in *Times Educational Supplement*. 1.4.83.
Warren, W. (1965) A study of adolescent psychiatric in-patients and the outcome six or more years later. *J. Child. Psychol Psychiat*. 6. pp. 1-17.
Weiner, I.B. (1970) *Psychological disturbance in adolescence*. Wiley, New York.
Werry, J. (1968) Developmental hyperactivity. *Pediat. Clin. North Am*. 15. pp. 581-599.
Werry, J (1972) Organic factors in childhood psychpathology. in Quay, H.C. & Werry, J. *Psychopathological disorders in childhood*. Wiley, New York.
West, A., Davies, J. & Varlaam, A. (1986) The management of behaviour problems: a local authority response. In Tattum D.P.: *Management of disruptive pupil behaviour in schools*. Wiley, New York.
West, D. (1977) Delinquency. in Rutter & Hersov. (1977) *op. cit*.
West, D. & Farrington, D.P. *Who becomes delinquent?* Heinemann, London.
West, D.J. (1979) (a) The Distribution of young adult delinquency and other social problems in relation to early social deprivation and family background. In M. Brown & N. Madge: *op. cit*.
Wheddell, K. & Merritt, F. (1988) *Positive teaching*, Postive Products, Cheltenham.
Whitting, J.W.N. & Child, I.L. (1953) *Child training and personality*. Yale Univ. Press, New Haven.
Widlake, P. (1972) Results of a reading drive. *Rem. Educ*. 7.1. pp. 1-16.
Widlake, P. (1986) *Reducing educational disadvantage*. Open University Press, Milton Keynes.
Widlake, P. (1990) Involving parents in the education of children with special educational needs. in Lane. D.A., & Dryden, W. (1990) *op.cit*.
Williams, M. (1970) *Brain damage and the mind*. Penguin, Harmondsworth.
Willmott, P. (1958) *Adolescent boys in east London*. Routledge & Kegan Paul, London.
Wine, J. (1971) Test anxiety and the direction of attention. *Psychol. Bulletin*. 76. 2. pp. 92-104.

Wolff, S. (1977) Non-delinquent disturbances of conduct. in Rutter & Hersov, (1977) *op. cit.*

Wolpe, J. (1973) *The Practice of behaviour therapy*. Pergamon, Oxford.

World Health Organisation (1973) *The international pilot study of schizophrenia*. Vol. 1. WHO, Geneva.

Yule, W. (1978) Behavioural treatment of children and adolescents with conduct disorders. in Hersov, Berger & Shaffer. (1978) *op. cit*

Zansmer, R.C.M. (1954) Treatment of tics in childhood. *Arch. Dis. Child.* 29. pp. 537-542.

Zuckerman, M. & Brody, N. (1988) Oysters, rabbits and people: a critique of race differences in behaviour by J.P. Rushton. *Per. Ind. Diff.* 9, pp. 1025-1033.

BIBLIOGRAPHY